ANTHROPOLOGY AND
THE RACIAL POLITICS OF CULTURE

Lee D. Baker

Anthropology and
the Racial Politics of Culture

Duke University Press   Durham and London

2010

© 2010 Duke University Press

All rights reserved

Printed in the United States of America on acid-free paper ∞

Designed by C. H. Westmoreland

Typeset in Warnock with Magma Compact display

by Achorn International, Inc.

Library of Congress Cataloging-in-Publication Data

appear on the last printed page of this book.

Dedicated to

WILLIAM A. LITTLE

AND SABRINA L. THOMAS

Contents

Preface

Questions

"Are you a hegro? I a hegro too. . . . Are you a hegro?" My mother loves to recount the story of how, as a three year old, I used this innocent, mispronounced question to interrogate the garbagemen as I furiously raced my Big Wheel up and down the driveway of our rather large house on Park Avenue, a beautiful tree-lined street in an all-white neighborhood in Yakima, Washington. It was 1969. The Vietnam War was raging in Southeast Asia, and the brutal murders of Malcolm X, Martin Luther King Jr., Medgar Evers, and Bobby and John F. Kennedy hung like a pall over a nation coming to grips with new formulations, relations, and understandings of race, culture, and power. As members of the Red Power movement occupied Alcatraz and took up armed resistance in South Dakota, members of the Black Power movement occupied San Francisco State University, demanding that black studies be incorporated into the curriculum. Yet even militant leaders could do little to abate the flood of so-called race riots that decimated black communities from Los Angeles to Washington, D.C., and no one could bring back the college students shot dead at Kent State and Jackson State.

My father was a pastor of an all-white Lutheran Church, and my mother was an instructor in the still-experimental Head Start program. Busy preaching, teaching, and raising three kids, my parents had little time to be involved in any organized movement. As good white liberals, however, they wanted to contribute something, get involved, and try to make a difference. My parents believed that adopting a child might be one way to make a small but important difference during the turbulent 1960s. Initially, they wanted to adopt an American Indian child from the nearby Yakama Reservation, but, as the story goes, some of my parents' black friends persuaded them that Indians were rather lazy and did not do well in school and advised my parents to adopt a black child instead. Apparently, my parents listened to these well-assimilated members of the rather small black middle class in Yakima because they decided to go black and not look back.

After dutifully requesting permission from the local Black Panther Party, they adopted me from a foster home in San Diego, California. At the age of three, I was plunked down in Yakima, which during the late 1960s was a hypersegregated town in eastern Washington State where the railroad tracks and the reservation demarcated strict residential color lines—red, black, and white.

We soon moved to Corvallis, Oregon, where I continued to ask questions and seek answers about race and culture, questions that were often prompted by school kids' rather cruel antics perpetrated against me and my blonde-haired, blue-eyed sister. The two of us were continually forced to explain how we could be siblings, being seven months apart in age and clearly of different races. Perhaps the real questions came from the exchange students our family hosted. The first was John D., who stayed with our family when I was in grade school; he was from Golivan, Alaska, a remote fishing village near the Arctic Circle. Even by fourth grade, John had a strong sense of his Inuit heritage and identity. The other student was Luza, who hailed from Bogotá, Colombia, and stayed with us for a year during my first year in high school. A member of an elite, wealthy family, Luza was smart, outgoing, and gracious. She immediately became the fifth sibling and made her way along with my brother and two sisters in our often busy and chaotic household. Each of these students stayed with our family for an extended period of time during my formative years, and each one left a deep impression upon me regarding culture and class, commonality and difference. In addition to these exchange students, our family was host to a constant stream of wayward international students from Oregon State University who would stay with us when the university was not in session or who would come over for holiday meals.

I have fond memories as a junior high school student of peppering Emi from Nigeria, Ahmed from Yemen, and Young from South Korea with endless questions. The bigger questions, however, came in high school, where the only diversity in an otherwise lily-white school was provided by the many Vietnamese, Cambodian, and Laotian students whose compelling stories of life in refugee camps and efforts to reunite with family members offered a somber and sober counterpoint to the frivolous, pedantic stories my classmates and I would come up with in creative writing exercises.

Although I was expected to perform a cultural blackness at school and assimilate my family's Swedish heritage at home, I walked a perilous cultural tightrope as I tried to navigate the full force of institutional racism and subtle forms of discrimination—on my own. School officials as well as my mother consistently explained to me that my placement in remedial courses and my many run-ins with the law were the direct result of my bad behavior. No doubt part of the reason *was* my behavior, but, lacking the cultural tools, folklore, and black family members to school me, I had no way of interrogating either the cause of racism or the effect it had on my smart-ass belligerency. My mother did work hard behind the scenes to abate the more flagrant forms of discrimination.

The idea that one has to learn to perform whiteness or model blackness was always at the forefront of my socialization. Together with the one other young black man in our high school, I worked hard at being black—befriending black college students at Oregon State and attending their parties. I also watched too much MTV. I naively but consciously modeled my behavior, dress, and "style" after my cultural heroes of the early eighties: the track star Edwin Moses, the music legend Prince, and Congressman Ron Dellums of California. My own cultural competence, however, was always called into question. Not because I was raised by a white family, but because I could not dance or play basketball. Although I was sensitive to the subtle distinctions between race and culture, I finally witnessed firsthand how race, culture, and power worked together in society when I had the opportunity to live as an exchange student with an Aboriginal family in Broome, Western Australia. I was seventeen years old and found myself suddenly in the middle of the Australian Outback. "These are black people," I said to myself, "but they are totally different from black folks in the U.S." Why, however, did they suffer from the same problems of substance abuse, police brutality, and poverty while embracing the same sense of family, rich social networks, and a sustaining pride in their culture? The similarities were stunning, the differences were stark, and I had many more questions than answers.

After returning from Australia and completing my senior year, I enrolled at Portland State University. Immediately, I declared my majors: anthropology and black studies. I thought I could use these tools to help

me answer the many questions I had about race, racism, and culture. Trying to synthesize African American studies and anthropology made intuitive sense to me. Both disciplines focused on culture, both privileged
history and theory, and both explored diasporas of people, examined the
diffusion of cultures, and tried to explain extant conditions in an effort to
effect change and better people's everyday lives. As a first-year student in
college, I was struck—and now, as a college professor, I am still struck—by
the fact that African American studies rarely, if ever, explores the experiences of Australian Aboriginals or American Indians, while anthropology
rarely explores the experiences of African Americans, especially when
compared to the attention anthropologists give to both American Indians
and Africans on the continent and throughout the diaspora. Although
these stark lacunae in both disciplines are changing somewhat as cultural
studies impacts both fields, I have never quite understood why sociology
gives so much attention to the analysis of African Americans and people
living within modern nation-states, and why anthropology gives so much
attention to the analysis of American Indians and people putatively living
outside of modern nation-states. I am still working out the retrospective
significance of these questions, and the chapters in this book directly and
indirectly seek answers to some of the questions I had more than twenty
years ago. These have been the questions of my lifetime. Although I have
certainly not yet answered them to my satisfaction, this book suggests
possible directions for exploring the history of specific anthropological
questions that turn on and around race and culture in the United States;
yet these specific questions are imbricated with the broader global questions of race and culture that led me to anthropology in the first place.

Acknowledgments

Funding for this research was provided by a Mellon Resident Fellowship at the American Philosophical Society Library, a Post-Doctoral Fellowship from the Ford Foundation, and the James B. Duke fellowship at the National Humanities Center. Further support was provided by the Dean of Trinity College of Arts and Sciences, the Provost, the Social Science Research Institute, and the Department of Cultural Anthropology of Duke University. This book was a long time in the making, and several arguments and preliminary ideas were worked out in articles that were previously published, which include "Franz Boas Out of the Ivory Tower," *Anthropological Theory* 4(1) (2004), 29–51; "Research, Reform, and Racial Uplift: The Mission of the Hampton Folklore Society 1893–1899," *Excluded Ancestors, Inventible Traditions: Essays Toward a More Inclusive History of Anthropology*, edited by Richard Handler, 42–80, vol. 9 of *History of Anthropology* (Madison: University of Wisconsin Press, 2000); "Daniel G. Brinton's Success on the Road to Obscurity, 1890–99," *Cultural Anthropology* 15(3) (2000), 394–423.

So many people have helped me with this project on my long journey toward completion. I cannot begin to properly demonstrate my heartfelt appreciation for guidance, inspiration, and motivation. I would like to both acknowledge and personally thank Sandy Graham, Dan Segal, Regna Darnell, Nancy Parezo, Leilani Basham, Michael Silverstein, Layli Phillips, Polly Strong, Marisol de la Cadena, Circe Sturm, Robert Warrior, Ralph Litzinger, Andrew Lyons, Alice B. Kehoe, Ty P. Kawika Tengan, Dana Davis, David Shorter, Eric Lassiter, Matti Bunzl, George Bond, Bayo Holsley, Carol Greenhouse, Maureen Mahon, Moira Smith, Noenoe K. Silva, George Stocking, John L. Jackson, Deborah A. Thomas, Nick Dirks, Jason Jackson, Richard Handler, Debra Wythe, Phil Morgan, Alan Goodman, Carol Spawn, Alex Pezzati, Roy Goodman, Beth Carroll-Horrocks,

Maria Vesperi, Ernie Freidl, Suzanne Shanahan, Steven Conn, Marla Frederick, Stephanie Evans, Brad Evans, Nancy Tolin, Rebecca Stein, David Rease, Cathy Davidson, Ada Noris, Jonathan Holloway, James Robinson, Jeffery Kerr-Ritchie, Brad Weiss, Kent Mulikin, Edward Carter, Moria Smith, Thomas Patterson, John Hope Franklin, J. Clyde Ellis, J. Kehaulani Kauanui, Theda Perdue, Randy Matory, Charlie Piot, Trina Jones, Faye V. Harrison, William A. Little, Nancy Scheper-Hughes, Elizabeth Chin, Arlene Davila, Ira Bashkow, Emily Choa, Brett Williams, Leith Mullings, Manning Marable, George McLendon, Anne Allison, Peter Lange, Bianca Robinson, Jim Peacock, Michael Elliott, Brian Kelly, Jonathan Marks, Alex Alland, Michael Blakey, Howard Margolis, William H. Tucker, John P. Jackson, Cathy Lewis, Gail Hignight, Bisa Meek, and Setha Low. Special thanks to Curtis Hinsley, Vernon J. Williams Jr., and Orin and Randy Starn. This book simply would not have been completed without the inspiration of Yaa and Quinton and the loving and steadfast support of my dear wife, Sabrina L. Thomas.

Introduction

"We are for a vanishing policy," declared Merrill E. Gates during his presidential address in 1899 to the influential reform group called the Lake Mohonk Friends of the Indian (1900:12). Gates was echoing the familiar refrain of Major Richard C. Pratt, the superintendent of the U.S. Indian Industrial School at Carlisle, who agreed, in part, with the idea that "the only good Indian was a dead one." As Pratt saw it, "All the Indian there is in the race should be dead. Kill the Indian in him, and save the man" (1973 [1892]:261). Pratt and Gates were important figures during the so-called assimilation era, when the federal government fused land allotment to industrial education in an explicit effort to quicken the slow processes of Indian evolution from savage pagan to civilized Christian.

In 1928, however, Lewis Meriam explained in his historic report on the failure of Indian policies that "some Indians proud of their race and devoted to their culture . . . have no desire to be as the white man is. They wish to remain Indians." He explained that many "intelligent, liberal whites who find real merit in . . . things which may be covered by the broad term 'culture'" advocate a policy that goes so far, "metaphorically speaking, as to enclose these Indians in a glass case to preserve them as museum specimens for future generations to study and enjoy, because of the value of their culture and its picturesqueness in a world rapidly advancing in high organization and mass production."

"With this view," Meriam reported, "the survey staff has great sympathy" (1928:86–87). With the help of John Collier, Franklin D. Roosevelt's politically savvy commissioner of Indian affairs, many of the recommendations Meriam and his staff made found their way into the Wheeler-Howard Act of 1934. Better known as the Indian Reorganization Act (IRA), this was sweeping New Deal legislation that was meant to curtail future allotments, empower tribal governments, and put structures in place to enable improved health, education, land acquisition, and cultural preservation (Medicine 1998:254). Broadly construed, this tumultuous period of explicit vanishing policies began with the passing of the Indian Religious Crimes Code (1883) and ended with the Wheeler-Howard Act (1934).

By employing stark and macabre metaphors, proponents of assimilation barely veiled their desires for the complete destruction of American Indian beliefs and cultural practices, albeit couched in the name of progress and the advance of Christian civilization. A generation later, however, cultural preservation and self-determination became the watchwords of federal policies governing Native Americans. Although the ultimate successes of the IRA varied, one can view this shift in terms of the federal government's promulgating of policies to first destroy and then protect American Indian culture. The dramatic shift in the policies of the Bureau of Indian Affairs (BIA) mirrored shifts in American popular culture, aesthetics, and attitudes toward traditional or authentic Native American cultures. The ascendancy and import of ideas like tradition and culture among American Indian groups, within state and federal governments, in vehicles of popular culture, and among philanthropists were congruent with the development of Americanist anthropology as it moved from embracing ideas of social evolution to articulating ideas of historical particularism and cultural relativism.

The world-renowned potter Maria Martinez (1887–1980), from San Ildefonso Pueblo, New Mexico, experienced the change in these ideas regarding culture in a telling way. As a young woman, she was exhibited at the Louisiana Purchase Exposition in St. Louis in 1904 as a primitive native on the bottom rungs of the evolutionary ladder, as evidenced by her quaint yet crude pottery. In 1933, however, Martinez received a special invitation to exhibit her highly touted pottery at the A Century of Progress International Exposition in Chicago. She fetched a bronze medal. Although her pots remained basically the same, American perceptions had changed; at the turn of the century, Indians were seen as on their way out, but by the 1930s they were seen as very much "in" (Jacobs 1999:3; Spivey 2003:167–68; Mullin 2001:91–172).

In this book, I explore anthropology in the United States and its emerging concept of culture as it played an increasingly important role in this dramatic shift in federal Indian policy and the broader public's understanding of distinctive cultures. At the same time, I investigate anthropology's concept of race, which also emerged as an important idea during this period. The anthropological concept of race, however, was less reliable, slower to stabilize, and often more paradoxical than that of culture (Williams 2006:16–47; Blakey 1999:33). Anthropology also had more competition in the arena of race than it did in the field of culture.

In each chapter, I have identified specific anthropologists who employed particular ideas of culture and race and document how these collide or collude with other ideas outside the academy. The intense public contestation of these collisions often produced unintended consequences that help to identify the motivations, investments, and commitments of the various stakeholders. Throughout the book, I attend to various publics, identifying when anthropology was lionized or reviled, and then try to understand the racial politics of culture animating both the anthropologists who pushed their science into public arenas and the public intellectuals who pushed back. Conversely, I illustrate how anthropology was pulled into the public arena and demonstrate how anthropologists pushed back. I try to focus on how the power of culture and the culture of power often ricochet off one another in unexpected ways and track the perception of anthropology as it made the significant transition from being a reliable narrator in the story of white supremacy to becoming an increasingly less reliable one.

I develop these stories about conflict and collision, collusion and cooperation that turn on ideas of race and culture to demonstrate that anthropology as discourse and discipline has played subtle, complex, and ambivalent roles in shaping the racial politics of culture in the United States. Focusing on the late nineteenth century and early twentieth, I argue that the role anthropology played in shaping popular conceptions of the culture for Native Americans was significantly different from the role it played in shaping popular conceptions of culture for African Americans. And I also argue that the role anthropology played in articulating notions of race had different implications from the role it played articulating notions of culture. Although the roles differed, I suggest the anthropological concept of race that was eventually used to address the Negro problem in the twentieth century emerged from the anthropological concept of culture that was used to understand American Indian languages and customs in the nineteenth century. In other words, to understand the development of African American customs, beliefs, rituals, practices, and art as "culture" in the United States, one must interrogate the way in which a diverse array of languages and customs were identified and described as cultures among American Indians.

Five fascinating and intertwined questions motivate and frame this research. First, anthropologists resisted studying Negroes and desired studying Indians, so why did many educated, self-proclaimed Negro elites desire the anthropological gaze while many educated, self-proclaimed Indian elites resist it? Second, anthropologists in the United States successfully fashioned a concept of culture by delimiting it from race, while articulating a concept of race by divorcing it from culture. Despite the left-leaning political motivations and even antiracist scholarship produced by Franz Boas and some of his students, how did anthropology in the United States so assiduously avoid or evade deliberate discussions and analysis of racism and structural inequality? Fourth, why did ideas of raceless culture never fully break free from their biological moorings (Harrison 1994; Mullings 2005; Steinberg 2007; Visweswaran 1998a)? Finally, how and why did an obvious division of labor emerge in social sciences in the United States that enabled anthropology to specialize in describing the culture of out-of-the-way indigenous peoples while empowering sociologists to specialize in explaining the culture of the many in-the-way immigrant and black people?

One of the reasons I do not or cannot fully answer these questions is that the problems that have always surrounded linkages and disconnects between concepts of culture and race stem from the fact that both are slippery social constructs, and people too often use one to explain the other or simply collapse the two. My hope is that these stories will help to delimit the limits, understand the contradictions, and offer a better understanding of the terms and conditions of race and culture which are deployed within explicitly political projects that get woven into the fabric of North American culture and become part of American history. My ultimate objective is to illuminate how anthropology helped to shape the racial politics of culture and the cultural politics of race that we are still grappling with today. In the balance of this lengthy introduction, I lay the groundwork for what I mean by the racial politics of culture and how that fits into the history of anthropology, while underscoring some of the differences between race and culture as they were used to describe difference, differently, among African Americans and American Indians.

The Racial Politics of Culture

As the United States relentlessly blazed a trail through Chinese exclusion, the Wounded Knee massacre, the Spanish-American War, acquisition of island territories, World War I, and the Great Depression, the field of anthropology emerged as a relatively powerful discipline as it explained, described, and preserved "peoples" who were out of bounds, culturally distinct, vanishing, and viewed as the primitive native (Appadurai 1988:36; Briggs 2002:481). This meant, with few exceptions, the description of the customs and behavior of American Indians (Hallowell 1960:15). During the same period, the United States came to terms with waves of immigrants from Europe, Asia, and the Americas, and people were forced to grapple with Jim Crow segregation, disfranchisement, citizenship, ghettos, and violent race and labor riots. Anthropology became popular when it explained and described "races" who were competing, crowding, reproducing, and being viewed as not worthy of the same rights and privileges as those men who were all created equal. And this meant, with some exceptions, the description of the brains and bodies of black people in the United States.

From the late nineteenth century to today, race and culture have routinely served as contentious fulcrums for particular political projects that range from claims of white supremacy to claims for citizenship, sovereignty, and civil rights. And since the late nineteenth century, anthropology has been the social science that has consistently studied race and culture. Anthropology has developed a symbiotic and at times parasitic relationship with popular conceptions of race and culture. The concepts of race and culture within anthropology have influenced popular understandings of these concepts, just as popular understandings of these concepts have influenced anthropology (di Leonardo 1998).

During the late nineteenth century, ideas of blood, civilization, nation, culture, and race were often used interchangeably because "there was not a clear line between cultural and physical elements or between social and biological heredity" (Stocking 2001:8). Culture was synonymous with civilization, and groups like the Kiowa and Navajo were identified as having achieved a stage of culture on the road to civilization that began at savagery, traveled through barbarism, and finally ended at the apex of culture: civilization. Race, language, and culture tracked together along an evolutionary road.

As recounted with almost catechistic alacrity in nearly every introduction to anthropology course, Franz Boas famously upended this presumption by demonstrating that one cannot rank-order the races because it is impossible to classify them. His most straightforward enunciation of this was his introduction to the *Handbook of American Indian Languages*, in which he demonstrated that "anatomical type, language, and culture have not necessarily the same fates; that a people may remain constant in type, but change in language; or that they remain constant in language and change in type and culture. If this is true, then it is obvious that attempts to classify mankind, based on the present distribution of type, language, and culture, must lead to different results according to the point of view taken . . . in the same way, classifications based on language and culture do not need at all to coincide with a biological classification" (Boas 1911a:11). This view of race, language, and culture gained traction inside and outside the academy. By the 1930s, it became a pillar of anthropological thought in the United States and influenced many Americans' understanding of "culture" as a plural noun and a modality that was not simply determined by race (Visweswaran 1998a:70). The Kiowa or the Navajo, for example, were viewed as historically distinct cultures that had particular traditions and languages that should be preserved, valued, and otherwise acknowledged in the wake of rapid industrialization.

Predicated on "the rejection of the traditional nineteenth-century linkage of race and culture in a single hierarchical evolutionary sequence," the anthropological concept of race as anatomical type largely independent of culture was, perhaps, more important than the anthropological concept of culture in the United States because it effectively complemented the powerful and seductive ideas of assimilation and racial uplift (Stocking 2001:46). On the one hand, this idea of race became a compelling argument for desegregation; on the other, it provided theoretical purchase for punitive policies to reform putative bad behavior.

If culture was not constitutive of race, the logic went, what was stopping people from acting white or getting culture, despite their color? Lucy C. Laney, an influential educator in Georgia, was fond of saying that discrimination in the Jim Crow South was bad, but she instructed people to "get culture, character, and cash, and the problem will solve itself" (Southern Workman 1899:364).

Although this concept of race served as a powerful critique of arguments for innate inferiority and superiority, the concept also enabled powerful figures to dismiss distinctive cultures and avoid addressing racism. The anthropological concept of race made it possible to promote the idea that regardless of their race, Indians, Negroes, and Orientals could and should learn to think, behave, and act like good white Protestants—white privilege would follow colored respectability, or so was the expectation.

This was the precise line of argument employed by the well-assimilated Japanese national Takao Ozawa when he filed for naturalization on October 16, 1914 (Ngai 2003:42). "That he was well qualified by character and education was conceded" by the U.S. Supreme Court, but it rejected his bid for citizenship because ethnologically he was not Caucasian and therefore not a "free white person" under immigration law [260 U.S. 189 (1922)]. The following year, Bhagat Singh Thind argued to the Court that he was "a high caste Hindu, of full Indian blood, born at Amrit Sar, Punjab, India." Anthropologically he was considered Caucasian and therefore eligible for naturalization (Jacobson 1998:234). The Court said, however, what it really meant was that "'free white persons,' as used in that section [of the statute], are words of common speech, to be interpreted in accordance with the understanding of the common man, synonymous with the word 'Caucasian' only as that word is popularly understood" [261 U.S. 214 (1923)]. Although some privileges were afforded to those responsible individuals who acted white, actual rights afforded white people never followed even the most sincere attempts to perform respectability. In this case, the Court did not heed anthropological findings, but it did have to contend with them and weigh the intellectual merit of anthropology against the broader impact of their decision.

By midcentury, policymakers, legislators, philanthropists, and Supreme Court justices embraced the modern anthropological ideas of race and culture. Most scholars credit this paradigmatic shift in American anthropology and eventually U.S. institutions with the charismatic and indefatigable leadership of Boas and his students, who "insisted on the conceptual distinction of race, language, and culture" (Stocking 2001:23). The way Boas and his students made these distinctions was often by a process of negation or proffering of a definition through delimitation (Stocking 2001:9). "Culture was expressed through the medium of language but was not reducible to it; more importantly, it was not race. Culture became everything race was not, and race was seen to be what culture was not" (Visweswaran 1998a:70).

Boas and his students eventually wrestled the "modern relativistic, pluralistic anthropological approach to culture" (Stocking 2001:23) from a racialized evolutionary hierarchy, but it took time. "Boas's success in critiquing racial anthropology was the product of a complex cluster of intellectual dispositions that, taken together, laid the foundation for the Boasian tradition" (Segal and Yanagisako 2005:13). As anthropology developed, its constitutive categories of analysis—race, language, and culture—slowly emerged as distinct objects of inquiry conceptually but, somewhat artificially, sutured together as the prime subject matter of a four-field anthropology.

Thanks to the scholarship of George W. Stocking, Regna Darnell, and others, the basic assumptions of Boasian anthropology are well known (Stocking 2001:24–48; Darnell 2000). Also known is the way Boas and his students simultaneously developed the concept of culture, challenged ideas of racial inferiority, and institutionalized anthropology within institutions of higher education (Darnell 1971, 1982, 1998, 2001; Stocking 1966, 1968, 1974).

Anthropology and anthropologists have been active, not always willing, participants in the messy race and culture wars that raged in the United States throughout the twentieth century and continue today. The modern anthropological concepts of race and culture that are, rightly or wrongly, credited to Boas's research and writing served as powerful tools to challenge white supremacy, curtail the vanishing policies imposed upon American Indians, legitimate distinctive African American beliefs and practices, and end racial segregation and disfranchisement. Although this is a powerful and important legacy of which anthropologists today might feel proud, the specific histories and the particular way in which anthropologists made these cumulative contributions were often ambivalent, usually contradictory, and never straightforward. More importantly, this legacy of American anthropology is the direct result of scholars, activists, lawyers, and government officials with little or no formal anthropological training having taken anthropology out of the academy to change the terms and conditions under which race and racism were constituted and cultures and languages were protected.

The School of Americanist Anthropology, Not the American School of Anthropology

During the first part of the twentieth century, anthropology in the United States became a successful and powerful discipline because it explained the culture of out-of-the-way indigenous peoples, influencing law and policy from the Philippines to Puerto Rico. Anthropologists had less success describing the culture of the many in-the-way immigrant and black people. That job went to sociologists committed to the study of assimilation and race relations. One of the foundational claims of sociologists and psychologists who studied race relations was that the races were neither inherently superior nor innately inferior to each other and that any aggregate differences between the races were the result of historical and environmental factors. This was the Boasian concept of race that was formed from the tailings of the crafted concept of culture (Baker 1998; Steinberg 2007:70; Myrdal 1964:146–50).

According to early twentieth-century sociologists, the unique mental and cultural traits of Negroes and Orientals flourished only as a result of racial prejudice, which prohibited integration and assimilation. Discrimination leads to segregation, the argument went, which leads to race consciousness, which leads to the propagation and perpetuation of social practices inimical to the ideals of the nation. According to the sociologist Robert Park, "The chief obstacle to assimilation of the Negro and the Oriental are not mental but physical traits. It is not because the Negro and the Japanese are so differently constituted that they do not assimilate. If they were given an opportunity the Japanese are quite as capable as the Italians, Armenians, or the Slavs of acquiring our culture and sharing our national ideals. The trouble is not with the Japanese mind but with the Japanese skin. The Jap is not the right color" (1914:610–11).

Sociology continued to hold the line regarding the value of assimilation, and this discourse contributed to the theoretical foundation for the movement to desegregate schools, the military, and neighborhoods, while anthropology developed its line regarding the value of particular cultures. That discourse became part of the theoretical basis for the drive to create day schools on reservations, cease land allotments, and incorporate tribal governments. In both cases, it was not easy, and the movements did not last long. Moreover, each discourse advanced constituent constructs that American Indians and African Americans continue to grapple with and negotiate today—essentialism, pathology, and authenticity.

While anthropology marshaled its nascent authority to describe the difference of exterior others, sociology marshaled its nascent authority to document the sameness of interior others. By the 1920s, both sociology and anthropology rejected notions of biological inferiority, but each embraced different ways of describing customs and behavior.

If we take Kamala Visweswaran's contentious account that "race was seen to be what culture was not" (1998a:70) as a starting point of Boasian articulations of race sundered from culture, then the ways in which late nineteenth-century anthropologists conceptualized ideas of the cultural as opposed to the strictly racial need to be scrutinized. Boas erected his powerhouse of anthropology that shaped the study of American race relations on the foundation of Americanist anthropology, or the ethnology of American Indian culture and language, which can be distinguished from the so-called American School of Anthropology, which propped up pro-slavery arguments (Fredrickson 2002:66–67). Framing twentieth-century formations of race and culture in this way has important implications in terms of identifying the role Native Americans played in the history of ideas and the construction of race. This frame also defines relationships between Native American, African American, and American studies, as well as each discipline's relationship to anthropology.

From Thomas Jefferson's and Peter S. Du Ponceau's efforts to collect American Indian vocabularies in the late eighteenth century to Charles Caldwell's and Samuel Morton's efforts to measure skulls to defend slavery in the mid-nineteenth century, anthropology in its many eighteenth- and nineteenth-century guises consistently examined African American brains and bodies and Native American customs and languages. Although there was considerable slippage and overlap, one can and perhaps should make a distinction between the American School of Anthropology and the School of Americanist Anthropology. The former was pioneered by Josiah Clark Nott, Samuel Morton, and Louis Agassiz and focused on brains and bodies to rank-order races, and the latter was pioneered by Albert Gallatin and Du Ponceau and focused on grammar and philology to categorize languages (Patterson 2001:7–23; Darnell 2008:37; Conn 2004:87). I argue that the Boasian concept of race was a product of the School of Americanist Anthropology, not of the American School of Anthropology. More specifically, it was a product of the product of Americanist anthropology.

Matti Bunzl demonstrates the influence of German scholars such as Johann Gottfried von Herder and Wilhelm von Humboldt on the early work of Boas (Bunzl 1996). Bunzl argues that Boas's critical approach to ethnology should be distinguished from that of Bronislaw Malinowski, who routinized the Self/"Other" dichotomy (Bunzl 1996; 2004). By extension, Bunzl distinguishes Boas from his contemporaries of both American schools who were obsessed with describing the "Other" and in a racialized hierarchy. Bunzl explains that "for Boas, the reason to explore cultural phenomena was not that they were 'Other' but that they were 'there'" (Bunzl 2004: 437). But who were there? For Boas, it was Indians.

The languages, customs, and folklore studied by members of the Bureau of American Ethnology (BAE), the American Folk-Lore Society, and Section H of the American Association for the Advancement of Science (AAAS) were overwhelmingly, but not exclusively, American Indian. According to calculations made by Brad Evans, for every ten articles in the anthropological literature addressing American Indians, there was one discussing American Negroes or Africans (2005:75). Boas made choices, and occasionally he wrote about people other than American Indians, but by and large the provenance of the cultural stuff he used to differentiate race from language and culture were his studies among indigenous folks in the Americas.

The anthropological concept of race that social scientists, lawyers, and journalists used to transform American race relations developed in tandem with the anthropological concept of culture used to understand American Indian languages and customs. This claim is based on Darnell's analysis that when Boas came to the United States, he extended the Americanist tradition that was pioneered by Gallatin but institutionalized by John W. Powell at the BAE (Darnell 1998:179). Although one could argue that W. J. McGee, Daniel G. Brinton, and Aleš Hrdlička were heirs to the American School of Anthropology, Darnell suggests that Frank Hamilton Cushing, James Mooney, Francis La Flesche, and the agents of the BAE were the real innovators of Americanist anthropology that developed during the first half of the twentieth century. Darnell is both clear and convincing in stating that "although Boas rejected the bureau's party-line evolutionary interpretation, he built his own historical particularist theory directly on the philological data accumulated under Powell's auspices" (2001:11).

Most scholars would agree with Paul Rabinow's suggestion that "Boas's arguments against racial hierarchies and racial thinking have thoroughly carried the theoretical day" (Rabinow 1992:60). Yet students of the history of anthropology rarely make the necessary connections between Boas's arguments for historical particularism that influenced the Wheeler-Howard Act (1934) and his arguments against racial hierarchies that influenced *Brown v. Board of Education* (1954). There is a relationship between Boas's arguments against racial hierarchies and his careful collecting and recording of Indian texts, grammars, and vocabularies. Moreover, there is a contingent relationship between the concept of culture that is pluralistic and distinctive and Americanist anthropology. Boas's critique of racialist science and the concept of culture is tethered to what William Y. Adams calls "indianology," which was the subject of much of early anthropology (1998:93).

Beginning with Lewis Henry Morgan through Powell and Frederic W. Putnam and continuing with Boas and his students, the primary focus of academic anthropological inquiry in the United States was American Indian languages, customs, and material culture (Adams 1998; Bernstein 2002; Bourguignon 1996; Browman 2002; Darnell 2001; Hallowell 1960:15; Patterson 2001; Stocking 1974; Yanagisako 2005). Erika Bourguignon has explained that from the beginnings of anthropology "until World War II and the subsequent great expansion of anthropology, most anthropologists were Americanists," and she emphasized that "the essence and primary task of American anthropology was the study of American Indians" (1996:7).

There is little argument with the fact that academic anthropology did not create this field of significance but instead traded on and legitimated a peculiar idea that describing, analyzing, and recording American Indian languages and customs was necessary and needed for the young nation to forge a distinctive American identity (Adams 1998:193; Conn 2004:91; Deloria 1998:94; Kasson 2000:218; Patterson 2001:32; Trouillot 2003:27; Yanagisako 2005:82). At the same time, the federal government needed to establish sovereignty over its land and was compelled to civilize the Indians. Both processes quickened a wicked and seemingly contradictory cycle of knowledge production and cultural destruction.

Michel-Rolph Trouillot forcefully enunciates, "The 'scientific' study of the Savage *qua* Savage became the privileged field of academic anthropology" (2003:18). As "anthropology came to fill the 'Savage' slot" (2003:19), it also came to fill the "salvage slot," and it is important to keep the latter in mind when discussing the former (2003:19). Anthropologists enthusiastically contributed to the knowing of American Indians that led to Janus-faced notions of utopia (Trouillot 2003), processed the raw material that enabled settlers to lay a legitimate claim to the land (Yanagisako 2005), and was party to the denial of American Indian coevalness (Fabian 1983). However, most anthropologists were sincerely motivated by the more mundane and scientific imperative to record and analyze disappearing languages and customs in the wake of the calamitous and destructive Civil and Indian wars.

Before the Great Depression, anthropologists were perhaps overly concerned with American Indian culture, while not being much concerned with African American culture (Bernstein 2002:554). Many African American intellectuals like Carter G. Woodson, Alain Locke, and James Weldon Johnson, however, were nevertheless interested in using anthropology to describe what they understood as a rich, distinctive culture that was historical and particular. At the same time, American Indian intellectuals like Zikala-Ša, Charles Eastman, and Simon Pokagon resisted and distrusted the often well-intentioned anthropologists. There were, of course, prominent American Indian intellectuals who supported anthropology, and several, like Arthur Parker, Ella Deloria, and La Flesche, became influential anthropologists. Likewise, there were many black social scientists who completely rejected anthropological concepts of culture. Nevertheless, an interesting pattern emerged from the late 1890s through the 1920s: African American intellectuals consistently appropriated anthropology to authenticate their culture, while Native American intellectuals consistently rejected anthropology to protect their culture.

Market Commodities and Museum Pieces

The various and conflicting roles that anthropology and specific ethnologists played as American Indian policies and attitudes changed over time were as varied as they were ambivalent, but what emerged was a unique and informative racial politics of culture that often pitted progressive white anthropologists and conservative Indian traditionalists against progressive Indian activists and conservative Christian reformers. A tug-of-war ensued over the meaning, value, and role indigenous cultures could and should have in the future of Native North America. Kinship and community, ritual and religion became central foci of contestation within heated debates over education, representation, land, and religious freedom. Well-meaning anthropologists were committed to "salvaging" cultures that were putatively disappearing by curating objects, narrating practices, and recording languages. These anthropologists were often allied with Native Americans committed to conserving and celebrating indigenous practices that resisted the assimilation project of the government and the civilizing mission of the reformers.

The so-called progressive Native North Americans were a diverse group of intellectuals whose work, faith, and zeal mirrored that of their contemporary and peer Booker T. Washington. They shared a belief in mutual progress, civilization, and an unwavering expectation that Indians were capable, even more capable than Negroes and east European immigrants, of assimilating American culture and partaking in all of the rights and responsibilities of U.S. citizenry. In 1911, six prominent progressives founded the Society of American Indians (SAI), a pan-Indian racial uplift group that resembled in many ways the National Association for the Advancement of Colored People (NAACP), organized two years earlier. Highly critical of the government's Office of Indian Affairs, the SAI fought for legal and political representation but set a course different from that of the Lake Mohonk Conference of Friends of the Indian and the Philadelphia-based Indian Rights Association. Unlike these white Christian reform groups, the SAI used Indian blood to police the boundaries of membership. From the beginning, the organizers were clear that Indians would run this organization (Maddox 2005:11). Drawing on older traditions of pan-Indian and intertribal cooperation, these Indian activists waged an explicit campaign against racism and oppression, often evoking Tecumseh, the early nineteenth-century Shawnee chief who tried to unite northern and southern nations in a military alliance to prevent further Westward expansion (Hertzberg 1971:36–37; Porter 2001:92). While there was consensus that the SAI should promote self-help by cultivating race consciousness, intertribal cooperation, and pride in Indian heritage, there was not a consensus that Indians should take pride in their culture, which was often viewed as "a real hindrance and obstacle in the way of civilization" (Eastman 1896:93).

In the broadest terms, the progressives shared with the supposedly conservative educators and reformers a faith in the benevolent ideals of progress embedded in social Darwinism and the civilizing mission. These Christian reformers were far from conservative. Committed to assimilation policies, this group of progressive reformers initially crusaded for the abolition of slavery. Following the Civil War, they extended their efforts to promote education for both Indians and Negroes, women's suffrage, settlement houses, and temperance (Hoxie 1984:ix; Utley 1964:154).

It is tempting to delineate the agendas of the SAI and anthropologists by suggesting that the anthropologists were contributing to a progressive yet nostalgic antimodernism by scientifically authenticating Indian behavior in an effort "to restore infinite meaning to an increasingly finite world" (Lears 1981:58), whereas the members of the SAI were simply chasing the allure and spoils of a modernism that too often used a bareback-riding brave as the trope with which to measure the advance of human progress. One can easily understand how members of the SAI combated stereotypes and oppression by employing a kind of strategic assimilation in which individuals sought to gain respect by embracing and performing respectability. However, these adjectives—modern and anti-modern, conservative and progressive—simply fail upon stricter scrutiny, and the debates over preservation and assimilation should not be reduced to "the crude calculus of interest and intention" (Comaroff and Comaroff 1991:7).

The racial politics of culture during the decades leading up to the New Deal were complicated and belie any "crude calculus," but anthropology played an important political role in authenticating the genuine culture many people, white and Indian, desired to perform, protect, and police (Sapir 1924:409; Deloria 1998:94). Anthropologists helped to engineer a timeless aboriginal Indian culture by subjecting Native Americans to what Curtis Hinsley calls "the museum process," which "constructed a meaning of Indian demise within the teleology of manifest destiny; it indirectly addressed the insistent doubts of Gilded Age Americans over the import of industrial capitalism; and it did so by encasing, in time and space, the American Indian" (1989:170). Hinsley argues that dehistoricization was the essence of the process, but entertainment and theater were key elements that cultivated and commodified desire, transforming "autonomous historical agents to market commodities and museum pieces." World's Fairs, Wild West shows, artifact and curio shops, tourist attractions, anthropology museums and publications, Indian folklore, novels, and ritual as well as the many youth camps where boys and girls played

Indian were all "public spaces for safe consumption of a newly dehistor-
icized Indian" (Hinsley 1989:170). In 1907 Boas suggested even that "the
value of the museum as a resort for popular entertainment must not be
underrated. . . . If a museum is to serve this end, it must, first of all, be
entertaining" (1907:621–22).

The consumption of a pacified and out-of-the-way Indian in Wild West
shows, World's Fairs, and museums needs to be juxtaposed with the consumption of a dangerous and in-the-way Negro in blackface minstrelsy,
professionally promoted lynchings, and buffoon-saturated advertising.
World's Fair organizers routinely turned down requests by African
Americans to erect Negro exhibits, and philanthropists simply rejected
requests to erect a museum to showcase African and African American
achievements. While many performers dressed up to offer allegedly authentic renditions of somber Indians, others blackened up to present exaggerated renditions of knee-slapping Negroes. Furthermore, there was
simply no African American analog to the Camp Fire Girls and Indian
Guides, organizations of young middle-class whites whose activities included dressing up to play Sambo.[1]

Although Mooney, Powell, and even Boas never spoke in terms of authentic and inauthentic, they routinely evaluated practices, languages, and
even phenotypes as being more or less conservative, aboriginal, or real.
Alexander Chamberlain suggested even that most primitives suffered
"insuperable neophobia," which served as something like a prophylactic
to prevent the decay of culture (1903:337). Each man attempted through
anthropological science to demarcate and determine what and who was
really Indian and what and who was not; whose culture was worthy of
study; and whose culture was lost and too far beyond the pale to be worth
investigation.

Ill Effects of Mind Poison

A turning point in this overall shift from assimilation to conservation was
the failure of the Hayden Bill to become law [H.R. 2614 (1918)]. This legislation was tied to the temperance movement, and it would have made
the use of peyote a federal offense. The U.S. House of Representatives
Subcommittee of the Committee on Indian Affairs debated this bill in
the so-called peyote hearings held in the winter of 1918, at the zenith of

the wider temperance movement (Hertzberg 1971:275). Just as these hearings commenced, individual states began to ratify the Eighteenth Amendment to the U.S. Constitution, which prohibited the sale, manufacture, or transportation of alcohol.

The hearings were one of the more dramatic moments when anthropology's authority to authenticate the Indian was seriously challenged by indigenous intellectuals and Christian reformers, but anthropological authority held fast to win the day. By briefly reviewing the debate, I hope to illustrate what I mean by anthropology's role in helping to shape the racial politics of culture, which is a key theme throughout this book and is nicely telescoped by the hearings' format. Although anthropologists helped to constitute a theory of culture that underwrote these dramatic shifts in federal Indian policy and beyond, they often did it by marshaling scientific authority to authenticate particular Indian practices as genuine, while explicitly and implicitly designating those practices they did not certify as fraudulent, broken, or simply not authentic.

American Indian intellectuals, several of whom were anthropologists, both challenged and contributed to this anthropological project that tenaciously debunked ideas of Indian racial and cultural inferiority by stressing how communal Indian cultures were unique and distinctive (cf. Hoxie 1984:142). Moments like the peyote hearings exemplify how anthropologists publicly described what culture is and privately delimited what race was not.

Freedom, justice, liberty, and equality—the so-called virtues of democracy—are among the powerful tools used by scholars, activists, lawyers, and politicians to make the United States a more perfect union. Unlike equality and justice, religious freedom is such an unambiguous and fundamental value held by so many Americans that it has rarely been evoked in struggles for equality. Even though bitter anti-Catholic and anti-Semitic movements have plagued the United States, the federal government never considered abrogating the First Amendment for Catholics and Jews—Indians, however, were different. The First Amendment states that "Congress shall make no law respecting an establishment of religion, or prohibiting the free exercise thereof," but in 1883 Congress passed the Indian Religious Crimes Code, which virtually outlawed all dances, ceremonies, and religious rites. Part of the government's efforts to assimilate the Indian, the code called for the imprisonment of practitioners and instructed bureau agents to focus their efforts on the "medicine men" (Irwin

1997:35). Combined with the fact that the peyote cactus can induce hallucinations or visions, the so-called peyote cult was one religious practice that generated a high level of controversy, persecution, and suspicion.

The peyote hearings of 1918 are a fecund site to analyze the tug-of-war over Indian culture and policy. First, the most important players involved in these issues squared off in one place. Zitkala-Ša, Charles Eastman, Francis La Flesche, James Mooney, and Richard Pratt all testified, and each person articulated his or her views by crafting responses to questions posed by members of the congressional committee while trying to debunk the testimony of the other witnesses.

The hearings were also an important pivotal point in the overall shift from assimilation to conservation, and many of the Indian progressives were split over the issue, revealing important fault lines and competing visions of the future (Swan 1999:6). Finally, the requisite mudslinging and name-calling revealed the role ethnology played in this high-stakes game of ethnographic authentication.

James Mooney (1861–1921), for example, was a white ethnologist from the Smithsonian Institution who was deeply committed to the rights and well-being of the Kiowa, Comanche, and Apache groups he studied. He argued at the hearings that "the use of this plant is not an ordinary habit, but . . . is confined almost entirely and strictly to the religious ceremony, excepting that it is frequently employed also for medicinal purposes" (Peyote Hearings 1918:69 [hereafter PH]).[2] In order to make this argument, Mooney decided he must first challenge the authority of Zitkala-Ša (1876–1938), a Yankton Lakota and secretary-treasurer of the SAI who was supported by powerful women in the temperance movement. She provided compelling testimony at the hearings against any use of peyote. Mooney, who supported the ceremonial and medicinal uses of peyote, went on the offensive, attacking her credibility by challenging her authenticity.

Zitkala-Ša launched a media campaign to coincide with the hearings, and it worked. The *Washington Times* ran a story that basically amounted to an interview of Zitkala-Ša (also known as Gertrude Bonnin) detailing the ill "effects of mind poison" (February 7, 1918:1). To accompany the story, the paper published an image of Zitkala-Ša in its front-page coverage of the hearing. Holding up a copy of the paper, Mooney explained to the members of Congress that the woman in the photograph "claims to be a Sioux woman," but she is wearing "a woman's dress from a southern tribe, as shown by the long fringes; the belt is a Navajo man's belt; the fan is a peyote man's fan carried only by men usually in the peyote ceremony" (PH 1918:63). Ostensibly, her gender bending and mixing of specific tribal elements on her body impeached her credibility and thus her claim to speak in the best interest of her people. As Mooney reminded the members of Congress, "An Indian delegate from a sectarian body or alleged uplift organization is not a delegate for his tribe" (PH 1918:149). Mooney implied that only the scientific eye of a seasoned ethnologist could identify these transgressions, which heightened his authority while diminishing hers.

The august General Richard H. Pratt could not let Mooney get away with promoting "these nightly orgies that have been described so graphically by the Bureau of Ethnology itself" (PH 1918:144). He challenged the scientific authority of ethnographic inquiry and implied that it was not the Indians but white anthropologists who were responsible for the growing use of peyote. In a heated exchange between Pratt and Mooney, Pratt addressed Mooney directly: "You ethnologists egg on, frequent, illustrate, and exaggerate at the public expense, and so give the Indian race and their civilization a black eye in the public esteem" (PH 1918:147).

Zitkala-Ša did not address Pratt or Mooney directly but chose to appeal to the conscience of the committee members. Calling peyote the "twin brother of alcohol, and first cousin to habit forming drugs," she pleaded, "Mr. Chairman, were the life of your loved one threatened by a pernicious drug, would you care a straw what the ethnologists had written about the drug; how many years they had studied the drug? No; because the civilized man has studied for centuries other habit-forming drugs; but that study does not warrant anyone giving it to another in the name of religion today" (PH 1918:164,165).

Charles Eastman, the esteemed Indian physician and Dartmouth graduate, took a different approach: He explained that the use of peyote "is not an Indian idea nor is it an Indian practice. It is more like what happened a few years ago during the ghost-dance craze, which, as we all know, was gotten up by irresponsible, reckless, and unprincipled people" (PH 1918:139). Eastman believed the use of peyote should be banned because it was not an Indian practice, but La Flesche reversed this argument to support its use as a sacrament. La Flesche was Omaha and an anthropologist who was elected in 1912 as vice president of the American Anthropological Association (AAA) (Mark 1982; Hoxie 2001:180). At the time of the peyote hearings, La Flesche was a member of the sai and disagreed with his sai colleagues Eastman and Zitkala-Ša on this issue. According to La Flesche, the use of peyote was part of a new, accommodating religion that helped Indians to avoid liquor and uplift the race. La Flesche argued, "The Indians who have taken the new religion strive to live upright, moral lives" (PH 1918:114).

At first blush, the contested but sincere beliefs for and against the use of peyote may seem like a dizzying array of contradictory statements and rhetorical jockeying. Upon closer inspection, one can identify the logic that bolsters each participant's political position. All the participants in these hearings had their own histories and political commitments forged in response to the assimilation policies promulgated by state and federal governments. The peyote hearings were but one example of many culture wars fought over well-meaning enterprises that too often turned on the lose-lose goal of either preserving or assimilating American Indian cultural practices. Mooney's hard line regarding who and what was genuine and what was authentic was typical of Americanist anthropology. It was also convincing. The Hayden Bill died in committee, and later that year Mooney helped to charter the Native American Church to strengthen legal protections for those who followed the peyote way (Willard 1991:35).[3]

In the wake of the hearings, some American Indians who were skeptical of assimilation began to see anthropology and anthropologists as allies in their fight to protect religious freedoms and resist the civilizing mission. At the same time, popular magazines and travel publications began in earnest to highlight sensitive yet romantic portrayals of Indian life—not as occupying the bottom rung of a ladder leading to civilization, but on Indians' own terms (Dilworth 1996; Jacobs 1999).

The spectacle of genuine and authentic culture that had not completely vanished was integral to the professionalization and popularization of the discipline during an era of progressive reform. Anthropology helped to shape an understanding of culture often underpinning rather unstable politics of race and culture that too often masked consistent and persistent racism and genocide (Churchill 1997). Ideas about culture also served as a central concept in attempts to empower Native Americans during the New Deal and African Americans during the New Negro movement; as well, the same concepts reappeared as critical elements of the Red and Black Power movements of the 1960s and 1970s.

Relationships between American Indian communities and anthropologists have often been tinged with ambivalence and derision (Deloria 1969:78–100). Despite, or, I suppose, in spite of, the less-than-amicable relationships, Americanists like Mooney and Boas consistently focused on customs, languages, and religions of American Indians that were very different from their own and explained them as legitimate practices that could be understood in terms of history and culture. They did not explicitly link these differences to ideas of race or to ideas of backwardness, inferiority, and illegitimacy.[4]

Does the Negro Have Culture?

One could see the appeal of this approach to Negroes, who were constantly barraged by experts like Nathan Southgate Shaler of Harvard University, who explained, in typical fashion, that "the Negro is not as yet intellectually so far up the scale of development as he appears to be; in him the great virtues of the superior race, though implanted, have not yet taken firm root, and are in need of constant tillage, lest the old savage weeds overcome the tender shoots of the new and unnatural culture" (1890:42). And while the inferiority of Negroes' race and culture was a constant refrain, the superiority of whites served to reinforce that hierarchy. For example, Frederick Hoffman, the esteemed actuary of Prudential Life Insurance, wrote in his influential article "Race, Traits, and Tendencies of the American Negro" that "it is not in the conditions of life, but in race and heredity that we find the explanation of the fact to be observed in all parts of the globe, in all times and among all peoples, namely, the superiority of one race over another, and of the Aryan race over all" (1896:312).

There has been a strong and long intellectual tradition among both American Indian and African American scholars of resisting and challenging racist and derogatory discourse and policies (Warrior 1995:1–44). These intellectual traditions of critique, vindication, and sovereignty were never homogeneous and often conflicted, as evidenced by the peyote hearings. Among African American communities, battle lines were often drawn identical to those within American Indian communities. Anthropologists were also called to assist, but it was difficult to outflank sociologists, who had long been busy describing African American customs, behaviors, and values in terms of race relations and racial uplift. As a result of occupying the so-called savage slot, anthropologists could exert scientific authority and push back organizations like the SAI and convince Congress, for example, not to prohibit the use of peyote and to pass the Indian Reorganization Act. Anthropologists, however, could not compete on the terrain of culture when it came to black people.

Early in the twentieth century, sociologists used anthropology to assert that Negroes were not biologically inferior, yet many sociologists employed Park's race relations cycle, which was explicitly teleological—moving from conflict to cooperation to accommodation and to its final destination, assimilation. It was the ultimate vanishing policy, under which any distinctive and particular custom or value expressed by an immigrant could and should be forever eclipsed by allegedly conventional habits and values (Baker 1998:168–77; Degler 1991:7; Lyman 1968:17).

Sociologists had the support of organizations like the National Urban League and the Rockefeller Foundation, which blindly promoted assimilation and racial uplift. Nevertheless, any practices or customs Negroes performed that differed from some mainstream norm were all too often explained in terms of deviance or pathology or simply as obstacles in the way of complete assimilation. Sociologists like Park, E. Franklin Frazier, and Guy B. Johnson leveraged the momentum of the progressive era, the mission of black colleges, and the sentiments of much of the Negro elite to convince the nation of the potency of racial uplift and the healing power of assimilation. Racial uplift and assimilation were not much more than euphemisms for evolution and civilization, minus the biological component. More importantly, this was assimilation without integration, racial uplift without equal rights. Although the approach was anti-African and elitist, it was radical, counterhegemonic, and pro-black because it was premised on the fact that racism, slavery, and poverty crippled the lives of black people.[5]

Viewed from the perspective of progressive-era sociology, anthropologists salvaged not only Indian relics, languages, and traditions, but also the very idea of culture from reformers like the founders of the SAI and the Lake Mohonk Friends of the Indian, who would have liked to see it all melt in the pot (Trachtenberg 2004:41). These Indian reformers were cut from the same cloth as the members of the Women's Club movement, Temperance Union, settlement house movement, and the Tuskegee machine—all of whom were joined in a global struggle to discipline, clean, educate, and civilize all of the dusky, swarthy people throughout growing empires (Anderson 2006). Each organization was committed to shaping modern reform by embracing the moral values of thrift, individualism, personal hygiene, hard work, and the Christian family. Americanist anthropology gained momentum during the progressive era too, but Americanist anthropology was articulated in a different register and often viewed as going hand in hand with protecting wilderness, creating national parks, preserving archaeological remains, and managing fish and wildlife. For example, the A A A linked the Parks Service with the B I A when it applauded the federal government's advancement of anthropology. The A A A reported in 1906 that:

> It is encouraging to note on the part of the National Government a better appreciation than ever before of the needs of anthropology. Among other evidences of this spirit is the recent enactment by Congress of the law . . . for the preservation of antiquities on public domain. . . . A step in a similar direction is the provision made by Congress at its last session for the establishment of the Mesa Verde National Park in Colorado, which contains some of the most important cliff-dwellings in the United States. . . .
>
> For many years the Office of Indian Affairs maintained a policy of trying to eliminate everything aboriginal from the American Indian by substituting there for something that originated with the white man, whether or not it was adapted to the Indian's needs. But the present Commissioner of Indian Affairs, Honorable Francis F. Leupp, who has long been an earnest student of the Indian problem, finds good in the aborigines that his predecessors seem to have overlooked, and is securing the means for encouraging some of the native industries. (American Anthropologists 1906:444)

By the early 1920s, anthropologists unequivocally asserted that American Indian groups maintained distinctive and particular cultures that should not be subjected to vanishing policies or federally sponsored assimilation schemes. Anthropologists were equivocal, however, when it came to the culture of American Negroes. For example, Boas asserted in 1911 that "the North American negroes, [were] a people by descent largely African; in culture and language, however, essentially European. While it is true that certain survivals of African culture and language are found among our American negroes, their culture is essentially that of the uneducated classes of people among whom they live, and their language is on the whole identical with that of their neighbors" (1911a:8). As late as 1925, Melville Herskovits offered his ethnological analysis of Harlem and concluded that it "was a community just like any other American community. The same pattern, only a different shade! . . . May it not then be true that the Negro has become acculturated to the prevailing white culture and has developed the patterns of culture typical of American life?" (1999 [1925]:353–54). In these instances, both Boas and Herskovits were trying to argue that blacks were not unlike whites and therefore should not be subjected to discrimination. Boas supported people like Woodson, who used the science of anthropology to authenticate Negroes' African heritage to empower black people to appreciate their heritage. Boas, however, was "absolutely opposed to all kinds of attempts to foster racial solidarity."[6] Furthermore, he favored cultural assimilation as an effective strategy to ameliorate the Negro problem (1905:87). Boas went beyond supporting a strategy of assimilation to advocate phenotypic miscegenation, explaining that "the negro problem will not disappear in America until the negro blood has been so much diluted that it will no longer be recognized just as anti-Semitism will not disappear until the vestige of the Jew as a Jew has disappeared" (1921:395).

But the question remained: Did the Negro have culture? And if Negroes did, was it worth salvaging, protecting, or cultivating? The answer to the question was not empirical but political. Whether one labels it the Herskovits/Frazier debate or the Boas/Parks division, two different discourses animated competing racial politics of culture, and both are woven into the genealogy and history of race in America. One pivoted on the value of cultural heritage, the other on racial uplift.

During the first half of the twentieth century, Boas and his students developed research that focused on the environment to explain the flexibility and essential equality of racial groups and the relativity of bounded traditional cultures. Although sporadically, they effectively used this understanding of race to help advance the civil and political rights of African Americans and, to a lesser extent, American Indians (Boas 1938 [1911a]; Benedict and Weltfish 1943; Powdermaker 1993 [1939]; Montagu 1952 [1942], 1951; Klineberg 1931; Redfield 1950:192–205). As I have argued previously, what eventually emerged in anthropology was a tightly knit discourse that aligned theories of racial equality with notions of historically specific cultural relativity. By solidifying the academic consensus that racial inequality was not based on biological inferiority, scholars and

activists interested in promoting racial uplift, assimilation, and integration were able to unravel the bundle and use the Boasian concept of race
as an unimportant biological type exclusively, discarding the other part
about the relativity or value of cultures (Baker 1998:177). For people promoting African American assimilation, this approach proved effective.
For people promoting American Indian assimilation, this approach failed,
in part because anthropologists were so effective at documenting cultures
of American Indians and less effective at documenting cultures of African
Americans. Yet for American Indians this effectiveness had a downside
too because anthropologists collectively failed to interrogate the tumultuous history of contact. Oftentimes anthropologists perpetuated the idea
that American Indians were trapped in time because they were trapped
on reservations. The sardonic upside, however, was that Indians trans-
mitted a pure, authentic, and healthy culture to their children; the tragic
downside for Negroes was that they inherited a dangerous, counterfeit,
and pathological culture from their parents.

Zora Neale Hurston perhaps best exemplified the contrasting ways in
which many anthropologists viewed the difference between Indian and
Negro culture when she wrote to Boas in 1927 that "the Negro is not living his lore to the extent of the Indian. He is not on a reservation being
kept pure. His negroness is being rubbed off by close contact with white
culture" (Kaplan 2002:97).

I argue that anthropologists' failure to view Negro culture as authentic as Indian culture helped to shape the racial politics of two dominant
views of culture that emerged in the United States between the two world
wars—one outlined by Boas at Columbia University, the other by Park
at the University of Chicago. Although scholars articulated elements of
these two visions of culture in analyzing immigrants, American Indians,
and people in the insular protectorates, the sharpest distinctions between
culture and behavior were drawn in analyzing African Americans.

Boas eventually came to view African American culture in terms of
that "peculiar amalgamation of African and European tradition which is
so important for understanding historically the character of American
Negro life, with its strong African background in the West Indies, the
importance of which diminishes with increasing distance from the south"
(Boas 1978 [1935]:x). Park, on the other hand, maintained that "the Negro,
when he landed in the United States, left behind him almost everything
but his dark complexion and his tropical temperament. It is very difficult

to find in the South today anything that can be traced directly back to Africa" (1919:16). Stated differently, Park believed that those Negroes who could and would assimilate had a legitimate claim to American culture, but those who suffered the full brunt of discrimination and structural inequality were simply mired in bad behavior and shackled by the legacy of slavery.

During the New Negro movement, intellectuals such as Herskovits, Arthur H. Fauset, Hurston, Arthur Schomburg, Woodson, and W. E. B. Du Bois often used Boas's work to authenticate the distinctive culture of the Negro (Gershenhorn 2004). Other scholars, such as Frazier, Charles Johnson, Ralph Bunche, and Guy B. Johnson, accepted the Boasian notion of racial equality but discarded the emphasis on cultural history. These scholars focused on class and extended the sociological view of Negro behavior advanced by Park (J. Holloway 2002).

The Boas-influenced heritage project privileged history, diffusion, and African cultural continuities, which, they argued, helped to shape African American culture. This approach was influential among many intellectuals of the New Negro movement and the Harlem Renaissance who liked to explain difference in terms of culture, not race (Lamothe 2008). Often discounting issues of class, these intellectuals used the idea of an African homeland to craft a complicated cultural identity, as opposed to claiming a simple racial identity. Too often, however, this approach reproduced naive ideas of alterity and simply produced another Other. Folklore, musicology, cultural history, and art history were approaches these scholars deployed in a collective effort to vindicate and validate the past as well as the present. For example, Schomburg argued, "The Negro has been a man without a history because he has been considered a man without a worthy culture. But a new notion of cultural attainment and potentialities of the African stocks has recently come about, partly through the corrective influence of the more scientific study of African institutions and early cultural history" (1968 [1925]:237). Scholars influenced by Park's approach focused on eliminating substandard housing, poverty, and racial segregation. These social scientists maintained that so many individual Negroes have been uplifted so far that they have collectively progressed far enough—especially among the educated elite—to take their rightful place among the higher civilizations of "mankind." Yet members committed to this uplift project were forced to explain why so many blacks could not or would not conform to proper standards of behavior, and they basically argued that the history of slavery, racism, disfranchisement, and segregation was simply an insurmountable obstacle that other immigrants did not face (Williams 1989:113–48).

One of the most influential proponents of uplift was Frazier. He explained the "simple Negro folk culture" as an "incomplete assimilation of western culture by the Negro masses," arguing that "generally when two different cultures come into contact each modifies the other. But in the case of the Negro in America it meant the total destruction of the African social heritage. Therefore in the case of the family group the Negro has not introduced new patterns of behavior, but has failed to conform to patterns about him. The degree of conformity is determined by educational and economic factors as well as by social isolation" (1927:166). Frazier also understood that ideas of culture were always already tied to racial difference and was critical of the Boasian approach because "Negro crime, for example, could be explained away as an 'Africanism' rather than as due to inadequate police and court protection" (Myrdal 1964 [1944]:1242).

These social scientists usually pointed to statistics that compared Negroes' deviations to a white standard, which underscored the high number of female-headed households and fictive kin relations, and these so-called deviant practices were conflated with high rates of crime, disease, and poverty. Together, they became indelible signs of deviant behavior or a pathological culture. Too often, the causal arrow pointed to the black mother or the matriarch as the catalyst for the calamitous experiences in black communities (Frazier 1939:89). Even at the height of the Harlem Renaissance, the heritage project was simply dwarfed by the uplift project. Even Du Bois's—what I would term—ethical humanity project could not compete with the powerful narrative of individual uplift and collective blame. Paralleling the lose-lose outcome of either assimilation or preservation among American Indians, Stephanie Y. Evans explains, the black "middle class was ultimately caught between the rock of primitivism and the hard place of bourgeois aspirations" (2007:65).

Perhaps the high-water mark of the racial uplift project's narrative was its inclusion in *The Negro Family: The Case For National Action* (1965), an influential report written by Daniel Patrick Moynihan, who was serving as the assistant secretary of labor under President Lyndon B. Johnson. Moynihan argued that "at the center of the tangle of pathology is the weakness of the family structure . . . it will be found to be the principal source of most of the aberrant, inadequate, or antisocial behavior that did not

establish, but now serves to perpetuate the cycle of poverty and depri-
vation" (1965). At the heart of the problem, according to Moynihan, was
a pattern of kinship that empowered women to head households, a pattern that Moynihan believed was inimical to gender norms and American
values and destructive of black manhood. Both sexist and racist, the well-
meaning and putatively liberal Moynihan used his report to help wage the
war on poverty and shape federal welfare programs. It was a hegemonic
paradigm, yet it was consistently challenged, for example, during the New
Negro movement of the 1920s and the Black Power movements in the
1960s. It was not seriously challenged, however, in the public's imagination or in federal policies until the women's and multicultural movements
of the seventies and eighties.

Versions of these two projects (uplift and heritage) continue today.
During 2007, Bill Cosby, for example, was on a media blitz blaming the
victim and promoting his book while recycling Frazier's dire mantra
that the problems black people face today stem from the fact that many
women are forced to head households. The crux of Cosby's latter-day uplift message can be reduced to the fact that "a mother can usually teach
a daughter how to be a woman, but as much as mothers love their sons,
they have difficulty showing a son how to be a man. A successful man can
channel his natural aggression. Without that discipline, these sons often
get in trouble at school because many teachers find it difficult to manage
their 'acting out behavior'" (Cosby and Poussaint 2007:4).

As for the heritage project, Rick Kittles has almost single-handedly
brought to life the Afro-centric idea with his company African Ancestry,
which markets itself with a catchy and deceivingly simple slogan, "Trace
your DNA. Find your Roots." The company really took off after Henry
Louis "Skip" Gates Jr. hosted a PBS documentary in which he used Kittles's
services to help celebrities such as Oprah Winfrey, Chris Rock, Whoopi
Goldberg, and T. D. Jakes map their DNA to identify the ethnic group in
Africa for which they could claim ancestry. In its confidence that with
"one simple test" you too can "determine your family's country of origin," Kittles's postmodern and high-tech approach to the heritage project,
ironically, takes one back to the nineteenth century, when biology and
culture were not yet sundered. For seven hundred dollars you can use
your biology to identify your culture.

The tension between uplift and heritage has been a staple within African American and Native American communities for generations, and

it serves as a key theme throughout this book on the racial politics of culture. In recent decades, anthropologists have scrutinized the concept of culture; at the same time, however, other disciplines, institutions, foundations, industries, media conglomerates, and social groups have institutionalized what can rightly be seen as a skewed but nevertheless anthropologically inflected idea of culture (Fabian 1983; Clifford 1988; Abu-Lughod 1991; Trouillot 1991; Visweswaran 1998; Briggs 2002; Evans 2005; Williams 2006). For example, people routinely speak of distinctive corporate or campus cultures, while talk radio pundits speak glibly about the culture inside the Beltway—as if members of Congress are the only people living in Washington, D.C. With the advent of the cochlear implant, some activists in deaf communities have decried the end of deaf culture, prompting the National Association of the Deaf to issue a statement recommending that parents of implanted children "receive education in deaf studies, including deaf heritage, [and] history of deafness and deaf people" (National Association of the Deaf 2000).

For better or worse, the concept of culture as most folks in the United States understand it is tethered to what Charles Briggs described as an epistemological land-grab during a period of history when the discursive terrain of the behavioral sciences was literally up for grabs (2002:481). However, despite the way anthropological analytics have been appropriated within popular parlance, anthropologists are not alone. Social psychologists have grappled with the way people use or misuse the term "identity"; sociologists bemoan the fact that the notion of deviance has been sorely overused; economists no longer hold sway over the compound term "cost-benefit"; and historians have always been leery of the way people throw around the word "history."

I understand the critique about bounded and essentialist ideas of culture, and I am often persuaded by the analysis. Moreover, I understand all too well the downside of essentialism as well as the danger of viewing culture as stuck and timeless, and I personally understand how a static notion of culture can bleed into ideas of authenticity and give life to a ridiculous line of inquiry that turns on a single question: Is Barack Obama black enough? It is this skewed appropriation of anthropologically inflected ideas of culture that sanctions and authorizes the so-called "Soul Patrol," the self-proclaimed culture cops who demarcate rather narrow boundaries of blackness. Even though this criticism of the culture concept is seductive, I still have to agree with that oft-cited line James Clifford penned some twenty years ago: "Culture is a deeply compromised idea I cannot yet do without" (1988:10).

Throughout U.S. history, anthropologically informed concepts of culture have been used to advance civil rights and achieve justice, but they have also been employed to defend segregation and maintain oppression. Many times it is difficult to sort out the intent and intentions from the truth or consequences.

Very little has been written documenting *how* anthropological concepts have been used in the service of political projects (cf. di Leonardo 1998). One reason I have chosen to write about this perspective of the history of anthropology is to address the paucity. I focus specifically on *how* and *why* anthropological concepts, particularly race and culture, have been lovingly adopted by some and disgracefully rejected by others; in each case it is often in the service of a specific political agenda.

Structure of the Book

The format of this book is influenced by George W. Stocking Jr., who has provided a generation of anthropologists with the big picture by his "ability to create 'vignettes' as opposed to painting the 'big picture'" (Stocking 2001:261). Stocking writes discrete yet thematically consistent and connected essays and weaves them into brilliant books. With regard to the vignette as method, he has been largely responsible for "raising it to the level of historiographic principle" (Stocking 2001:261). I too have found writing discrete vignettes that are connected by an overarching theme a powerful method that allows me to dive deep into a story while covering quite a bit of ground in one book. The structure of this book is pretty simple.

The first two chapters are on anthropology and the racial politics of culture, and the last two are on anthropology and the cultural politics of race. The chapters on culture compare and contrast how anthropology was used to promote racial uplift among African Americans and to contest it among American Indians. Chapter 1 looks at the Hampton Folk-Lore Society and its relationship to early anthropology, and chapter 2 looks at the World's Columbian Exposition of 1893 and the way in which American Indian groups resisted the anthropological exhibits. In both cases, white reformers played a critical role in shaping the terms and conditions of those relationships.

The chapters on race compare and contrast anthropology first as a booster of white supremacy and then as a detractor. Chapter 3 examines D. G. Brinton, who moved from studying the linguistics and philology of American Indians to examining the brains and bodies of American Negroes and as a result became an influential academic, in part because he became a reliable narrator for the story of white supremacy. Finally, I explore Boas's so-called conspiracy to destroy the white race, which was galvanized in the wake of the crisis in Little Rock in the fall of 1957.

I did not necessarily try to identify representative cases, but I hope I identified illustrative cases that highlight not only the limits and contradictions, but also the possibilities and potential that anthropology as a practice, discourse, theory, and discipline can represent in the complex world where culture, race, and justice matter in people's everyday lives.

(1)

Research, Reform, and

Racial Uplift

Playing Dead Twice in the Road (version d)

Once a fox heard a rabbit had outwitted a wolf. He decided not to be friends to her any more. But Mis' Rabbit came and begged his pardon, and it was granted. Mr. Fox offered to go hunting with Mis' Rabbit; but the rabbit was lazy and played off sick, and staid at Mr. Fox's house till he was very near ready to come back. Then she ran way down the road, and curled up and played off dead. Brer Fox came 'long and looked at her; but he thought probably she had been dead too long, so he passed on. As soon as Brer Fox was out of sight, Mis' Rabbit jumped up and ran through the field and got ahead of him, and laid down again to fake Mr. Fox. This time he looked at her and looked into his bag. His bag was large enough to accommodate one or two more, so he put Mis' Rabbit in, and put his bag in the grass, and went back to get the other rabbit. Before he was around the corner Mis' Rabbit jumped up and ran home with Mr. Fox's game. So Mr. Fox found no game when he returned.

But one day Mis' Rabbit was walking along, and she asked Mr. Fox what he killed. He said he killed a lot of game, but he had learned a headful of Har'sense. She laughed and went on.

—ANDREW W. C. BASSETTE, 1903

This folktale, with its distinctive pan-African trickster motif, was written and recorded by Andrew W. C. Bassette, who was a member of the Hampton Folk-Lore Society (HFS), founded in 1893 by Alice M. Bacon (Bacon and Parsons 1922:76). The educators and graduates of Hampton

Normal and Agricultural Institute formed the society to salvage and record cultural practices of rural blacks to demonstrate that industrial education succeeded in fostering the so-called Christian civilization of its graduates—in part by using folklore to evaluate how much African heritage remained to be rooted out. "Playing Dead Twice in the Road" was one of hundreds of tales, jokes, and conundrums Bacon compiled into the society's many notebooks of fieldwork during the last decade of the nineteenth century.

Bassette's story was written in 1903 and eventually published in 1922 in an article in the *Journal of American Folk-Lore* (*JAF*) titled "Folk-Lore from Elizabeth City County, Virginia." Although Bacon died in 1918, the authors of the article were given as A. M. Bacon and E. C. Parsons, and it was the last article in an issue devoted exclusively to Negro folklore. In her preface, Parsons noted that "two decades ago or more, Miss A. M. Bacon conducted a folk-lore society in Hampton Institute. Some of the material recorded was published in 'The Southern Workman.' Through the kindness of Miss Herron of the Institute the unpublished material was given to me to edit, and appears in the following" (Bacon and Parsons 1922:251). The following seventy-seven pages of that article included the remaining unpublished notebooks of the HFS.[1]

Among her many initiatives, Elsie Clews Parsons underwrote, organized, and guest-edited fourteen single-theme issues of the *JAF* dedicated to African and African American folk traditions between 1917 and 1937 (Deacon 1997:173, 282–83). Leonora Herron, librarian at the Hampton Institute, had been the secretary of the HFS, which from its inception to its end in 1899 had found in the American Folk-Lore Society (AFLS) one of its staunchest supporters. An occasional coauthor with Bacon in the *JAF* in the 1890s, Herron thus had a personal connection with Bacon, the AFLS, and its journal, and presumably that is why she turned over an old notebook of Negro folklore to Parsons, a rich white lady who conducted ethnographic fieldwork in Zuñi (Herron and Bacon 1896a, 1896b; Waters 1983:3).

Along with nearly two dozen other articles on African ethnology and African and African American folklore, Bacon's and Parsons's article of 1922 was cited in Alain Locke's *New Negro* (1968:444) in 1925. Yet in that volume, such folklore was not, as it were, the same rabbit as the one collected by the HFS—for the purpose of Locke and his associates was to demonstrate that New Negro intellectuals were succeeding in empowering new understandings of black culture, in part by using folk-lore to embrace their African heritage. Thus the New Negro rationale for collecting folklore in the 1920s was virtually the opposite of the HFS rationale in the 1890s. This one tale was first used to articulate the uplift project, and two decades later it was used to bolster the heritage project. And while the United States endured tumultuous changes during these periods, what is important to my argument here is that black educators and white reformers turned to anthropology and encouraged ethnologists to help articulate the uplift narrative for African Americans while at the same time, as we will see in the next chapter, white reformers and Indian activists turned against anthropology and spurned ethnologists to help articulate virtually the same narrative regarding uplift for Native Americans.

Several scholars have noted how anthropology was employed during the Harlem Renaissance and used in the service of the heritage project (Hutchinson 1995:61–77; Huggins 1971:28–30; Lewis 1997:102; Possnock 2000:210). None, however, makes the case better than Daphne Lamothe in *Inventing the New Negro: Narrative, Culture, and Ethnography* (2008). Yet few historians of anthropology have specifically explored the role of the field in the late nineteenth-century club and racial uplift movements within African American communities. The divergent ways in which the black and white crusaders for uplift and boosters of heritage interpreted Negro folklore over the course of two decades suggest that anthropologists and anthropology in the United States played different roles during different historical periods. In short, the ethnology of Negro culture was used in diverse ways to play a small but significant part in the complex and ever-changing racial politics of culture.

General Armstrong's Racial Project for Reconstruction

One way to better understand the relationship between early anthropology and the bootstrap-pulling uplift project galvanized by Hampton's favorite son, Booker T. Washington, is to turn to Washington's mentor and early benefactor, the tireless founder of the Hampton Institute, General Samuel Chapman Armstrong. Although the educational component of the project flourished in the efflorescence of Reconstruction respectability and enduring Southern sensibilities, it was a product not of the American

South, but of American empire. Armstrong learned the strategy of using industrial education to develop Christian civilization from his father in the Sandwich or Hawaiian Islands in the 1840s. This is also where he learned how to use folklore as a yardstick to measure it.

The American Board of Commissioners for Foreign Missions was founded in 1810 to proselytize the so-called colored races, and it launched its Hawaiian campaign in 1819. In 1831, General Armstrong's father, the Reverend Richard Armstrong, graduated from Princeton Theological Seminary and vowed to be among the number of missionaries the board was sending to the South Pacific that year, so he asked the seminary's principal, Archibald Alexander, to write him a letter of recommendation that testified to his "pure zeal for the glory of God" and his commitment to the "salvation of the heathen" (Engs 1999:2). To serve abroad, however, he had to be married, so he asked Clarissa Chapman, a recent graduate of Westfield Normal School and a teacher at the Pestalozzian Infant School in Brooklyn, New York, to be his bride. The two devout Presbyterians were married and set sail the following November on an arduous voyage to Honolulu, where they were stationed for less than a year before they assumed a difficult mission in the Marquesas Islands, which they soon aborted. Upon the Armstrongs' return to Hawai'i, the missionary board stationed them and their growing family in Haiku, a small community in the remote upcountry of Maui. They spent seven difficult but successful years on Maui, and as a result of his successes Reverend Armstrong was appointed to the powerful and storied Kawaiaha'o Church in Honolulu. During his years on Maui, Armstrong observed that the natives were in need of "steady industrial occupation."[2] As he ministered to the health and welfare of the populace, he convinced Kanaka Maoli to build schools, churches, sugar plantations, and sawmills.

Armstrong was shrewd and rose through the ranks of the missionary and government agencies. Closely associated with other powerful Protestant missionaries like Richard Williams and Gerritt P. Judd, he became the minister of public instruction in the islands, a member of the House of Nobles, a member of the King's Privy Council, and a close advisor on both spiritual and policy matters to King Kamehameha III (Lindsey 1995:1–2; Talbot 1969:3–37; Armstrong 1909:1–4; Engs 1999:10). Armstrong was perhaps best known for his creation and administration of the many missionary and government schools expounding his philosophy of moral and industrial education, which above all aimed to civilize the natives. He

outlined his teaching philosophy in a letter responding to his appointment by King Kamehameha III as minister of public education in 1847:

> No sphere of labor sir, would be more congenial to my feelings, than the
> department of public instruction, and I may add, no branch of the govern-
> ment, seems to me of more vital importance to the welfare, of the Hawaiian
> race than this. Education, intellectual, moral, and physical, is the great lever
> by which philanthropists of every land, are seeking to redeem and elevate
> the mass of people. *Here* it is of peculiar importance, where the glory and
> safety of the nation must depend in so great a degree upon the proper train-
> ing of the young. If depopulation here is to be arrested; if the vices which
> are consuming the natives are to be eradicated; if an indolent and thrift-
> less people are to become industrious and thrifty: if Christian institutions
> are to be perpetuated, the work must be accomplished mainly where it has
> been so prosperously begun, *in the education of the young.* (Armstrong 1887:
> 29–30)

Writing to his daughter in 1844, Richard Armstrong explained why the
"inhabitants" were in need of this type of education: "Had they skill and
industry they might abound in every good thing. . . . But, poor creatures,
they will not very soon shake off the low wretched habits of their former
state. Their government, until recently, was one of the worst forms of
despotism . . . and in those days *a character* was formed which will not
soon be entirely reformed. When I look over this valley, I think what a
Little Yankee skill would do here?"[3] Armstrong even complained that the
"king himself is as near to being an animal as man can well be & most of
the high chiefs are ignorant, lazy, and stupid." His remedy to help advance
what he called "Christian civilization" among these near-animal heathens
was to improve "the heart, the head & the body at once." As he surmised,
"This is a lazy people & if they are ever to be made industrious the work
must begin with the young. So I am making strenuous efforts to have
some sort of manual labor connected with every school . . . without industry they cannot be moral."[4]

The combination of morality, industry, and church was not a novel
philosophy of education. Mrs. Armstrong, for example, had been an
instructor in a school modeled after the philosophies of Johann Hein-
rich Pestalozzi, who incorporated similar values in his curriculum, and
her influence over her husband's philosophies is not well known. What
made Richard Armstrong so successful as an educator, missionary, and

confidante to the king was his intimate knowledge of the traditional language, customs, and folklore of his charges. Using his genuine respect of Hawaiian language and culture, he became an important facilitator of the Great Awakening during which thousands of Hawaiians converted to Christianity by the mid-nineteenth century. Even King Kamehameha IV, who detested the influence of missionaries, noted that Armstrong "was an eloquent preacher in the Hawaiian language" and commented on "his accurate knowledge of the Hawaiian language, and the facility with which he wielded the pen of a translator" (Armstrong 1887:57–58). In fact, Armstrong's institutional efforts to increase education increased Hawaiian language literacy, which helped to facilitate Kanaka's distinctive tradition of protesting against colonialism and imperialism through poetry and prose, often waged within the pages of Hawaiian-language newspapers (Silva 2004:45–86).

As Richard Armstrong labored at his mission to make Puritans out of Polynesians, he often used cultural markers to demonstrate how far Kanaka Maoli supposedly had come, suggesting, for example, that the natives "have better clothes than they used to have" and explaining that "we rarely see a native now unclad or even wearing native kapa." But he also used such markers to show how much civilizing work remained to be done, lamenting that the natives "still live in small and filthy grass huts, destitute of every comfort, and herding together often a dozen sleeping on mats in one small house without even a partition, and some of them, as if to make bad worse, keep their dogs and ducks in the house during the night" (1887:63).

During their final year on Maui in 1839, Mrs. Armstrong gave birth to Samuel Chapman Armstrong, the sixth of their ten children. Samuel grew up close to his father, and in a memoir titled "From the Beginning" explained how Richard Armstrong's philosophy of education shaped that of Hampton. Comparing the Lahaina-luna Seminary, which taught Greek and Latin, to the Hilo Boarding and Manual Labor School, Armstrong remarked that "as a rule the former turned out more brilliant, the latter less advanced but more solid men. In making the plan of Hampton Institute that of the Hilo School seemed the best to follow. . . . Hence came our policy of teaching only English and the system of industrial training at Hampton. Its graduates are not only to be good teachers but skilled workers, able to build homes and earn a living for themselves and encourage others to do the same" (1909:4–5).

In 1860 Samuel Armstrong left Hawai'i to attend Williams College, where he came under the influence of its president, the philosopher and missionary Mark Hopkins. As the Civil War erupted, he answered Abraham Lincoln's call for Union Army volunteers. Accepting a commission as captain, he recruited and trained Company D of the 125th Regiment of New York. Promoted to major and then to colonel, Armstrong was put in command of the 9th Regiment of U.S. Colored Troops, and in March of 1865 Lincoln made the twenty-six-year-old Hawaiian citizen a brevet brigadier general.

Although Armstrong demonstrated great leadership and courage in the battle to preserve the Union, he confessed to his mother that "the Union is to me little or nothing." He explained that he "was a foreigner, a Sandwich Islander, who had no local sympathies." He saw "the great issue to be that of freedom or slavery for 4,000,000 souls" (Talbot 1969:115–18), but as he told his Williams classmate Archibald Hopkins, "I am sort of [an] abolitionist, but haven't yet learned to love the Negro." His most consistent reason to fight was rooted in his faith that God did not intend for the souls of people to be bought and sold: "I go in, then, for freeing them more on account of their souls than their bodies, I assure you" (Talbot 1969:86). In a less searching letter to Hopkins, he castigated those who fought for honor or God, saying, "That's all poppy cock." Armstrong provided a set of more quotidian reasons: "I say *strike*, in order that you may get $100 or so per month, see the country, wear soldiers' clothes, save the land from anarchy, rescue the Constitution and punish the rebels—long live the Republic!"[5]

As the war ended, he searched for a mission in life, both personal and Christian. As a commander of Negro troops, he had been impressed by "their quick response to good treatment and to discipline," and he was convinced that African Americans yearned for education because he witnessed how his soldiers were "often studying their spelling books under fire" (Armstrong 1909:6). Immediately after the war, the commissioner of the Freedmen's Bureau, General Oliver Otis Howard, appointed Armstrong as the superintendent for the tidewater area of Virginia; its headquarters was the small town of Hampton. General Armstrong's jurisdiction was populated with a large number of formerly enslaved people, and his area quickly became a bellwether for radical Reconstruction experiments as missionaries, bureau agents, and the new freedmen and -women negotiated competing agendas, policies, and plans.

After the war, the American Missionary Association took the lead in establishing schools for African Americans in the South (Jewell 2007:29–62). Armstrong used his access to both government and missionary resources to establish a coed industrial and normal school for Negroes, and it soon became independent of both the missionary association and the government. It opened in 1868 with two teachers and fifteen pupils but grew quickly. Armstrong often touted his brand of industrial and moral education, known as the Hampton idea, as "the only way to make them good Christians" (1909:12). The Hampton idea found powerful support among philanthropists, missionaries, and the nation's political and industrial leaders. Although interest was generated by Hampton's civilizing mission, white backers were also attracted to its political and economic components which, as they saw it, would foster regional stability by discouraging students from participating in party politics while encouraging the efficient exploitation of their labor (Spivey 1978:22). As George Fredrickson explains, Hampton's financial backers "anticipated that blacks would make a more effective contribution to general prosperity and individual white profit making if they were taught useful skills" (1971:216). The method and message Armstrong used to teach African Americans how to become civilized and virtuous was simple and consistent: "Work, *work*, work" (Southern Workman 1874:163). The majority of black colleges followed Hampton's model, and when Hampton's own graduate, Booker T. Washington, reproduced Armstrong's model at Tuskegee Institute in the late nineteenth century, it became *the* most influential model for black schools (Fredrickson 1971:216).

Armstrong not only created the blueprint for Washington's popular industrial education, with its concomitant policies of racial accommodation and cultural assimilation, but also helped to shape the federal government's policies regarding Native American assimilation through education. Between 1878 and 1893, Hampton "experimented" with Indian education, again employing the notion that industrial education helped to civilize the savages (Lindsey 1995; Robinson 1977; Adams 1995:28–59). In 1878, Captain R. H. Pratt, who, after the Civil War, commanded black troops and Indian scouts on the Great Plains, searched without success for a school to continue the education of a group of Indians under his control. General Armstrong welcomed the opportunity to extend Hampton's civilizing mission to American Indians and invited Pratt to bring them to Hampton. The experiment was seemingly so successful that

President Rutherford B. Hayes announced in his State of the Union address the following year that the Department of the Interior would reproduce Armstrong's Hampton idea for Native Americans.

Initially, Hayes voiced his concerns about hostile Indians but assured Congress and the nation that the "vast majority of our Indian population have fully justified the expectations of those who believe that by human and peaceful influences the Indian can be led to abandon the habits of savage life and to develop a capacity for useful and civilized occupations." He then extolled the virtues of "the experiment of sending a number of Indian children of both sexes to the Hampton Normal and Agricultural Institute, in Virginia, to receive an elementary English education and practical instruction in farming and other useful industries, [which] has led to results so promising that it was thought expedient to turn over the cavalry barracks at Carlisle in Pennsylvania to the Interior Department for the establishment of an Indian school on a larger scale" (Hayes 1966:1390). That year, 1879, Captain Pratt along with some American Indian students from Hampton started the Carlisle Indian Industrial School. Like Tuskegee and Hampton for Negroes, Hampton and the Carlisle School became defining institutions for education policy to assimilate Indians (Adams 1995; Hampton Normal and Agricultural Institute 1893; Makofsky 1989; Robinson 1977). According to C. Kalani Beyer, in 1880, Samuel Chapman Armstrong went back to Hawai'i to help reestablish even more strict— English-only—industrial training schools, and he even "had a great deal of influence in determining the curriculum" at the new Kamehameha Schools (Beyer 2007:36). Carlisle, Tuskegee, and Kamehameha were each influenced, in part, by Samuel Armstrong's Hampton idea, which was modeled after the supposed success of civilizing the savages at the Hilo Boarding School founded by David and Sarah Lyman in 1836 (Goodyear-Ka'opua 2005:82–90). David and Sarah Lyman together with Richard and Clarissa Armstrong were part of the same contingent of young, zealous missionaries the American Board of Commissioners for Foreign Missions sent from New Bedford to Honolulu on the whaler *Averick* in November of 1831. Although uncertain about their mission in the South Pacific, these young couples became enduring agents of American empire.

Samuel Armstrong's gospel of industrial education was even spread to Africa. With close ties to the American Missionary Association, Hampton provided many recruits for the association's work of converting and educating West Africans. In reports published in the *Southern Workman,*

Hampton graduates who became missionaries routinely testified that the Hampton idea in Africa was helping the Lord in the "upbuilding of his kingdom" (White 1878:54; Sharps 1991:121).

Mary Francis Armstrong, Samuel Armstrong's wife, explained that the general's unparalleled success in establishing his school stemmed from the fact that he "brought from Hawai'i to Virginia an idea, worked out by American brains in the heart of the Pacific, adequate to meet the demands of a race similar in its dawn of civilization to the people among whom this idea had first been successfully tested" (Armstrong and Ludlow 1874:22–23; see also Kaplan 1993:16). General Armstrong deployed a transnational and transracial discourse about civilization, assimilation, Christianity, and industrial education to build an institution that defined dominant approaches to the education of African Americans, Native Americans, Kanaka Hawai'i Maoli, and even Africans. And like his father, General Armstrong realized that understanding the folklore and cultural practices of these peoples would facilitate his civilizing mission.

Bedeviling Christian Civilization

Armstrong explained the role of what he called "comparative ethnology" in an introduction to a series of reports published in the *Southern Workman* for 1878, which explored Negroes' "firm belief in witchcraft and conjuration" from Virginia to Florida. He compared the way Negroes and Sandwich Islanders practiced the "tangle of superstition, demonology, and fetish worship," which he described as "a combination of Salem and Central Africa." After discussing the parallels between the Hawaiian "'kahuna' or native witch-doctor" and the Negro conjure doctor, he concluded that both groups had "the same love of the supernatural, and dense ignorance of the laws of living" and that the Negroes thus possessed the "elements which form the soil for a growth of superstition as rank and as fatal as that which is helping to depopulate Hawaii" (1878:26).

The reports on conjure doctors were intended "to throw light upon the mental condition of the masses of this people, and the kind of work that must be done among them if they are to be raised to civilization or even saved from extinction" (Armstrong 1878:30). These reports provoked a flurry of published responses. Orra Langhorne, a regular contributor to the *Southern Workman*, reminded readers that conjure doctors were "evidently a legacy handed down to [American Negroes] from their sav-age ancestors. I sometimes think such ideas are growing with them, in spite of their chances for education." She used these reports to articulate a common theme sounded during the Reconstruction period, that slavery provided a veneer of civilization that was therapeutic for the Negro but dissipated once slavery ended: "My husband, who lived in what natives know as 'old Virginia,' says there was always a great deal of superstition among the slaves of this section, but it was held in check by their own-ers, who always forbid the discussion of such subjects, and by the laws which prevented the assembling of negroes in large gatherings, except for religious worship, even that being restricted. Now there is no check of that kind and the belief of the more ignorant colored people in 'conjuring, witches, &c,' is astonishing" (Langhorne 1878:67). As if to illustrate Lang-horne's contentions, a member of Hampton's junior class offered compel-ling examples of the good and ill work of conjure doctors and closed his letter to the editor by saying, "I believe in the conjure Drs. And all this that I have written I can vouch for my self" (Armstrong 1878:31). Armstrong's faith in the civilizing mission of Hampton Institute prompted him to comment, "Two years more in the school will change his ideas, it is to be hoped" (1878:30).

Other responses to the reports focused not on the practices described but on the utility of their publication. For example, W. I. Louis, a Hamp-ton alumnus teaching in Spartansburg, South Carolina, was upset with the reports, stating, "I fail to see what is gained by your repeating this dark legend of a by-gone day." He wanted the *Southern Workman* to re-port "facts that are elevating, facts that will inspire even the humblest." Louis concluded by noting that "our days of childhood are (if not, they should be) fast taking their flight, and the advent of manhood is at hand" (Armstrong 1878:35).[6]

This letter provoked perhaps the most spirited response from the gen-eral; he described why the *Southern Workman* frequently published eth-nographic accounts by missionaries and folklore from around the world.

> It is time for every man who loves his people to lay aside sensitive feeling
> and go to work with all the aid he can get. And the first step of all is to make
> known the true state of the case. When a general begins a campaign, the first
> point is to get a true map of the country, and spy out all the enemy's forces
> and know the strength of every battery. It is not the beauty of his banners and

his martial music that will win the victory, but knowledge of the work before
him, and hard fighting. . . . let us not be afraid to face our own faults and fol-
lies, to drag them into the light where they will show for what they really are.
(Armstrong 1878:35)

Combining espionage with exorcism, folklore, and ethnology became
a way of demonstrating how Hampton succeeded at civilizing students,
and it also demonstrated the need for continual financial support of this
institution that was so committed to uplifting the race. More importantly,
the *Southern Workman* reports of the cultural practices of Native Americans, Hawaiians, West and South Africans, and African Americans were
used in the service of a complicated racial project that articulated a putatively progressive discourse about an individual's ability to rise to a state
of civilization, during a period when many scholars argued that every
member of these groups was doomed to eternal savagery.

The graduates and educators of Hampton, Fisk, Howard, and other
black schools explicitly used the terms of this discourse in their programs
of racial uplift. These self-described Negro elites most often framed their
pejorative descriptions of their less civilized neighbors in terms of class,
but the HFS did so in terms of culture. Virtue, chastity, and cleanliness
were key signifiers of civilization that black elites embraced while chastis-
ing vice and sensuality. For example, Booker T. Washington was fond of
remarking, "In all my teachings I have watched carefully the influence of
the tooth-brush, and I am convinced that there are few single agencies
of civilization that are more far reaching" (1902:75).

Uncivilized blacks were the ones who believed in conjure doctors, told
the animal stories, sang the work songs, and gyrated their bodies in ring
shouts and juke joints. They were also the field hands, manual laborers,
domestics, and washerwomen who never had the opportunity to attend
one of the normal schools in which strict discipline and obsession with
proper behavior convinced students they had become civilized. And it
was the uneducated and less refined souls who were held responsible for
the vice, promiscuity, and debauchery associated with all black Americans. Moreover, many Negro elites found the main culprit of their neighbors' cultural degradation in African cultural patterns. The notion that
African culture underpinned the behavior of uncouth black people was
so routine that it provided a useful shorthand for one Hampton graduate,
who complained about the rural school district of his first teaching job.

Displeased with all of the "drinking, swearing and fighting," he reported, "when I came here I thought that there was as much Africa here as I cared to witness" (Southern Workman 1876:46; see also Hunter 1997:175).

Not all folk customs were seen as bad or viewed as degrading. In fact, the so-called plantation melodies were viewed as redemptive, and the animal stories were often seen as entertaining. Armstrong himself was ambivalent, and he loved moving spirituals. As he disclosed to his wife, "These songs are but the cry of their desolate hearts unto their God—once uttered in long agony of their oppression and now sung by their children as the songs of their home and nation. Their music," he explained, "makes the matter of civilization a puzzle. . . . Should we educate them out of all this . . . that was needed to carry them through slavery?" (Engs 1999:76).

During the 1870s and 1880s the boosters of the uplift project combined ideas from many sources. They employed referents from the Bible that resonated with the ideas of Adam Smith, Herbert Spencer, Jean-Baptiste Lamarck, Lewis Henry Morgan, and E. B Tylor to foster the idea that individuals could work hard and attain civilization while unloading the cultural baggage of African savagery. As General Armstrong explained, however, in order to civilize the Negroes, reformers had first to "spy out" those Africanisms which bedeviled the uplift project and debilitated the health and welfare of the poor. His approach influenced Alice Mabel Bacon and, through her, the HFS.

Theory and Practice of the Hampton Folk-Lore Society

Alice Bacon was born in 1858, the youngest daughter of Leonard Bacon, an influential abolitionist, professor at Yale Divinity School, and long-standing pastor of the First Church of New Haven. Her brother Francis was a professor of surgery at Yale and married Georgeanna Woolsey, who was the cousin of Yale's president, Theodore Dwight Woolsey. Georgeanna was the sister of Jane Stuart Woolsey, who supervised nurses during the Civil War and established nursing training schools in New York City and New Haven. Jane was stationed in Virginia during the final campaigns of the Civil War, and General Armstrong persuaded her to come to Hampton Institute in 1868 to direct the Girls Industrial Department, where she stayed until 1872. She left Hampton to become the first resident-director of Presbyterian Hospital in New York City. Jane was accompanied by her sister-in-law, Rebecca Bacon, who became Armstrong's assistant principal (Waters 1983:5).

In 1870, just two years after Hampton was under way, Rebecca Bacon brought her twelve-year-old sister, Alice Mabel Bacon, for "a year at Hampton . . . among the pleasant, sweet-voiced, kindly faced Negro girls, whom even in her Northern home she had learned to know and trust" (Bacon 1909:75). During that year she earned the nickname "junior professor" because she even instructed some the students. She also formed a lifelong commitment to Hampton, vowing to come back and teach at the school (Waters 1983:5). In 1882 her mother died and, now twenty-four, Alice Bacon applied for a post at Hampton, where she taught for five years. At the invitation of her childhood friend Countess Oyama, she left Hampton to spend a year in Japan, where she worked to help westernize the schools for elite Japanese women (Waters 1983:6; Sharps 1991:32). Returning to Hampton in 1889, she worked to establish Hampton's Dixie Hospital to provide health care to the needy in the area and nursing training for students at Hampton Institute.

Bacon conducted case studies of individual people in communities in the surrounding Elizabeth City County to assess the need for the hospital. In an effort to raise funds for the hospital, she wrote an essay for the *Southern Workman* that included graphic descriptions based on her case studies. Her essay reflects both her missionary sensibility and the type of language that was expected by her audience of philanthropists and "the better class of colored people" who were "anxious to co-operate" in establishing the hospital (Bacon 1890:124).

The essay was published under her occasional column titled "Silhouettes," and it opened by describing "the poorest and most ignorant of the colored people" who lived "in the little slab cabins with their mud chimneys, where father, mother, children of both sexes, and frequently adult lodgers of either sex, are thrown together at all times under all circumstances." She surmised that this "life must be more the life of the savage than that of civilization. . . . That the Negroes are by degrees moving upward, that every year more and more of them lift themselves a little above the merely animal life of the roughest plantation hand, is a fact that none but the most pessimistic can doubt, but to those who are working among them the question often arises, what can we do that will help to relieve, on some measure, those who from years or by reason of infirmities can never lift themselves out of the squalor and misery about them?" (1890:124).

All they needed, she proposed, was basic medical attention and the "healing gift of Christian civilization." One of the challenges she identified in offering health care was the difficulty of establishing who was needy and who was not. According to her, the people seeking aid could "be roughly divided into two classes, those who suffer without complaint, and those who complain without suffering, for these people are like the lower animals in that a small ailment will often produce groans and cries, where a great one will be endured with pathetic dumbness" (1890:124).

After describing near-miraculous recoveries from serious ailments that could have been cured at their outset with basic medical aid, she made her pitch: "This is the work that is already begun, and it is this work that we wish to establish on a permanent foundation, and to increase so that it may include within its scope not only the work in the cabins but also a hospital in which we can nurse the sick who can not be cared for in their own homes, and a training-school in which colored girls can be trained for either missionary or private nursing" (1890:124). She continued conducting interviews and writing case studies but soon discovered that one of the chief obstacles to delivering medical care and advancing Christian civilization to those she euphemistically called the cabin people was their tenacious belief in conjuring and superstitions. In her view, sociological and anthropological research ought to be used as an aid in missionary and health work (Waters 1983:36).

By 1893, Bacon's efforts were joined by those of some Hampton alumni, students, and faculty who began to see the need to salvage the songs, stories, and African survivals that made up Negro folklore. Combining Armstrong's commitment to espionage and exorcism with a desire for historical preservation, Bacon published a call to form the HFS in the form of a circular letter, reprinted in the *Southern Workman* for December 1893:

> Dear Friends: The American Negroes are rising so rapidly from the condition of ignorance and poverty in which slavery left them, to a position among the cultivated and civilized people of the earth, that the time seems not far distant when they shall have cast off their past entirely, and stand as an anomaly among civilized races, as a people having no distinct traditions, beliefs or ideas from which a history of their growth may be traced. If within the next few years care is not taken to collect and preserve all traditions and customs peculiar to the Negroes, there will be little to reward the search of the future

historian who would trace the history of the African continent through the years of slavery to the position which they will hold a few generations hence. Even now the children are growing up with little knowledge of what their ancestors have thought, or felt, or suffered. The common school system with its teachings is eradicating the old and planting the seeds of the new, and the transition period is likely to be a short one. The old people, however, still have their thoughts on the past, and believe and think and do much as they have for generations. From them and from the younger ones whose thoughts have been moulded by them in regions where the school is, as yet, imperfectly established, much may be gathered that will, when put together and printed, be of great value as material for history and ethnology.

But, if this material is to be obtained, it must be gathered soon and by many intelligent observers stationed in different places. It must be done by observers who enter into the homes and lives of the more ignorant colored people and who see in their beliefs and customs no occasion for scorn, or contempt, or laughter, but only the showing of the first child-like, but still reasoning philosophy of a race. . . . To such observers, every custom, belief or superstition, foolish and empty to others, will be of value and will be worth careful preservation. The work cannot be done by white people, much as many of them would enjoy the opportunity of doing it, but must be done by the intelligent and educated colored people who are at work all through the South among the more ignorant of their own race, teaching, preaching, practising medicine, carrying on business of any kind that brings them into close contact with the simple, old-time ways of their own people. (Bacon 1893:180–81)

Bacon's initial rationale for continued research on the so-called cabin people was to make missionaries more efficient health-care providers, and she effectively articulated this rationale in her later work (Bacon 1895a, 1895b; Herron and Bacon 1896a, 1896b). But the emphasis on cultural preservation so evident in her statement of 1893 spoke to another, perhaps less obvious motivation: the urgency with which Bacon enjoined the graduates to go out and salvage disappearing Negro lore stemmed from the educators' need to demonstrate the success of the Hampton idea, which it fit neatly into complementary efforts initiated by historians and collectors salvaging the traditions and relics of the "old south" after the calamitous Civil War, and ethnographers and curators salvaging Indian languages and artifacts in the wake of the decimating wars and epidemics.

The best way to demonstrate their success at civilization was to show it. Hampton and Carlisle effectively crafted before and after images to depict a narrative of their success at making progress. Native Americans were initially photographed adorned in ceremonial attire or wrapped in a woolen blanket. For the after shot, the girls were given starched linen dresses and the boys pressed military uniforms. Freighted with immense symbolism, it was a dramatic presentation of the schools' success at civilizing their charges (Adams 1995:45). Hampton also tried this approach with images of black Americans. Most notably, Frances B. Johnston's photographs of Hampton students that were used for the institute's exhibit at the Exposition Universelle in Paris in 1900. The self-styled "greatest woman photographer in the world" and photographer of choice of five United States presidents, Johnston was commissioned by Hampton to mount the exhibit at the Paris World's Fair. Johnston's stunning images of young Hampton students and old cabin people framed Hampton Institute as a utopia of progress and promise, while outside its storied walls was a dystopia of squalid conditions, rampant lynchings, and widespread disfranchisement. Unlike the beads and buckskin that indexed American Indian advancement, Johnston used material culture and technology to demonstrate African American progress (Patterson 2000:62).

In Bacon's call in 1893 for a folklore society, she seemed to suggest that the society might be the last opportunity of Hampton educators to record the "ignorant people," before the impact of common schools eclipsed the remaining folk culture. Armed with a record of African American folklore that was no longer practiced, the educators at Hampton would be able to reproduce the popular before and after images used to raise money for their Indian program.

Bacon's call for the formation of the HFS was greeted with great enthusiasm. Letters of support came in from all corners of the intellectual community. The popular Harvard geologist Nathan S. Shaler supported the effort. Although Shaler routinely spoke about Negroes' inherent inferiority, he chimed in to offer his best wishes. On the other side of the political spectrum was the author, abolitionist, suffragist, and former colonel of Negro troops Thomas Wentworth Higginson, who suggested that Hampton students would be acting as scientists, which would "enlarge their lives and dignify their position." Booker T. Washington approved heartily of the plan, as did T. Thomas Fortune, publisher of the *New York Age*. Even the venerable Southern historian and folklorist George Washington

Cable supported the venture and offered his service (Bacon 1893:179–80; Southern Workman 1894:5).

Although the *Southern Workman* published only ringing endorsements, some evidence suggests that African American supporters of the society held more cautious views of its promise. For example, the missionary, educator, and early pan-Africanist Alexander Crummell strongly supported the formation of the society, but he warned that its members must offer a positive, not a negative, interpretation of their African heritage. "The truth," he explained, has been "the dinning of the 'colonization' cause into the ears of the colored people—the iteration of the idle dogma that Africa is THE home of the black race in this land; has served to prejudice the race against the very name of Africa. And this is a double folly:—the folly of the colonizationists, and the folly of the black man; i.e. to forget family ties and his duty to his kin over the water" (Southern Workman 1894:5). Another activist, educator, and author, Anna Julia Cooper, also commented on the philosophical foundation of the organization:

> What you say is true. The black man is readily assimilated to his surroundings and the original simple and distinct type is in danger of being lost or outgrown. To my mind, the worst possibility yet is that the so-called educated Negro, under the shadow of this over powering Anglo-Saxon civilization, may become ashamed of his own distinctive features and aspire only to be an imitator of that which can not but impress him as the climax of human greatness, and so all originality, all sincerity, all *self*-assertion would be lost to him. What he needs is the inspiration of knowing that his racial inheritance is of interest to others and that when they come to seek his homely songs and sayings and doings, it is not to scoff and sneer, but to study reverently, as an original type of the Creator's handiwork. (Southern Workman 1894:5)

The comments by Crummell and Cooper suggest that even at the formation of the first black folklore society, some African Americans understood that folklore could provide a positive interpretation of their African heritage or a scientific basis to identify and preserve their distinctive culture. Still, they did little to influence the twenty or so Hampton students, teachers, and alumni who made up the society. Most Hampton graduates did not question their desire to ascend to a civilized state, and even more perhaps loathed any association with Africa. However, not all members uncritically accepted the entire Hampton idea, particularly the segregated dining facilities on campus: "Public documents as well as private letters reveal that the students at Hampton consistently challenged the racial politics latent in the Hampton Idea" (Moody 2006:100).

Two of the society's elected leaders, Robert R. Moton and Daniel Webster Davis, even made a departure from the espionage and exorcism outlined by Armstrong and adopted by Bacon (Waters 1983:45). Moton used the folklore and the society to challenge the "contempt and derision" of the minstrelsy industry, which transformed black folk songs, stories, and sayings into laughingstock buffoonery and thereby crystallized stereotypes for all African Americans (Lott 1993). Challenging those who made the "experience of the Negro a joke for white audiences," Moton reported to the annual meeting of the AFLS in 1894 that folklorists need to distinguish between "real folk-music" and those popular songs that were an "imitation by white 'nigger minstrels'" (1976:146).

Recent scholarship by Shirley C. Moody carefully explores the diverse approaches specific members of the society took toward interpreting and collecting folklore. Highlighting the close relationship with the society of the visionary scholar Anna Julia Cooper, Moody makes a compelling case that particular members of the HFS argued that folk culture made African American culture distinctive, and it ought not be patently condemned, thus anticipating the way New Negro scholars used folklore during the 1920s and 1930s (2006:68–133). In addition, Ronald Sharps has argued that the HFS's approach amounted to a form of "applied folklore" (1991:65).

The core of the HFS was a group of young men and women who graduated from Hampton and went on to work in business, education, and medicine. By better understanding the practices and lore of their clients, patients, and students, these young professionals believed they could contribute to racial uplift by developing more efficient ways to sell, heal, and teach. More generally, the society's work, as published in Hampton's *Southern Workman*, formed part of an uplift discourse that was integrated into a complicated transnational racial project whose proponents engaged in a racial politics of culture that shaped communities from Hawai'i to Hampton, from Perth to Pretoria.

Although missionary efforts to civilize people of color made little distinction with regard to the savage state of Indians, Hawaiians, and Negroes, their methods and rhetoric served remarkably well to make distinctions between individuals within each group who had supposedly reached a state of civilization. Specifically, the putatively civilized people of color in the late nineteenth century used the discourse that homogenized difference between groups to mark the heterogeneity within their group—describing and inscribing a distinction between themselves, the civilized, and those others, the uncivilized.

As the next section shows, the AFLS participated in and scientifically validated this racial project by supporting and collaborating with the HFS. From its inception in 1893 until 1899, when Bacon left Hampton to return to Japan and the society lost momentum, the HFS found in the AFLS important support.

Theory and Practice of the American Folk-Lore Society

William Wells Newell (1839–1907) was born in Cambridge, Massachusetts. The son of a Unitarian minister, he graduated second in his class of 1859 at Harvard and then enrolled in Harvard's Divinity School to pursue the ministry. Instead of serving a parish, he joined the Union Army during the Civil War as part of the Sanitary Service. After the war, he followed in his father's footsteps as a Unitarian minister but quickly learned he was ill suited as a man of the cloth and better suited as a man of letters. In 1871, he earned a master's degree and moved to New York City to open a private elementary school. In New York, Newell became fascinated with the games children played and began transcribing and recording them. His patient research and scrupulous attention to detail resulted in his most celebrated book, *Games and Songs of American Children* (1883). In 1884, he decided to leave his private school in New York and return to Cambridge to pursue his scholarly interests as a financially independent scholar and help to organize a national folklore society.

In the spring of 1887, Newell drafted a circular letter that outlined the scope of "a society for the study of Folk-Lore, of which the principal object shall be to establish a Journal, of scientific character." He organized prominent scholars in anthropology and literature to sign the letter and commit to participating in the society. On January 4, 1888, in Cambridge the AFLS was officially incorporated (Newell 1888:3); from the beginning, Newell was the central and most prominent figure in the organization. He served as permanent secretary of the society and the editor of its journal from 1888 to 1900. While the other officers had responsibilities in the university, museum, or elsewhere, Newell was able to devote considerable time and money to the development of the fledgling society (Bell 1973:10).

In the first issue of the journal, Newell explained the society's various departments, or divisions. The first division was Old English Lore, and he explained that old ballads, fairy tales, historical reminiscences, and beliefs in witchcraft were quickly disappearing. But with the advent of the folklore society, "there is reason to hope that some of these may be saved from oblivion" (Newell 1888:4). "The second division," he continued, "is that belonging to the American negroes." Newell explained that "the origin of these stories, many of which are common to a great part of the world, has not been determined." He believed that the animal stories should be "recorded as complete as possible," and he also directed the society to make thorough studies of "negro music and songs" because, as he put it, "such inquiries are becoming difficult, and in a few years will be impossible." He finally emphasized that the "beliefs and superstitions that exist among this people need attention, and present interesting and important psychological problems connected with the history of a race, who for good or ill are henceforth an indissoluble part of the body politic" (1888:5). Another division Newell discussed in terms of progress and the civilizing mission included the "traditions of the Indian tribes. A great change is about to take place in the condition of the Indian tribes," he wrote, "and what is to be done must be done quickly. For the sake of the Indians themselves, it is necessary that they should be allowed opportunities for civilization; for our sake and for the future, it is desirable that a complete history should remain of what they have been, since their picturesque and wonderful life will soon be absorbed and lost in the uniformity of the modern world."

Despite such predictions concerning the course of modern civilization and the fate of colonized peoples within it, Newell did not advocate that the AFLS make any political interventions or that its editors use the journal to promote policy positions. In this, he was less ambitious than Bacon and the HFS; he was resigned to the fact that "all that a single journal can hope to accomplish is to print a few articles of limited extent, to stimulate inquiry, keep a record of progress, and furnish abstracts of investigations" (1888:6).

The first president of the AFLS was Francis J. Child, a professor of English at Harvard University and an authority on English and Scottish ballads. He, however, retired from the organization within a year. Although none of the initial members of the governing council of the AFLS were affiliated with Harvard's Peabody Museum of American Archaeology and Ethnology, Newell wanted to make folklore a science and distinguish it from literature, so he turned to anthropology and established a link with Boas, who, in the fall of 1889, had assumed a position at Clark University in Worcester, Massachusetts. As chair and secretary, respectively, of the council, Boas and Newell worked together to change the character of the organization from a literary society of wealthy enthusiasts and reformers into a scientific organization of credentialed ethnologists. Newell admired and deferred to the young academic from Germany, and "gave Boas virtually a free hand in publishing his own materials and those of his early students" (Darnell 1973:28). Boas took full advantage of this opportunity and published much of the material he collected in the Pacific Northwest. Although Boas chose more prestigious venues to articulate his theoretical and methodological positions (Boas 1887a, 1887b, 1889, 1895, 1896a), he used the JAF to formulate his work on diffusion (1891b, 1896b).

The concept of diffusion was also important to Newell (Newell 1888:7; 1895), but he had more pressing issues: he needed to recruit enough people to sustain the journal and the society. He explained to Boas that his "efforts to enlarge circulation" had taught him that "the general public is very indifferent" and that "vanity is the only spring of action which can be relied on. . . . If you write to ten men that the Council of the American Folk-Lore Society wishes their cooperation, one out of those ten will feel flattered, and join. I have got eight subscribers out of the 80 letters, one from you, and one from Prof. Crane! The other letters are to hear from. I think, if names of about thirty New Yorkers of prominence and fortune were sent to me, men identified with the geographical and historical societies, and I wrote them, some would unite with us."[7]

Newell needed the support of wealthy enthusiasts, but he was concerned that attempts to enlarge the society would inhibit its professionalism. Newell expressed this tension in another letter to Boas about "Dr. Mann of Brooklyn," who wanted to join the society. Newell deemed it necessary to "exclude him from a learned society" and even felt that "it would be a nuisance to have him in a Brooklyn local society." He suggested that the prickly issue of membership "might be averted, should the need arise, by making such a society elective. However, as our society is pretty promiscuous, perhaps it would be harsh to keep him out."[8] Newell only toyed with the idea of an elective society, focusing his efforts instead on securing wealthy and responsible collectors and professional anthropologists. As secretary and editor, he was able to set rigorous standards for the scholarship published in the society's organ. With well-attended annual meetings, a scholarly journal, and growing numbers of both amateur and professional scientists, Newell's launching of the society was perceived as a success. The AFLS also emerged as a formidable anthropological organization. Daniel Garrison Brinton, from Philadelphia's Academy of Natural Sciences, served as its president in 1889, followed in 1890 by Frederic W. Putnam from Harvard, in 1891 by Otis T. Mason from the United States National Museum, and in 1892 by the director of the BAE, J. W. Powell (Darnell 1973:38). Newell used the presidency to gain the support of the various leaders in American anthropology, which in turn gave the budding society increased visibility and validity. From the beginning, however, Newell structured the office of the president in a way that limited its power. The executive officer of the society was the secretary, and the editor of the JAF controlled everything that was printed under the society's name. Those two offices were filled by Newell, who often deferred to the wishes of Boas, the chair of the society's governing council.

By 1893 Newell had distinguished himself as a skilled administrator and editor within the closely knit anthropological circles, but he also wanted to distinguish himself as a folklorist and folklore as its own discipline, not an adjunct to anthropology or English (Darnell 1973:28; Bell 1973:11–13). When Bacon organized the Hampton society, Newell saw an opportunity to develop the Negro department of the journal and thus to pursue a topic that few anthropologists were then exploring. He was "a personal friend" of one of Hampton's trustees, and there was considerable overlap between the founders of the AFLS from the Boston area and supporters of the Hampton idea, well before the HFS was even formed (Newell 1983:187). At the first annual meeting of the AFLS, the Boston-area members elected to its council included Mary Hemenway, Thomas Wentworth Higginson, and Alice C. Fletcher.

Mary Tileston Hemenway (1820–94) was one of Hampton's chief benefactors. Her philanthropic support enabled Armstrong to launch the *Southern Workman*, buy more land, build Virginia Hall, and underwrite the popular Hampton Student Singers, who often performed in her Boston parlor, the same parlor where Boston-area members of the AFLS convened. She supported research on and reform for both Native and African Americans, and her philanthropic support of anthropology enabled Frank Hamilton Cushing to direct the Hemenway Southwestern Archaeological Expedition (Lindsey 1995:50; Hinsley 1989:178–90; Hinsley 2003:7–18; Armstrong and Ludlow 1874:139; Sharps 1991:31, 38; Ludlow 1909:122; Newell 1890:2, 9).[9]

Alice C. Fletcher (1845–1923) was also elected to the council. Although she could not, as a woman, attend Harvard, she was one of the first women to receive professional training in anthropology, studying with Putnam at the Peabody Museum of American Archaeology and Ethnology. An enthusiastic supporter of the Hampton idea and a frequent contributor to the *Southern Workman*, she worked to recruit Indian students to both the Hampton Institute and the Carlisle School. In addition, her longtime collaborator Francis La Flesche was a graduate of Hampton's Indian program (Fletcher and La Flesche 1911; Lindsey 1995:198; Adams 1995:303; Newell 1890:9). Thomas Wentworth Higginson (1823–1911), a Unitarian minister and Boston-based radical reformer, was also elected to the AFLS council. A champion of both racial uplift and women's suffrage and a longtime supporter of Negro normal schools, he wrote one of the initial letters of support for Hampton's folklore society.

Newell wasted no time incorporating the members of the HFS into the AFLS. On May 25, 1894, he traveled to Hampton to deliver the keynote address for Hampton's first folklore conference, which followed the spring commencement exercises. Speaking to "trustees, teachers, officers and graduates of the school," he gave a talk entitled "The Importance and Utility of the Collection of Negro Folk-Lore," which struck a note that resonated more with General Armstrong's notion of civilization than with Boas's ideas about diffusion. He began by explaining, "I came from Cambridge, in the hope of forwarding an undertaking which appears to me most meritorious, and of promoting the work of the Negro Folk-lore societies, a movement which is significant in regard to the present intelligence and rapid progress of Southern Negroes" (Newell 1983:186). He then asked, "What is Negro Folk-lore?"

> It is that body of songs, tales, old-fashioned religious beliefs, superstitions, customs, ways of expression, proverbs, and dialect, of American Negroes.
> Lore means learning; folk, as I shall here use the word, means race.

The Folk-lore of Negroes in the United States then, is the learning or knowledge peculiar to the Negro race. It is that mass of information which they brought with them from Africa, and which has subsequently been increased, remodelled, and Anglicized by their contact with the whites.

All this body of thought belongs to the past. It is vanishing in proportion to the progress of Negro education; it fades away before the light of such institutions as Hampton; it is superseded by more advanced ideas, habits, morals, and theology. (Newell 1983:186)

This interpretation of folklore was part of a larger theory of civilization. According to Newell, "Each race has its distinctive customs, ideas, manners; civilization has but one set of customs and ideas for all races. The race is formed to be merged in the unity of races, as rivers flow to disappear in the ocean." Nevertheless, he believed that a race needed a record or memory of the past. Evoking the before and after pictures of the Indian students, Newell argued that Negroes should be able to demonstrate "the height to which they rose, the depth through which they have passed. . . . For the sake of the honor of his race, he should have a clear picture of the mental condition out of which he has emerged: this picture is not now complete, nor will [it] be made so without a record of songs, tales, beliefs, which belongs to the stage of culture through which he has passed" (1983:187–88).

Newell went on to describe various types of Negro folklore that needed to be collected, focusing on the value of the music. When he broached the subject of "spirits and demons," he argued, recalling Armstrong and Bacon, that "the best way to correct superstitious notions is to collect and study them. When all are gathered and made to elucidate each other, what is false and absurd is at once seen to be false and absurd. Thus, in order to get rid of a disgraceful custom, or of an ancient credulity, the best way is not to try to ignore its existence, but to face and find out what it is" (1983:189).

Working with Bacon, Newell arranged for a delegation from the HFS to participate the following December of 1894 at the annual meeting of the AFLS in Washington, D.C. Bacon's call to form the society was printed in December of 1893, and exactly one year later members of the HFS were sailing up the Chesapeake to the nation's capital to deliver papers alongside Boas, Cushing, J. Walter Fewkes, Newell, "and others equally well known along the lines of ethnological research" (Southern Workman 1895:30). Otis T. Mason chaired the meeting, which was hosted by the Anthropological Society of Washington and the Woman's Anthropological Society (Journal of American Folk-Lore 1895:5).

The HFS delegation consisted of Robert Moton, F. D. Banks, William E. Daggs, and J. H. Wainwright. It was on this occasion that Moton challenged the appropriation and distortion of Negro music by minstrels. His paper, "Negro Folk-songs," was premised on a single question: "Whether there is to-day a distinct and original music existing among the Negroes." Although Moton explained that "our work is not to discuss that question, but to furnish material gathered at first hand from the plantation songs of the south, that to some minds at least, seems to show that whenever or wherever that music may have originated, it is today a part of the life and heart of the colored people of the south, a true body of folk-songs" (1976:145). He did, however, make a strong case that the "true body of folk-songs" was distinct and original. He carefully analyzed and categorized the difference between "real folk-music" and the ridiculous imitation of folk music perpetrated by minstrels, which "have tended to bring the whole subject of Negro music into contempt and derision" (1976:146). Moton also distinguished the real or authentic music from the popular music written by whites but associated with black singers, which included such songs as "Old Kentucky Home" and "Swanee River." Finally, he included what he called "the war songs that were sung through the streets of all northern cities during the war" as the last category of spurious renditions of the real (1976:146). This left work songs, dance songs, spirituals, and shouts to form the "true body of folk-songs."

As Moton delivered his paper, his HFS colleagues joined him to form a quartet that performed a selection from each type of music he analyzed. Although Moton embraced the beauty and distinctive character of much of the music, he created temporal distance between himself and his colleagues when discussing examples of the Juba. Moton explained that "in some of these, the rhythmic expression is mainly through the beating of feet and patting of hands, while the vocal expression is simply a rude chant. The whole effect of this music, if music it can be called, is as barbarous as if rendered in African forests at some heathen festival" (1976:148). Despite its barbarity, the quartet performed it for the good of science and the integrity of the authentic.

Moton presented his paper in association with his backup performers on Thursday afternoon during the scientific session. That evening,
between eight and ten o'clock, anthropologists performed music for
each other. For example, "Mr. Frank Hamilton Cushing sang several Zuñi
songs, and Rev. J. Owen Doresy those of Sioux. Miss Alice C. Fletcher,
with Mr. La Flesche, sang Omaha songs connected with the ritual of the
Peace Pipe." Scheduled in the evening and after a reception, this blend of
science and entertainment was meant to be a light diversion to the otherwise heady scientific program. The real attraction, however, was "Dr. J.
Washington Matthews [who] presented, by means of phonograph, Navajo
songs." The fact that Moton delivered his paper during the scientific session, as opposed to being shunted to the more entertaining reception, is
noteworthy because it means the AFLS explicitly resisted Jim Crow segregation and the perception that performance of Negro folk music was to
be consumed as minstrelsy.

The performance by Moton and company was such a success that Newell and Thomas Wilson asked for an encore performance and recorded
it on phonographic cylinders, "which was found to reproduce the songs
with considerable exactness." As Bacon reported in the *Southern Workman*, "It is to be hoped that [at] sometime the Hampton Folk-Lore Society
will be able to secure a phonograph of its own" (Moton 1976:146).[10] The
HFS was off to a strong start, with powerful backing from the nation's
leading folklore society. Each month they convened to decide among such
topics as courting stories and hag stories, healing and medicine, jokes
and proverbs, or work songs and dance songs. The next month they presented or performed the work done since the last meeting and chose the
topic for the upcoming month. Each month the society's collections were
published in the "Folklore and Ethnology" department of the *Southern
Workman*.

Almost every year between 1893 and 1899 the HFS held a major conference that coincided with commencement exercises, attracting such notable participants as William Scarborough, a professor of classics at Wil-
berforce University, and Anna Julia Cooper, the author of *A Voice from
the South* (1892), who earned a B.A. from Oberlin and a PH.D. from the
Sorbonne. The HFS also developed an elaborate network of corresponding members who taught in the small schools scattered throughout the
rural South. Corresponding members submitted their collections to the

HFS secretary, who read them during meetings and then published them in the *Southern Workman*.

Bacon became an integral member of the AFLS and was elected to its council in 1897 along with Mason and Brinton. Members of HFS routinely participated in the meetings of the AFLS, and Bacon and her colleagues published several collections in the *JAF*; often Newell would simply reproduce the "Ethnology and Folklore" department of the *Southern Workman* in the *JAF* department called the "Folk-Lore Scrap-Book" (Baltimore Sun 1897:8; Banks 1894; Journal of American Folk-Lore 1894; Showers 1898; Herron and Bacon 1896a). Bacon sincerely appreciated the atheistic value of the animal stories and plantation melodies and understood the historical imperative to collect and preserve even the conjure remedies. It appears, however, that her work among some of the more forward-thinking members of the AFLS did not sway her from her commitment to use the study and description of cultures in the same way missionaries had used it for years—to learn how to civilize their charges (Mead and Bunzel 1960:59). In "Work and Methods of the Hampton Folk-lore Society," a paper presented in 1897 and published in the *JAF* in 1898, she reiterated that the HFS was sustained by "a strong desire on the part of some of those connected with the Hampton work to bridge over, if possible, the great gulf fixed between the minds of the educated and the uneducated, the civilized and the uncivilized—to enter more deeply into the daily life of the common people, and to understand more thoroughly their ideas and motives" (1898:17). "Our interest in folklore is used," she explained, "not so much to help us in interpreting the past as it is to aid us in understanding present conditions, and to make it easier for us to push forward the philanthropic work that Hampton is doing" (1898:17).

After a brief overview of the society and a quick discussion of the type of material they collected, she described the difficulty of transcribing a "weird melody chanted at baptism" or a "complicated negro religious ritual" and appealed for help to the AFLS: "If we can only secure and preserve them by some other method than that of writing them down.... If we can obtain a graphophone, and thus make records not only of songs, but sermons, prayers, etc. and so gather, as we cannot now gather, some complete records of entire religious services, we are convinced that through this means we may add much to the common fund of knowledge of the negro music" (1898:20).

Newell believed that providing Hampton Institute with the latest scientific technology would help to advance the science of folklore. Writing to Boas shortly before the AFLS meeting in New York City in 1898, Newell explained that he had "promised to procure a graphophone for . . . Miss Alice M. Bacon, of the Hampton Institute, [who,] as you know, takes a great interest in negro music." Since Boas would "be in a position to know the best recording instrument," Newell asked him to "order an instrument of this sort, if you think that form the best, to be shipped at once to Miss Bacon . . . with fifty cylinders, and send the bill to me." Bacon, Newell explained, "already has a great body of collections of tales, &c, and I hope will be able to prepare a volume suitable for publication in the series of Memoirs. If this instrument can be got to Hampton at once, Miss Bacon will send, or bring, a number of cylinders to our meeting. I think that would have an excellent effect toward exhibiting the scientific energy of our Society."[11] Boas did not respond to the first request, and now, with the meeting less than two weeks away, Newell wrote Boas again about the high-tech graphophone, which was a new and improved phonograph. Reiterating the urgency, Newell exclaimed, "I want them to get cylinders for the meeting."[12] Forty-eight hours later, just days before the meeting, a testy Newell pleaded with the man he had supported for so many years: "I should like to have the instrument sent to Hampton at once, and the bill to me. . . . Pray send the machine at once."[13]

During the month of December, Bacon was eagerly awaiting the graphophone. By December 21 she realized that even if it came, she could not make the recordings. She wrote to Newell, "I am afraid that it will be impossible for us to get up anything with its aid for the annual meeting." Instead, she proposed the real thing, and offered up

a most delightful paper by Prof. D. W. Davis of Richmond, on "Echoes from a Plantation Party," which may be worth studying up on. Davis is a full blooded Negro, a teacher in Richmond and the authority of a number of dialect processes. He takes a real interest in the old customs of his own people, and has been at considerable pains to collect all he can. . . .

I asked him if he would be willing to describe it [his paper] in New York at the annual meeting and he says that he can. . . . The songs are a great part of it. It is rather better than a phonographic reprint as he gives it.[14]

Newell did not give up on the graphophone or on Boas. Two months after the New York meeting, he again pestered Boas: "Pray let me know if you have been able to send the graphophone to Miss A. M. Bacon at

Hampton Institute as directed by me. If you do not wish to take the responsibility of sending it, I will write direct to the Columbia Graphophone Company."[15] The correspondence between Newell and Boas is incomplete, but the tone of the preceding letter suggests Boas agreed to do it but never followed through. Newell then turned to Putnam for advice and counsel about the proper graphophone to send, but as he explained to Boas in one final plea, "Prof. Putnam says that it is not safe for me to order the instrument, as it is very easy to get instruments which are practically worthless. He thinks I had better leave it to you. But he also says that perhaps they will not forward the instrument without previous payment. If so, I will remit a check. . . . As you are interested in musical collection, I hope you will not think this too much trouble; it seems to me that here is an opportunity."[16]

It appears the HFS never got its graphophone. One can only speculate as to why Boas ignored such a simple request. What we do know is that he began seriously engaging African American issues after 1905—before then it probably was not a high priority.

Bacon left Hampton in 1899 to return to Japan and administered a school for young women, and the HFS was not sustained in her absence. Her major literary contributions remain those on Japanese women (Bacon 1891). Moton left Hampton to be one of Booker T. Washington's chief lieutenants and succeeded Washington as Tuskegee's president. Leonora Herron remained as Hampton's librarian. Bacon died in 1918, but the notebooks of folklore she collected to promote racial uplift were republished in 1922 to promote Negroes' African heritage.

Lifting as We Climb

The HFS developed as the progressive era waxed and the Gilded Age waned. During that period, the tidewater region of Virginia was marked by increased lynchings and restrictions on black male suffrage, and the routinization and legalization of Jim Crow segregation. Under the leadership of Bacon, the work of the HFS can be seen as cut from the same cloth as Jane Addams and the settlement house movement or the founding of the Kamehameha Schools—a tapestry of thrift, self-reliance, morality, and Christian faith. The HFS does not, however, fit neatly within the discursive practices of progressive era reformers, the black women's club movement, or the black men's self-help leagues. Although its members grappled with identical issues and emulated many of these other groups' practices, they are distinguished from the others by the particular attention they paid to ideas regarding culture, as well as class, to articulate the ideology of racial uplift.

The former students of Hampton who made up the bulk of the membership of the society viewed themselves as part of a Negro elite who shared faith in Jesus and a moral obligation to uplift the race. Shouldering the responsibility of what would have amounted to a talented 2 percent, these "college-bred" Negroes of the late nineteenth century promulgated a complex ideology of racial uplift inflected by gender and class distinctions (Du Bois and Dill 1969). Black ministers, educators, journalists, doctors, and social workers used rhetoric, research, and writing to combat egregious and dehumanizing claims that African Americans were inherently inferior and not capable of assuming the rights and responsibilities of citizenship or civilization.

Imbued with the optimism and progressive spirit of the age, these black leaders enlisted the support of white political and business leaders to foster racial progress, primarily through a trickle-down theory of education. College graduates would fan out across the South, teaching students in small schools the Victorian and Yankee ideals taught to them by missionaries and reformers. The idea was to improve the material conditions of blacks and demonstrate that they were capable of citizenship and civilization, indeed of humanity. The efforts to show racial progress, however, were largely predicated upon identifying distinctions between those blacks who rose to a civilized state and those not quite there, and such distinctions often turned on status or class distinctions.

The National Association of Colored Women, founded in 1896, struck the keynote of this ideology with their motto "Lifting as we climb," which had been something of a credo for years among educated black folks (Evans 2007:61–69). The catchwords, however, signified a distinction between the lifters and the lifted, the climbers and the pulled. As Kevin K. Gaines has argued, "Generally, black elites claimed class distinctions, indeed, the very existence of a 'better class' of blacks, as evidence of what they called race progress" (1996:xiv). Gaines further argues that "the attempt to rehabilitate the image of black people through class distinctions trafficked in claims of racial and gender hierarchy." These hierarchies created obvious tensions: "On the one hand, a broader vision of uplift signifying collective social aspiration, advancement, and struggle had been the legacy of the emancipation era. On the other hand, black elites made uplift the basis for a racialized elite identity claiming Negro improvement through class stratification as race progress, which entailed an attenuated conception of bourgeois qualifications for rights and citizenship" (1996:xv).

Although proponents of uplift did not advance unified themes about racial progress, the idea that the race would progress toward a civilized citizenry served as a unifying theme as people searched for various ways to create an authentic and respectable black middle-class subjectivity (Higginbotham 1993:14–15). Proponents did not want to mimic whites or become white; they believed the Negro had special gifts to contribute to civilization and was indeed more moral and upright than the vast majority of white folks. Like the Kanaka elite or members of the SAI, these Negro promoters of racial uplift saw themselves as being what Noenoe K. Silva has described as "ultracivilized" (2004:179).

Through essays, pamphlets, newspaper articles, poetry, and books, Ida B. Wells, Booker T. Washington, Anna Julia Cooper, Robert Moton, W. E. B. Du Bois, Frances Ellen Watkins Harper, Mary Church Terrell, James Corrothers, Paul Lawrence Dunbar, and a host of others announced to the world, "We are here!"—right here, in the Christian brotherhood of civilization (Alexander 1997:67; Eversley 2004:3–20).

The HFS was also articulating racial uplift ideology. They, too, were propounding the notion "We are here." But it was not the temporally static "We are here, right here." It was a "We are (up) here, not (down) there." Knowingly or not, HFS members used an anthropologically inflected folklore to plot the perceived temporal distance between the college-bred Negroes and the cabin people. Although this folklore helped to demonstrate how far they had come in the race to progress, it was ultimately deployed to document how quickly they were closing the gap and to measure the success of lifting as they climbed.[17]

The HFS provided an additional dimension to the idea of racial uplift by inserting notions about stages of culture. By explicitly distinguishing the low and savage African culture from the high and civilized Christian culture, they appropriated the comparative method of evolutionary anthropology to bolster a politics of culture that advanced the status of many individuals as citizens. After all, it was Tylor who suggested that based on customs and behavior, not race, "we may draw a picture where there shall be scarce a hand's breadth difference between an English ploughman and a negro of Central Africa" (1920:7). Like the tricksters they studied, members of the HFS were arguing, without explicitly stating it, that despite perilous poverty, demeaning segregation, savage lynch mobs, and widespread disfranchisement, behavior and character, not inherited characteristics, could elevate not only one, but *all* into Christian civilization. This conviction simply flew in the face of the most powerful science of the day.

Twenty years later, well after Boas's critique of the comparative method, members of the New Negro movement appropriated Boasian ideas of diffusion and the particularity of cultures to bolster a very different politics of culture that advanced the idea of a proud African heritage. Although the HFS no longer existed, the material they had collected was recycled into this very different racial project during the New Negro movement.

(2)

Fabricating

the Authentic

and the Politics

of the Real

On January 29, 1919, Zitkala-Ša wrote as the secretary-treasurer of the SAI to "Brigadier-General R. H. Pratt" lambasting the ethnologist James Mooney of the Smithsonian Institution for his "peyote propaganda" and his efforts to assist followers of the peyote way with "chartering their so-called peyote church to evade possible peyote prohibition." Soliciting the good general's assistance, she explained that "prompt action should be taken to disarm him of his government position." Zitkala-Ša was particularly concerned with the fact that "Mr. Mooney . . . is paid by the Government for his services along ethnological lines. This work takes him into the heart of Indian communities. It appears that he takes advantage of these field trips to encourage peyote eating among the tribes."[1] Pratt had been after Mooney for a long time. He had collected letters and affidavits documenting Mooney's statements that "he was in favor of the Indians having Peyote" and that "he was not in favor of laws prohibiting it." Using a blue Crayola crayon, Pratt highlighted a section of a letter from T. J. Davis, "Missionary to the Cheyenne Indians," who recalled that Mooney stated, "Peyote is a good thing for them." The missionary accused Mooney of encouraging "these old customs" simply to then "go back to Washington and write them up."[2]

Pratt was an unlikely ally of Zitkala-Ša because she hated him. For many years the two clashed over boarding school education. As a young woman, she had been an instructor for Pratt at Carlisle but grew more and more disenchanted by a pedagogy that systematically sought to discipline and control the lives of young people by driving a wedge between young and old, traditional and civilized Indians. After she left Carlisle in 1899 to pursue her passion for music at the New England Conservatory of Music, she also began to write. She wrote a series of impassioned short stories for the *Atlantic Monthly* that indicted the method and form of education being imposed on Indian children at Carlisle. In "An Indian Teacher among the Indians," she flat out rejected their pedagogy to embrace the wisdom of her mother, who "had never gone to school" (1900:384). Using an unnamed first-person narrator, Zitkala-Ša blurred the genres of autobiography, fiction, and campfire story to highlight the atrocities perpetrated upon the young people at Indian boarding schools, detailing how she came to doubt the sincerity of some of the instructors and the mission of the schools. Using the voice of the young teacher's mother, Zitkala-Ša wrote, "Beware of the paleface. . . . He is the hypocrite who reads with one eye 'Thou shalt not kill,' and with the other gloats upon the sufferings of the Indian race" (1900:385). After returning from the reservation to "the school in the East," the teacher began to scrutinize "the large army of white teachers in Indian schools," describing in detail "an opium-eater holding a position as a teacher of Indians" and "an inebriate paleface [who] sat stupid in a doctor's chair, while Indian patients carried their ailments to untimely graves" (1900:385). In a stunning indictment of the civilizing mission, Zitkala-Ša concluded her story by questioning "whether real life or long lasting death lies beneath this semblance of civilization" (1900:386).

There was little doubt that her "school in the East" was Carlisle, and Pratt was furious. His school's paper responded to the article noting that "her portraits are either so exaggerated as to be untrue or are pure inventions" (Pratt 1900:2). For several years, Zitkala-Ša continued to write stories critical of the civilizing mission and the boarding school movement, and Pratt continued to use his power and influence to curb the impact she had on the public's imagination (Spack 2001:187–88). Yet Pratt's bellicose trashing of Zitkala-Ša's literary work actually increased her motivation to write more critically. In 1901, she explained how she hated Pratt in a letter to her fiancé, the renowned physician and Pratt protégé Carlos Montezuma. "Col. Pratt has used his pull against me," she wrote, "because my think is not his think—nor my ways his ways and just the hate of him frees me to work again even when I would most like to fold my hands."[3] Almost twenty years later Zitkala-Ša humbly requested Pratt to use his pull *for* her, asking his assistance to help prohibit the use of peyote and remove Mooney from his government post.

Framing the Politics of the Real

In this chapter, I focus first on the life, fieldwork, and writing of James Mooney and then on his, Putnam's, and Boas's contribution to the World's Columbian Exposition of 1893. I focus specifically on Mooney to illustrate my point that the political implications of the anthropology of Indians and culture were significantly different from the anthropology of Negroes and race, which I take up in the next chapter with the rise of Daniel G. Brinton. Brinton, as noted earlier, abandoned his work on American Indian languages to chase the professional spoils that followed in the wake of an anthropology of race that supported white supremacy and Negro inferiority. There is an interesting asymmetry between the career trajectories of Brinton and Mooney. Both scholars used anthropology to engage public issues: Brinton was supported by public people and embraced by private institutions as he continued his research on race, while at the same time Mooney was marginalized by public institutions and challenged by private people as he continued his research on Indian cultures. Despite his tireless crusade for religious freedom and Indian rights, American Indians and their so-called friends privately conspired to bring him down, and in part they succeeded (Moses 2002:145–53). Leading "the cry for Mooney's scalp" was Richard Henry Pratt (Moses 2002:148). Unlike Armstrong, who saw some value in ethnology for advancing the Hampton idea, Pratt felt nothing but contempt for ethnology and ethnologists and saw the whole enterprise as anathema to the Carlisle idea, and in Pratt's eyes Mooney was the most contemptible ethnologist at the bureau.

I demonstrate how the pattern of preserving and exhibiting traditional Indian cultures while ignoring and erasing Negro folk cultures was firmly established by the late nineteenth century. I also show how white reformers and indigenous intellectuals tried to derail anthropologists' efforts to showcase the Indian, while African American intellectuals protested the fact that they were denied a showcase at all. The HFS and its close relationship with the AFLS was not typical. During the late nineteenth century, anthropologists did little to support, exhibit, or study African

American cultural patterns and processes, while they engaged in Herculean efforts to collect, preserve, and exhibit American Indian cultures. Despite the outcries of reformers and American Indian intellectuals, ethnologists played a critical role in cementing a racial politics of culture in which out-of-the way Indians had a culture worthy of preservation and exhibition while in-the-way Negroes did not.

James Junior Goes to Washington

Mooney is generally considered a pioneer of public anthropology, and while he might not be deemed the father of the anthropology of engagement, he should at least be considered the wacky uncle (Cook 2003:195). His tireless Indian advocacy, his lucid and politically engaged prose, and his commitment to reciprocity and collaboration with people whom he loved and labored with seem to be at the forefront of a type of engaged anthropology that has always been an important approach to the field, and recently has received increased attention (Borofsky 2000; Sanday 2002; Lamphere 2004; Lassiter 2005a, 2005b; Lyon-Callo and Hyatt 2003). Mooney was a committed and engaged fieldworker, but he was also dogmatic and fiercely protective of what he considered the real or true Indian life ways. In his zeal to police authenticity, he often engaged in actions that might be termed fabricating the authentic or producing the real (Hinsley 1990). Although excellent biographical work has been done on Mooney, no one has used his style of salvage and fabrication of American Indian cultures as a counterpoint to the HFS's style of salvage and erasure of African American culture to draw connections and distinctions between the ways the culture of blacks and Indians were described and exhibited (Moses 2002; Hinsley 1981; Cook 2003).

One of the best examples of the stark differences between the black and Indian representation in the late nineteenth century was the 1893 World's Fair, whose organizers systematically and unapologetically produced American Indian culture for popular consumption, while at the same time purposely prohibiting the showcasing of the culture of African Americans—either their culture of uplift or traditional folk culture.

Who was James Mooney Jr., and why did he personally incur the wrath of Zitkala-Ša, a noted author and the secretary-treasurer of the SAI? He was born on February 10, 1861, in Richmond, Indiana. Steeped in Irish folklore and Catholic catechism, he and his two sisters were raised by his devout mother, who was widowed shortly after his birth. Like many children of Irish immigrants during the mid-nineteenth century, James Jr. grew up in a stark landscape of poverty and prejudice, yet developed a strong sense of Irish pride by listening to stories about the mystic and mythic landscapes of the Emerald Isle, the kings who reigned at the Hill of Tara, and the heroic feats of St. Patrick.

By the age of twelve, Mooney developed a keen interest in Native American communities as he excelled in Richmond's public schools. As the very last tribes were brought under the discipline of the reservation system, Mooney began to catalogue the name and location of each Indian tribe in the United States. His interest in American Indians continued to develop throughout his high school career, which culminated in his valedictory speech in 1878 in which he addressed the need for a humane and effective federal Indian policy, one that could be implemented only after careful study of tribal cultures (Moses 2002:1–6).

After graduation, Mooney taught school for a couple of years, wrote for the local paper, and became involved with Irish famine relief and land reform (Moses 2002:6). He continued to be interested in American Indians, and in June of 1882 he boldly wrote to Major John Wesley Powell, the director of the newly formed BAE, to ask him for a job (Moses 2002:7; Hinsley 1981:147). Powell ignored Mooney, but in a last-ditch effort Mooney traveled to Washington to track Powell down and introduce himself. Powell eventually acquiesced and offered Mooney a staff position.

Powell explained to Mooney that he had to serve as a volunteer until the next fiscal appropriation. Mooney started at the bureau on April 24, 1885, compiling a list of tribal names, their synonyms, and languages (Moses 2002:17). Mooney joined the bureau when it was doing some of its most important work and Major Powell was at the high-water mark of his career as an ethnologist and bureau director. This was also the period when Henry L. Dawes was beginning to make headway in the legislative process that would result in the Dawes Act of 1887.

John Wesley Powell made his mark in Washington as a geologist and surveyor, scientist and adventurer during the 1870s as he emerged as a storied Washington insider (Darnell 1971; Darrah 1951; Stegner 1954; Worster 2001). Although he is viewed as a founder of the conservation movement in the West, he was also the first person to institutionalize anthropology in the United States by mobilizing a corps of paid professionals at the bureau (Seigel et al. 2003:1; Hinsley 1981:151). The BAE was originally authorized by Congress in the spring of 1879 when it consolidated various geographical surveys into the U.S. Geological Survey.[4] Although the bureau was chartered under the auspices of the Smithsonian Institution to extend its mission "for the increase and diffusion of knowledge," Powell used the application of knowledge as the justification he gave Congress for the bureau's inception (Smithson 1826:3). In short, ethnology could help to solve the so-called Indian problem.

Important segments of Powell's surveys of Colorado, the Rocky Mountains, and the Great Basin were detailed descriptions of various Native North American communities as well as an analysis of the often tense relationships between indigenous and settler groups in the Great Basin and desert Southwest.[5] In a report Powell wrote to help reform the way the federal government managed its public lands, he included a prospectus for the bureau by demonstrating the utility of having a stand-alone agency to help scientifically solve the Indian problem: "The rapid spread of civilization since 1849 had placed the white man and the Indian in direct conflict throughout the whole area, and the 'Indian Problem' is thus thrust upon us and it *must* be solved, wisely or unwisely. Many of the difficulties are inherent and cannot be avoided, but an equal number are unnecessary and are caused by the lack of our knowledge relating to the Indians themselves" (1878:15). In keeping with his military background, surveillance, reconnaissance, and intelligence were key rationales Powell offered Congress to justify this federal bureau of investigation. He indicated that ethnology could provide intelligence about Indians because their practices "must necessarily be overthrown before new institutions, customs, philosophy, and religion can be introduced" (1878:15). Powell's blueprint for the bureau was twofold; on one hand it would serve Indian agencies by supplying information to help manage and control dissimilar tribes, while on the other it would serve Smithsonian science by conducting research on disappearing societies. Powell outlined how "the field of research is speedily narrowing because of the rapid change in the Indian population now in progress . . . and in a very few years it will be impossible to study our North American Indians in their primitive conditions except from recorded history. For this reason ethnologic studies in America should be pushed with utmost vigor" (1878:15).

The bureau produced original research within the survey under the rubric of natural history. The discovery, description, and cataloguing of

Indian languages, customs, and kinship terminologies soon filled the elaborate annual reports, which highlighted the collective work of the bureau as well as that of individual staff members. As director, Powell set the tone and tenor. The year Mooney joined the bureau, Powell was president of the Anthropological Society of Washington. Powell's presidential address was entitled "From Savagery to Barbarism," and he sketched out his vision for a nomothetic anthropology and his ideas about the road to civilization.

There is little doubt Powell viewed himself as heir apparent to the legacy created by Lewis Henry Morgan and E. B. Tylor, while making a not-so-subtle distinction between himself and Herbert Spencer, who coined the phrase "the survival of the fittest." Powell opened his address to what must have been a rapt audience by confidently stating, "It is a long way from savagery to civilization." This telling line underscored the difference between the bureau's view of Indian advancement and that of the members of the Lake Mohonk Conference, namely, Pratt and Senator Dawes. These reformers believed in a relatively short road to civilization augmented by education and programs that would enable rapid assimilation.

Powell's main message was that he had a new and improved way to measure the progress from savagery to civilization. Powell began by challenging "the most noteworthy attempt hitherto made to distinguish and define culture-stages," which he credited to "Lewis H. Morgan in his great work entitled 'Ancient Society [1877]' " (1885:171). Powell's basic argument was that "the separation between savagery and barbarism" was greater than Morgan or Tylor had surmised and that people stayed within the stage of savagery longer but then sped through the other stages faster with the help of racial and cultural mixing, or what he termed "a return to homogeneity" (1885:194). As Powell optimistically reasoned, "Civilization overwhelms Savagery, not so much by spilling blood as by mixing blood, but whether spilled or mixed, a greater homogeneity is secured" (1885:194). Powell was not very specific in terms of temporality, but he was clear that "human evolution has none of the characteristics of animal evolution. It is not 'by the survival of the fittest' in the struggle for existence, but it is by human endeavor to secure happiness" (1885:195).

Although Powell's long road out of savagery differed from that of Dawes and Pratt, he agreed with them that assimilation was the best way to solve the Indian problem. Reporting to Congress on public lands west of the Rocky Mountains, Powell went so far as to suggest that "the sooner this country is entered by white people and the game destroyed so that the Indians will be compelled to gain a subsistence by some other means than hunting, the better it will be for them" (1874:8). In important ways, however, his ideas about an overall trend toward homogeneity or a type of equality and his dismissal of the notion of the survival of the fittest contrasted markedly from those of people like Andrew Carnegie, the well-known steel baron, who argued, "We accept and welcome, therefore, as conditions to which we must accommodate ourselves, great inequality of environment, the concentration of business, industrial and commercial, in the hands of a few, and the law of competition between these, as being not only beneficial, but essential for the future progress of the race" (1889:654–55). The theoretical orientation of the bureau when Mooney came on board was decidedly grounded within an evolutionary framework, but it was not the tooth-and-nail social Darwinism of Carnegie and Spencer or the strict racial hierarchy embraced by Brinton. Pratt and Powell embraced a Larmarckian-inflected notion of evolution, popular among reformers and educators (Stocking 1987:234–36). This is not to say that the bureau challenged white supremacy. Powell was quick to assert that when discussing "the evolution of barbarism into civilization it becomes necessary to confine the exposition . . . to a large extent, to one great stock of people—the Aryan race" (1888:109).

Although Mooney did not stray far from these theoretical lines, his Irish background gave him a different perspective on the way people respond to cultural, political, and physical oppression. According to Curtis Hinsley, "From these roots came the central questions of his anthropology: How do oppressed people transmit the binding elements of their culture from one generation to the next? How do those who are defeated and dispersed nonetheless preserve identity and tradition?" (1981:207). Both Hinsley and L. G. Moses make a compelling case that Mooney's commitment to Irish heritage and nationalism influenced his careful ethnography with an emphasis on history, oral tradition, and mythology because he was well aware that political and cultural disintegration resulting from conquest and displacement were historical facts, not the result of inherent worth or moral decay. Moreover, he was particularly attentive to the trauma inflicted upon persons who were forced to assimilate (Hinsley 1981:205–6; Moses 2002:20–21). Yet the tenacious grip with which he held onto Irish folklore, customs, and spirituality was perhaps also partly responsible for his obsession with the exotic and authentic, which contributed to his self-assigned role as the arbiter of real Indians. An interesting tension runs through Mooney's work. For example, he could not accept Zitkala-Ša's "costume" as a creative salute to the pan-Indian political movement, and he simply dismissed the Lumbee tribe of south central North Carolina as "five thousand mongrels" who "seek to prove their descent from the lost colony of Roanoke" (Mooney 1891a:394). However, he was unique among his peers because he came to see Indian cultures as dynamic and changing in response to extreme conditions. Although the peyote religion in the 1890s was as much of a hybrid pan-Indian movement as the SAI's movement, he could support the use of peyote because it was not imposing the trauma of assimilation.

Mooney quickly distinguished himself at the bureau. He was twenty-six years old and the youngest person on Powell's staff when the director sent him off to investigate the southernmost dialects of the Iroquoian language found among the so-called Mountain Cherokees of the Great Smoky Mountains. Mooney, however, envisioned a much broader scope for his research.

The Difference Is Only Relative

Mooney arrived in western North Carolina in the summer of 1887—an important moment in the extremely tumultuous history of the Eastern Band of the Cherokee Nation. The Eastern Band resisted the genocidal Indian removal policies, or the infamous Trail of Tears of 1838–39. The history of this resistance is complicated and dramatic, but some Cherokees had acquired land under a treaty of 1819 and insisted on remaining in North Carolina, while others hid or outmaneuvered army troops in the mountainous forests. Still others quietly "passed" as they worked to eke out a hard living in southern Appalachia. In 1895, the official census numbered the Eastern Band at just under fifteen hundred people (Mooney 1900:179; Finger 1984).

Historically, the Cherokee were consistently viewed as the most assimilated of the so-called Five Civilized Tribes, but the communities in western North Carolina were always more isolated and less acculturated than their friends and relatives in South Carolina, eastern Tennessee, northern Alabama, and north Georgia (Finger 1984:3–4). By the time Mooney arrived, however, many of the traditional practices were no longer being sustained. In fact, several scholars have noted that Mooney's interest in the folklore, medicine, and spiritual practices of the Eastern Cherokee actually revived and renewed interest in preserving and sustaining these practices (Finger 1984:153; White 2001:15).

When Mooney arrived at Qualla Boundary, which straddles the banks of the Oconaluftee River in the westernmost corner of North Carolina, he described the Eastern Cherokee as the "purest-blooded and most conservative of the Nation" (1900:157) but went on to note:

> As a people they are peaceable and law-abiding, kind and hospitable, providing for their simple wants by their own industry without asking or expecting outside assistance. Their fields, orchards, and fish traps, with some few domestic animals and occasional hunting, supply them with food, while . . . they procure what additional supplies they need from the traders. The majority are fairly comfortable, far above the condition of most Indian tribes, and but little, if any, behind their white neighbors. In literary ability they may even be said to surpass them. . . . All wear civilized costumes, though an occasional pair of moccasins is seen, while the women find means to gratify the racial love of color in wearing of red bandanna kerchiefs in place of bonnets. The older people still cling to their ancient rites and sacred traditions, but the dance and the ballplay wither and the Indian day is nearly spent. (1900:180–81)

The Eastern Cherokee were not like the exotic Navajo, Zuñi, or Ojibwa, who were the subjects of detailed ethnographic description and depiction that filled the pages of the annual tomes compiled by the bureau. Many of the Eastern Cherokee were God-fearing Christians who worked hard in the mountains of North Carolina, weaving their history and heritage with that of their southern Appalachian neighbors.

Mooney was not, however, concerned with outward appearances (at least this time); he was more concerned with documenting, discovering, and salvaging the tribe's history, folklore, and religion. True to form, he began by compiling a list, this time of all of the indigenous plants used by the Cherokees for food and medicine, but "it soon became evident that the application of the medicine was not the whole, and in fact was rather the subordinate, part of the treatment, which was always accompanied by certain ceremonies and 'words' " (Mooney 1891b:310).

Mooney's painstaking approach to fieldwork mirrored the participatory-observation model pioneered by bureau ethnologists like Frank Hamilton

Cushing, who worked with Zuñi, and Washington Matthews, who worked
with Navajos. Like Cushing and Matthews, Mooney employed a research
strategy that revolved around a complex negotiation of persistence, pa-
tience, indirection, exchange, flattery, and language competence (Hinsley
1981:210). Although Mooney had the offices of Chief N. J. Smith (who had
worked in Washington with J. Owen Dorsey at the bureau) at his disposal,
he had a difficult time winning the trust of powerful men and women
who quite literally held tribal secrets, in the form of notebooks and manuscripts written some thirty years earlier. Securing these sacred notebooks
was not easy, and Mooney was unscrupulous in his methods of gaining
under generally false pretenses the trust and confidence of the people
who held the sacred manuscripts. Mooney eventually succeeded in per-
suading the Cherokees to sell him the writings, which are, he reported,
"now in the possession of the Bureau of Ethnology" (Mooney 1891b:306).
"Mooney's [initial] field success," Hinsley explains, "was attributable in
part to the fact that he astutely but sympathetically took advantage of the
social disintegration and economic poverty of the Cherokees" (1981:210).
His first major publication for the bureau was a translation and analysis
of these manuscripts written in the unique Cherokee syllabary and aptly
titled "Sacred Formulas of the Cherokees" (1891b).

In "Sacred Formulas" Mooney candidly reported how he obtained his
sacred secrets as well as each of the secret manuscripts. His most reliable informant was a spiritual leader named A'y^{ñn} inĭ, or "Swimmer." Although Swimmer was "willing to tell anything in regard to stories and
customs," he would not sing the songs Mooney requested because "these
songs were part of his secret knowledge" (1891b:311). Mooney threatened
to fire Swimmer because "he was paid to tell all he knew" (1891b:311).
Mooney tried to explain to Swimmer that "the only object in asking about
the songs was to put them on record and preserve them, that when he
and the half dozen old men of the tribe were dead the world might be
aware [of] how much the Cherokees had known" (1891b:311). Many of the
elders objected to this rationale. As Mooney recounts, "Among other ob-
jections which they advanced was one which, however incomprehensible
to a white man, was perfectly intelligible to an Indian, viz: That when he
had told everything this information would be taken to Washington and
locked up there, and thus they would be deprived of the knowledge. This
objection was one of the most difficult to overcome, as there was no line
of argument with which to oppose it" (1891b:311). After failing to appeal to

Swimmer's sense of obligation, financial or otherwise, Mooney attempted
to "appeal to his professional pride [which] proved effectual, and when he
was told that a great many similar songs had been sent to Washington by
medicine men of other tribes, he [Swimmer] promptly declared that he
knew as much as any of them, and that he would give all the information
in his possession, so that others might be able to judge for themselves
who knew most" (1891b:311). Eventually, Swimmer produced his secret
notebook, and Mooney struck a bargain such that Swimmer could copy
all of his formulas and Mooney would buy the original (1891b:312).

To Mooney's amazement, it included "just those matters that had proved
so difficult to procure. Here were prayers, songs, and prescriptions for the
cure of all kinds of diseases—for chills, rheumatism, frostbites, wounds,
bad dreams, and witchery; love charms . . . fishing charms, hunting
charms. . . . It was in fact an Indian ritual and pharmacopæia" (1891b:312).
Although Mooney attempted to acquire other notebooks that summer,
he would have to wait until his return the following year. He returned to
Qualla Boundary during the summer of 1888 and explained that "by this
time the Indians had several months to talk over the matter, and the idea
gradually dawned upon them that instead of taking their knowledge away
from them and locking it up in a box, the intention was to preserve it to
the world and pay them for it at the same time" (1891b:313). In addition,
Mooney "took every opportunity to impress upon them the fact that he
was acquainted with the secret knowledge of other tribes and perhaps
could give them as much as they gave"(1891b:313). In fact, Mooney did not
limit the reciprocity of information to his knowledge of American Indian
folklore and formulas; he frequently shared his knowledge of traditional
Irish stories, songs, and remedies, and boasted to his informants, "I am a
great conjurer too" (Moses 2002:24). In many respects, Mooney's tactics,
ambition, and genuine love for both the Cherokee and their cultural practices emerge as one of many examples of the type of love and theft that
leavened both blackface minstrelsy and ethnographic research.

Swimmer had informed Mooney that all of the spiritual leaders as well
as deceased former leaders of the tribe possessed these notebooks. Upon
his return, Mooney began in earnest to follow up on his leads. One particular manuscript that he wanted to procure was written by Gahuni, who
"like several others of their shamans, combined the professions of Indian
conjurer and Methodist preacher" (Mooney 1891b:314). Gahuni had died,
but his living relatives dutifully kept his manuscripts of secret formulas,

rites, and spiritual practices. Although Mooney had some difficulty obtaining the manuscripts from people who did not possess a "mercenary disposition," he eventually persuaded the kinfolk of several deceased spiritual leaders and obtained four manuscripts (1891b:313). Although Mooney confronted "one or two shamans" who refused to sell their notebooks, he was confident that his collection of sacred material "comprised by far the greater portion of the whole quantity held by the Indians, and as only a small portion of this was copied by the owners it can not be duplicated by any future collector" (1891b:318).

Another problem Mooney faced during this collecting expedition was ferreting out what was aboriginal and what was not. Many of what he called manuscripts of sacred formulas also contained what he termed "miscellaneous books, papers, and pictures" as well as "Scripture extracts" (1891b:314, 315). The case of the Inâli Manuscript was an example of how Mooney was forced to authenticate what was Indian and what was not, what was sacred and what was profane. Inâli, or "Black Fox," according to Mooney, "was a full-blood Cherokee, speaking no English, and in the course of a long lifetime he had filled almost every position of honor among his people, including those of councilor [lawyer], keeper of the townhouse records, Sunday-school leader, conjurer, officer in the Confederate service, and Methodist preacher" (1891b:314–15). Mooney explained that Black Fox had assembled a massive manuscript collection and did not distinguish between letters from his Confederate comrades, records from the town hall, or his certificate from the Methodist Episcopal Church to preach the gospel. He simply kept a record of his notable and noteworthy achievements and memories, along with the tools of his many trades, which included useful biblical scriptures and sacred formulas. Even the daughter of Black Fox, who was the keeper of the archive, did not distinguish between the articles. To her, it was all important and all secret, and she wanted it preserved in the bureau's library. Mooney was really only concerned with the formulas.

Eric Lott's work on minstrelsy focuses on the ambivalence of both the actors and the audience as it relates to a fabricated blackness. Lott explains how "minstrelsy's mixed erotic economy of celebration and exploitation" animated racial and sexual anxieties and ambivalence. "The very form of blackface acts—an investiture in black bodies—seems a manifestation of the particular desire to try on the accents of 'blackness' and demonstrate the permeability of the color line" (Lott 1993:6). Lott loosely terms this ambivalence "love and theft." In some respects, love and theft were integral to fieldwork based on participant observation, collecting objects for museums, or inscribing the grammar of a particular language; moreover fieldwork was a clear investiture in traditional or aboriginal culture while trying on the accents of Indianness.

Like many of Mooney's relationships with American Indians, his initial fieldwork among the Cherokee was tinged with ambivalence—love and theft—and it was not always clear who was using whom. Moreover, the fact that these formulas and spiritual practices were kept secret but not separate from other material that was kept secret but not considered sacred begs larger questions about secrecy, memory, and sacredness among Eastern Cherokee. Perhaps these formulas and rites were sacred, as in spiritual, divine, or holy, but not hallowed, needing protection for fear of desecration, or perhaps Mooney never received the most hallowed formulas. Whatever the case, Mooney sifted and sorted, edited and judged the material, so that he could set "forth in the clearest light the state of the aboriginal religion before its contamination by contact with the whites" (Mooney 1891b:318).

Mooney's analysis of the manuscripts was compelling, and he demonstrated that he did not share Powell's belief in the wide gulf between savagery and barbarism. He also engaged in a type of comparative method that did not compare one savage to another but showed the close proximity of Indian religions to Christianity. Although he did not question evolution per se, he did argue for a type of relativism. In a stunning analysis published a year after the massacre at Wounded Knee, when the Dawes Act and the boarding schools were fully engaged in vanishing policies to assimilate American Indians, Mooney describes the importance of viewing American Indian religious practices holistically, historically, and relative to one another, as opposed to seeing them as stages within a hierarchy. As Mooney observed,

> These formulas furnish a complete refutation of the assertion so frequently made by ignorant and prejudiced writers that the Indian had no religion excepting what they are pleased to call the meaningless mummeries of the medicine man. This is the very reverse of the truth. The Indian is essentially religious and contemplative, and it might almost be said that every act of his life is regulated and determined by his religious belief. It matters not that some may call this superstition. The difference is only relative. The religion of

today has developed from the cruder superstitions of yesterday, and Christianity itself is but an outgrowth and enlargement of the beliefs and ceremonies which have been preserved by the Indian in their more ancient form. When we are willing to admit that the Indian has a religion which he holds sacred, even though it be different from our own, we can then admire the consistency of the theory, the particularity of the ceremonial and the beauty of the expression. So far from being a jumble of crudities, there is a wonderful completeness about the whole system which is not surpassed even by the ceremonial religion of the East.'(1891b:319)

Powell, however, was moved neither by such cross-cultural comparisons nor by Mooney's assertion that the Cherokee religion was closer to Christianity than most people would like to admit. In his introduction to the annual report in which Mooney's ninety-page manuscript was published Powell set limits on the scope of Mooney's claims by suggesting that the ethnologist "naively compares the pharmacopæia of savagery with that of civilization," but in fact the work only "deals with the use of plants by the Indians for the healing of disease" (1891:xxxix). Despite the fact that Mooney clearly stated that the Cherokee were "savage," only "a child in intellect" (1891b:329), and believed that it was "a matter of fact" that "the medicine man's knowledge of herbal remedies is about on a level with that of the ordinary farmer's wife" (1890:44), Powell felt compelled to reiterate his evolutionary sequences, making sure the reader understood that these Indians were at the bottom, but rising. As Powell saw it, the Eastern Cherokees' "zootheism is not a permanent state of philosophy, but only a stepping-stone to something higher" (1891:xl). Drawing on the widely shared view that Cherokees had a long history with the civilizing process, Powell remarked, "A mythology with its religion subject to the influences of an overwhelming civilization yields first in its zoomorphic elements. Zoic mythology soon degenerates into folk tales of beasts, to be recited by crones to children or told by garrulous old men as amusing stories inherited from past generations" (1891:xl). Powell's overall conclusion was that Mooney merely "sets forth the vestiges of a once powerful organization" (1891:xxxix).

Although Powell appreciated the material Mooney brought back to the bureau, Mooney never received the recognition he thought he deserved and remained on the margins, never becoming a bureau star like the much-vaunted Cushing. Nevertheless, Mooney pressed on under difficult circumstances both in the field and at the Smithsonian to write two of the bureau's most influential monographs, *The Ghost Dance Religion and the Sioux Outbreak of 1890* (1896) and *Myths of the Cherokee* (1900), his six-hundred-page memoir of the Cherokee Nation. His initial field experience on the Qualla Boundary in 1886 indeed set the stage for his later, more notable work, but it also galvanized his commitment to preserve and conserve spiritual practices that were subjected to the government's vanishing or assimilation policies. The experience also strengthened his commitment to use history as a way to explain changing and emergent American Indian practices like the Ghost Dance and peyote meetings.

During his initial fieldwork at the Qualla Boundary, Mooney developed three facets of his research and writing that would serve as his greatest strength, while also creating the most controversy: intensive fieldwork tethered to the historical record, editorial authentication, and a penchant for comparing whites to Indians.

Mooney lived side by side with and engaged in the everyday life experiences of his informants and the people he studied. He pioneered intensive participatory fieldwork in the 1880s, which would later become the standard methodology of anthropologists during the twentieth century. "They like me," he told a reporter in 1893, "because I come to them in sympathy, eager to preserve all that is sacred to them while the missionary and the agent come to do away [with] and destroy their traditions." Mooney explained how "unless you live with a people you cannot know them. It is the only way to learn their ideas and study their character. . . . But it is not a pleasant life," he continued, "and a white can hardly expect to endure the exposures and privations more than twenty years. Besides, savages are always dirty, and many of their habits and tastes are revolting to a civilized man. Only an absorbing ethnologic interest makes it possible to endure what a scientist must in exiling himself from civilization" (McCabe 1893).

This type of intensive fieldwork actually allowed him to command some authority within the bureau, and Mooney generally chose to live with and study only the most conservative or traditional Cherokee, and later, the Kiowa and Apache (Moses 2002:44–46). Inevitably, this contributed directly to the second facet, which included the editorial license that he took when describing the image of the real or genuine Indian. In some cases he fabricated images and sounds of people outright in order to shape them into what he perceived as genuine.[6]

In his *Myths of the Cherokee* (1900), for example, Mooney emphasized ball play, herbal medicines, and what he considered traditional customs, while he avoided discussing the factionalism, alcoholism, and high rates of mortality that plagued the Eastern Cherokee (Finger 1984:153). He also gave short shrift to the wake of turmoil created by the Eastern Band's Confederate troops while virtually ignoring the role that free and enslaved blacks played in shaping the Cherokee Nation, merely enumerating the number of "Negroes" in the censuses that he included in the text (Mooney 1900:125; Perdue 2003; Sturm 2002; Finger 1984:90–100; Inscoe 1989:59–114).

Although Mooney was quite clear that he had to sift and sort, delete and edit the material influenced by Europeans, he could not conceive of the fact that African American folklore could have any role in shaping Cherokee folklore, nor could he edit out the many animal and tar baby stories that formed a large corpus of Cherokee lore. In one case, he was actually struck by a Cherokee who told one of their many rabbit and tar baby stories in a way that was virtually identical to one in Joel Chandler Harris's *Uncle Remus, His Songs and His Sayings* (1880). Mooney explained, "The negro, with his genius for imitation and his love for stories, especially of the comic variety, must undoubtedly have borrowed much from the Indian in this way, while on the other hand, the Indian, with his pride of conservatism and his contempt for a subject race, would have taken but little from the Negro . . . there can be no suspicion of negro influences" (1900:233).[7]

By reading *Myths of the Cherokee*, one gains a better perspective on why Mooney was so committed to preserving this ideal of the Indian. He noted that not much history or ethnology was written about the Cherokee because they "are so advanced along the white man's road as to offer but little inducement for ethnologic study" (1900:11). But Mooney's goal was to demonstrate that, despite a tumultuous and violent history and "change indeed in dress and outward" appearances, "the heart of the Indian is still his own" (1900:12).

This theory directly contradicted the theory of Pratt, Armstrong, and even Powell, all of whom believed that, once the outward appearances changed and the folklore died out, the heart and mind changed in lockstep along some evolutionary path toward civilization. It is quite telling that a book about Indian "myths" in 1900, published by the bureau, did not directly address the question of evolution. Rather, the entire first half of the manuscript was a detailed history of wars, settlement patterns, alliances, treaties, chiefs, removal, and government policies that impacted both the Cherokee who were removed to Oklahoma and the ones who defiantly remained in North Carolina.

Mooney's history and folklore remain definitive and vital to the Cherokee Nation today. The *Cherokee Phoenix and Indian Advocate*, the official magazine of the Cherokee Nation, routinely publishes the stories he collected for *Sacred Formulas* and *Myths of the Cherokee* in its arts and culture section, and in an article in 2002 describing Mooney's overall impact the publication noted that his ability to "gain acceptance by the Cherokee people" helped to give "the world a unique glimpse into Cherokee life at the time." Calling *Myths of the Cherokee* a "fascinating book," a *Phoenix* staff writer reminds readers that "it can be purchased from the Cherokee Gift Shop by calling 1-800-256-2123" (Cherokee Phoenix 2002:58). Mooney's *Myths of the Cherokee* also continues to serve as an important source for the popular melodrama *Unto These Hills: Outdoor Drama of the Cherokee Indians* and an outdoor museum where members of the Eastern Band demonstrate Cherokee arts, crafts, and dances in a replica of an Oconaluftee Indian Village. After the casino, these are two of the most popular tourist attractions in Cherokee, North Carolina.

Hinsley frames why Mooney turned to history and never fully embraced the idea that evolution was the engine of progress: "Mooney came to the BAE with a critical edge that was soon sharpened by work among a defeated but persistent people. The remarkable fact is that Mooney, perhaps because he lacked a thorough grounding in Powellian philosophy or a variant evolutionism, saw the persistence in Cherokee defeat. Mooney's own persistence and struggle may have been determinative. For him, nothing came easily. . . . To him the human world was enigmatic, an accidental series of affairs, anything but a progressive rise to civilized reason" (1981:215). Although Mooney viewed science as the epitome of civilization, there is evidence that he did not hold the religion or superstition practiced by supposedly civilized people in high regard, which may explain why he was quick to compare Indian myths to those of Christians. In a suggestive footnote, Mooney used a favorite tactic of Ida B. Wells, the successful antilynching crusader who liked to highlight the savagery of so-called civilized Christians (Wells-Barnett 1899:7).

In an article about the folklore of the South, Mooney described the lucky rabbit's foot and how it is rendered even luckier if the rabbit is caught in a graveyard or near the gallows. Albeit in a footnote, Mooney passionately described a lynching or "execution" in Cobb County, Georgia, in 1889 by depicting a "man hanging in mid-air, writhing in the agonies of death, while 3,000 people scattered over the hill-sides and safely ensconced in the top of trees." Mooney then detailed how a rabbit was scared out of the bushes by the "drop" of the body, and a thousand boys and men scrambled to catch the rabbit because of this association between death and luck. Indignantly, Mooney concluded, "What a picture of unfeeling barbarism and superstition in this Christian year of Grace!" (1889:100).

Mooney rarely disclosed his emotions in his published work, but it was this type of heartfelt righteousness that motivated his subtle but damning indictment of federal Indian policies within the tempered prose, dense history, and circuitous narrative that make up his *Ghost Dance Religion* (1896). In the spring of 1890, Mooney had completed his fieldwork in North Carolina and was writing "Sacred Formulas." He was also planning a trip to Indian Territory (present-day Oklahoma) to continue his work with Cherokees who were removed from the southeastern states, and this was the work that finally culminated in 1900 in *Myths of the Cherokee*.

Mooney was, however, forced to shelve his notes on the Cherokee for almost a decade when he was asked to investigate the millennial Ghost Dance in the territory. On December 29, 1890, while Mooney was en route by train to the territory, Big Foot's division of Miniconjou Ghost Dancers from the Cheyenne River Agency in South Dakota clashed with the Seventh Cavalry of the U.S. Army at the Pine Ridge Agency, near the bed of a dry creek called Wounded Knee.

Like Grain before the Sickle

In the span of two years, the Ghost Dance religion spread and was especially popular among the American Indians of the Great Plains and Rockies, who had suffered violence, death, and near starvation while confined to reservations. It spread quickly as far east as the Missouri River, north to the Canadian border, west to the High Sierras, and south to northern Texas. Early in 1890 it reached the Dakotas. The simple message of Wovoka, the professed Paiute Prophet, gave hope to those who felt hopeless in the face of food shortages verging on famine and difficult adjustment to life on the reservation, whose land area, population, and resources seemed to shrink with each passing year. Wovoka instructed communities to dance and bathe together as well as to work hard, do no harm, not lie, not fight, and "be good and behave always." If they followed these prescripts, Jesus would come and take them away from the white people, give their land and buffalo back, and reunite each person with his or her deceased relatives. He instructed them not to be afraid of the end of the world because "there will be no sickness" and everyone will "return to [being] young again" (Mooney 1896:781).

Shrouded in secrecy, the Ghost Dance received considerable media attention and caused alarm among whites, who pushed for federal military intervention while government agents moved to arrest the spiritual leaders who were spreading the teachings and leading the frenzied dances.

During December of 1890, agency police began in earnest to subdue the Ghost Dance movement in South Dakota. The press followed the events closely. William "Buffalo Bill" Cody even chimed in to indict his former star attraction, explaining to a reporter from the *New York Times* that "of all the bad Indians . . . Sitting Bull is the worst" (*New York Times* [hereafter *NYT*], November 25, 1890:5). On December 15, 1890, agency police arrested Tatanka Iyotake, the famed Lakota chief Sitting Bull, under the pretense that he was organizing a final fight under cover of the Ghost Dance. The police botched the arrest, and Sitting Bull was killed near the Grand River. The next day the *New York Times* reported on the front page that Sitting Bull was "the most unrelenting, the most hostile . . . and the most desperate foe of the whites of any chief of modern times" (*NYT*, December 16, 1890:1).

About forty followers of Sitting Bull left the Standing Rock Agency after his murder. Many believed in the Ghost Dance and feared for their lives, so they sought refuge in the Badlands. This contingent eventually joined with a group of Miniconjou Lakota under the leadership of Si Tanka (Chief Big Foot), a longtime advocate of policies of assimilation. His group of mostly women and children from the Cheyenne River Agency, however, were also devout Ghost Dancers. Together with the contingent from Standing Rock, they tried to make their way south to the Pine Ridge Agency for safety and to avoid further confrontations. Traveling at night to avoid detection, Big Foot's beleaguered party crossed more than 140 miles of freezing, windswept South Dakota terrain. On December 28, the ever-vigilant army discovered them about five miles from Wounded Knee. Once off the reservation, Chief Big Foot and his party were considered hostile, despite the fact that Big Foot surrendered peaceably to an army detachment who moved the group to a camp overnight at Wounded Knee Creek. During the night, the 7th Cavalry got reinforcements, and 470 soldiers controlled 400 Sioux. They surrounded Big Foot's camp and placed four Hotchkiss mountain guns on a low hill to the west. Following the overnight encampment, the band was surrounded and a scuffle broke out as the cavalry disarmed the party. A shot was fired from within the group, and a soldier fell. From close range the soldiers fired into the group of exhausted, hungry, cold men, women, and children. The men fought hard with hatchets, knives, and clubs, but the soldiers' barrage of hundreds of rifles and the continuous close-range shelling simply massacred the party. As General L. W. Colby recalled at the time,

> It was the desperate death struggle of brave men against three or four times their number, who believed that they were all to be massacred, and who determined to sell their lives as dearly as possible. The slaughter was terrible; rifles rang; hatchets whizzed through the air; soldiers shouted. . . . The Hotchkiss guns were turned upon them, regardless of women and children, and the repeated volleys from the carbines brought them down like grain before the sickle. The camp, valley and hill-sides seemed but a sheet of flame over which the smoke rolled in clouds. Big Foot, himself, rose from his sick bed, and came to the door of his tepee only to fall dead pierced with many bullets. The surviving Indians now started to escape to the bluffs and canyons. The Hotchkiss guns were turned upon them, and the battle became really a hunt on the part of the soldiers, the purpose being total extermination. (1892:156–57)

Although the exact number of Lakota dead is unknown (Mooney was probably pretty close when he estimated nearly 300), 144 Lakota, including 44 women and 16 children, were buried in a mass grave the following spring when the weather permitted the army to return. About 30 soldiers were killed, but many of the soldiers were killed by friendly fire in the rain of bullets and shrapnel that indiscriminately pounded the encampment.[8] Rocky Bear, a leader among the Oglala Lakota, reminded an investigator at the time that

> the cause of the trouble is the same old story. The Great Father sends his agents here to make treaties with us. The white man came and we were driven out. We are promised things, but they never come. The Great Father

promises to give us food, money, farming tools, and to educate our children, in exchange for our lands, but forgets to do it. Treaties are only a lot of lies. The Government never kept any treaty it ever made with us. We have always been robbed and lied to. We did not commence the fight. We know that will do no good, but the government takes our lands and puts us here where nothing can be raised, and our wives and children suffer for food; they are cold and hungry. Then they send soldiers to kill us, and the Agents lie about us after they rob us. If my people could get what the Government agreed to pay us, they would all be fat and there would be no trouble. The Great Father knows this, and the white people know this. (Colby 1892:188)

The massacre, army incompetence, and the blatant disregard of agency officials and missionaries moved Mooney to anger. He held nothing back as he described the scene of the aftermath in a measured but indignant tone:

On New Year's day of 1891, three days after the battle, a detachment of troops was sent out to Wounded Knee to gather up and bury the Indian dead and to bring in the wounded who might be still alive on the field. In the meantime there had been a heavy snowstorm, culminating in a blizzard. The bodies of the slaughtered men, women, and children were found lying about under the snow, frozen stiff and covered with blood. Almost all the dead warriors were found lying near where the fight began, about Big Foot's tipi, but the bodies of the women and children were found scattered along for 3 miles from the scene of the encounter, showing that they had been killed while trying to escape. A number of women and children were found still alive, but all badly wounded or frozen, or both, and most of them died after being brought in. Four babies were found alive under the snow, wrapped in shawls and lying beside their dead mothers, whose last thought had been of them. They were all badly frozen and only one lived. . . . It is a commentary on our boasted Christian civilization that although there were two or three salaried missionaries at the agency not one went out to say a prayer over the poor mangled bodies of these victims of war. (1896:876–78)

Mooney's *Ghost Dance Religion* was a tour de force. He meticulously researched the history of the dance and religious doctrines and even secured an interview with Wovoka. Mooney's investigative report of what he called "the butchery" was exhaustive. He often sandwiched copies of original source documents between his narrative prose (Mooney

1896:870). In this sense, the manuscript itself served as an archive of salvaged material—ethnographic and historical. A full third of the five-hundred-page tome was composed of an appendix which was a catalogue of detailed lists of the various dances, prayers, rites, and songs and how these practices varied between groups and regions. The appendix also included musical scores, drawings, and detailed translations for each song.

Mooney went beyond narrating an archive to put the Ghost Dance religion in the context of other pan-Indian religious revivals that occurred against a backdrop of agony and defeat, but for which hope, redemption, and some great miracle could rescue people from imminent demise.[9] Mooney did not stop there. Throughout the texts, Mooney employed a novel trope for his time, one that made Christianity seem strange and exotic while making the Ghost Dancers seem normal, familiar, and even logical. Peppered throughout his texts are references that compare aspects of Christianity to those of the Ghost Dance. In his opening paragraphs he confidently explained that "the doctrines of the Hindu avatar, the Hebrew Messiah, the Christian millennium, and the Hesûnanin of the Indian Ghost dance are essentially the same, and have their origin in a hope and longing common to all humanity" (1896:657). Even when he referenced the diversity of dances and variations between tribes, Mooney surmised that "the differences of interpretation are precisely such as we find in Christianity, with its hundreds of sects and innumerable shades of individual opinion" (1896:777).

There were other instances in which he directly opposed Powell and others at the bureau who maintained a commitment to the wide gulf between savagery and civilization, not to mention American exceptionalism. Mooney, for example, hinted that it was obvious this type of religion would flourish in the United States: "In a country which produces magnetic healers, shakers, trance mediums, and the like, all these things may very easily be paralleled without going far from home" (1896:783).

The Ghost Dance Religion and the Sioux Outbreak was included as the second volume of the Fourteenth Annual Report of the Bureau of American Ethnology for 1892–93. In Powell's introduction to the report, he reproduced the same line of criticism he had when he introduced Mooney's *Sacred Formulas of the Cherokee* five years earlier. This time he was even more adamant and less obtuse. Powell was getting pressured from all sides, including the secretary of the Smithsonian, Samuel P. Langley, who warned Powell that Mooney's work afforded "ill-wishers of the Bureau a powerful means of attack" (Hinsley 1981:218). Powell's criticism focused on Mooney's comparative method: "It may be observed that caution should be exercised in comparing or contrasting religious movements among civilized peoples with such fantasies as that described in the memoir; for while interesting and suggestive analogies may be found, the essential features of the movements are not homologous . . . and whatever the superficial resemblance in the movements, there is strong resumption against their essential homology" (1896:lx–lxi). Mooney's subtle critique of Christian civilization, overt sympathies for Indians who resisted assimilation, and tepid embrace of evolutionary schemes challenged the very foundation of the assimilationist programs promulgated by the same government who employed the errant ethnologist. Mooney understood the limitations of ethnology during the 1890s but could not transcend them.

The contemporary literary critic Michael A. Elliott has pointed out that Mooney was writing a type of tragic realism and notes that "this strategy comes at a price. While Mooney's account resists casting Ghost Dance adherents as ignorant barbarians and refuses to see the Wounded Knee massacre as the end of a backward race, the work's circular emplotment does not make an easily available entry point for historical agency, either on the part of the Ghost Dancers or the government that reacted so fearfully to them" (1998:214). Elliott continues by suggesting that "Mooney's narrative strategy demonstrates that the power of ethnography lies in the act of differentiation between what is *real* and what is not (1998:216). James Clifford captures the ambivalence and the disquieting politics of Mooney's work when he explains that "ethnography, a hybrid activity, thus appears as writing, as collecting, as modernist collage, as imperial power, as subversive critique" (1988:13).

Although Mooney's unique comparative method raised concern at the bureau, it was his pedantic commitment to the real and his routine dismissal of blended identities or practices that raised the most concern in reformers and Indian activists. In practice, these two facets of Mooney's work (a sincere commitment to authentic rendition and routine rejection of everything else) were not separate. Another way to understand why Mooney was so despised by some activists was the fact that he did not consider those American Indians who advocated uplift to be authentic. His dismissal of Zitkala-Ša during the peyote hearings is one such case, but during the World's Fair in Chicago in 1893, Mooney became embroiled in a controversy with another self-assertive woman. This time

it was Emma C. Sickels, an educator and reformer whose disagreement
with Mooney over how to exhibit Native Americans led to her accusa-
tions in the *New York Times* that the bureau was advancing "one of the
darkest conspiracies ever conceived against the Indian" (*NYT*, October 8,
1893:19; see below).

"The Civilized, the Half Civilized, and the Savage Worlds to Choose From"

After the ravages of the great fire of 1871, Chicago's political and business
leaders made their bid to host the World's Columbian Exposition of 1893,
a bid for national prominence. After the city won the fierce competition
with New York, millions of dollars poured in to support the construction
of elaborate fairgrounds in Jackson Park. Highly skilled sculptors and architects were contracted to erect a majestic city within a city that evoked
the grandeur of past civilizations while showcasing the latest advance-
ments and refinements in science and technology as well as in music and
art. The city within a city quickly received an apt moniker, the "White
City." Over the course of its six-month operation, the fair drew more than
twenty-seven million spectators.[10]

Typical of the extravagant promotion surrounding the fair, one of the
architects wrote in *Atlantic Monthly*, "The exposition will furnish to our
people an object lesson of a magnitude, scope, and significance such as has
not been seen elsewhere. They will for the first time be made conscious of
the duties, as yet unfulfilled, which they themselves owe to the civilization
of the century" (Van Brunt 1893:579). The fair was to be didactic from beginning to end, and the new science of anthropology was to play a central
role in the overall educational experience, while Buffalo Bill's Wild West
was shunted aside because it putatively lacked both sophistication and
educational value (Moses 1991:210). At least, that was the plan.

After the fair managers denied the appeals of William Cody and his
financial partner Nate Salsbury to perform their Wild West show within
the bounds of the fairgrounds, the two entrepreneurs immediately leased
a tract of land just opposite the elevated train stop where many visitors
entered the fair. They built an elaborate stadium, executed crafty publicity
campaigns, and produced a show that was quite literally second to none.
Cody's Chicago season netted profits of up to a million dollars and capped

off a season that was one of the most successful in the history of outdoor theater (Kasson 2000:99).

In the early planning stages of the fair, Frederic Ward Putnam was appointed to head up Department M, "Ethnology and Archaeology." At the time, Putnam was the director of the Peabody Museum of American Archaeology and Ethnology at Harvard College, and he possessed considerable experience curating museum displays culled from his large archaeological expeditions throughout the desert Southwest and the Ohio River valley (Browman 2002; Baker 2002:6–7). In an article in the *Chicago Tribune* on May 30, 1890, Putnam explained the plans, concept, and pedagogic value of the enormous exhibit. Putnam wanted to produce for "the Exposition a perfect ethnographical exhibition of the past and present peoples of America and thus make an important contribution to science." Marveling at exhibits produced by the ethnographical department "at the World's Fair at Paris last year," Putnam embraced its theme of the advance of civilization, which depicted the evolution of architecture from "the primitive shelters of savages to the elaborate dwellings of barbaric times, and finally to the early classical architecture." Putnam called it a "a grand conception" that could "impress upon the mind the trials and struggles through which the civilization of today has been attained." Putnam envisioned an even grander exhibit to express this theme and outlined how he was for "the first [time] bringing together on a grand scale representatives of the peoples who were living on the continent when it was discovered by Columbus, and by including as thorough a representation of prehistoric times as possible, the stages of the development of man on the American continent could be spread out as an open book from which all could read" (1890:13).

The former Illinois congressman George R. Davis appointed Putnam to the post. Davis was the director-general of the Washington-based World's Columbian Commission, which was organized to oversee each state's contribution to the fair as well as that of the federal government and to help coordinate the participation of foreign governments. The commission was continuously at odds with the Chicago-based World's Columbian Exposition, which had charge of the initial construction and production as well as the day-to-day operation of what was then the largest fair to date. The dual governance of the exposition created complications in authority at all levels, and Putnam became ensnared in their fight for power, which contributed to his perpetual struggle with cost overruns, construction delays, and space. Putnam eventually oversaw the completion of his "anthropological building," which was the first time that archaeology, ethnology, and physical anthropology were housed, literally, under one roof and termed anthropology. To assist in these efforts, Putnam recruited an impressive team of assistants and associates who worked hard to get the exhibit ready for the public (Dexter 1966:316–23).

Alice C. Fletcher (1838–1923) was one of the first applied anthropologists, a former student of Putnam and a certainty to be appointed to the coveted position of chief assistant. She explicitly used science to help shape public policy and became influential in implementing the Dawes Act, most notably with the Omaha. One of the few bridges between the Lake Mohonk Friends, Captain Pratt, General Armstrong, Putnam, and Francis La Flesche, she was a logical choice for Putnam to name as chief. But in the end her gender, her steadfast belief in assimilation, and her close ties to Christian reformers precluded her from obtaining such a prestigious appointment (Mark 1980:62–95, 1988:211; Visweswaran 1998b:103; Thomas 2000:67–70). She was appointed as a member of the department and was listed simply as being responsible for "Indians in the Western United States" (Dexter 1966:332).

Instead of Fletcher, Putnam appointed Boas as chief assistant and charged him with overseeing the physical anthropology exhibits. Boas had just resigned from Clark University in Worcester, Massachusetts, but hoped he could continue his research on growth and development at the fair (Baker 2004:33; Cole 1999:154). Boas offered fairgoers an interactive experience with this new science. Describing his exhibit, he wrote, "A number of instruments are shown in operation, and measurements of visitors who present themselves are taken" (1893:609). Within the laboratories of the Anthropological Building, visitors had the opportunity to quite literally measure up to "the well known statues of the Harvard boy and [Radcliffe] girl" or compare their measurements to the "very full collection of crania and skeletons" used to demarcate and classify the "anatomy of human races" (Dall 1893:225; Boas 1893:609).[11]

Boas was also influential in developing and organizing the static or mannequin displays inside the Anthropological Building as well as the dynamic or living group displays that made up a "small colony of Indians, who live in their native habitations near the Anthropological building" (Boas 1893:609).[12] Putnam organized dozens of agents, many of whom were "naval and military officers" to recruit participants for the living ethnological exhibits or to send him artifacts for the exhibit (Ralph 1892:209). In the end, representatives of some twelve tribal groups came and performed dances, rites, and customs and sold art, crafts, and other items in hopes of earning some cash, in what Michaela di Leonardo calls "ethnological zoos" (1998:6). Unlike the touring actors in Buffalo Bill's Wild West, these performers were not paid and were always on stage. Even the most quotidian routine, like cooking, eating, cleaning, or caring for a youngster, was a performance under surveillance of the touristic or voyeuristic gaze of curious onlookers.[13]

"In the flush of the Columbian Exposition," Rosemarie Bank explains, "display cases, photographs, and reconstructions indoors led seamlessly to living peoples in the Department's 'Ethnographical Exhibit'" (2002:594). The seamlessness was by design. The live ethnographic performances were choreographed in such a way as to reconstruct remnants of some authentic past from long ago and far away. As Boas described it in 1893, "Nowadays it is difficult to obtain good collections, which show native industries entirely unaffected by our civilization." Conflating good with authentic or even prehistoric, Boas explained that the dynamic or living exhibits "have the advantage over archælogical collections" because "the implements can be seen in actual use and . . . the meaning of ceremonial objects and of ornaments can be learned from the people who use them" (1893:608).

The living life group genre of exhibition, under the express aegis of academic anthropology, had its grand debut in the United States that year in Chicago. Putnam's and Boas's ethnological exhibits were explicitly set up to challenge the evolutionary scheme that simply arrayed specific artifacts or industries from savage to civilized with no regard to context or geographic distribution. However, the various commercial displays of exotic people along the Midway Plaisance as well as the academic displays around the Anthropological Building made anthropology at the fair seem more like a creation of Barnum than Putnam.

The Midway Plaisance was officially under Putnam's direction and designated as part of the ethnological exhibits. Dominated by the 260-foot Ferris wheel, the midway was a mile-long strip of food, fun, and fantasy. Juxtaposed against the palatial and civilized White City, the midway was home to the savage and uncivilized brown village. There were simulated villages, streets, and bazaars that formed a veritable kaleidoscope of peoples and cultures. On the midway were an "American Indian Village" and the popular "Dahomeyan village," which was next to "the Cairo street." There were also "villages" from Tunis, Lapland, Java, Samoa, and, not to be missed, was the "encampment of Bedouins" (Dall 1893:225; Kasson 2000:95; Bank 2002:595).

Although Putnam's and Boas's emphasis on cultural areas, life groups, and the environment would later have a significant impact on twentieth-century anthropology and museum display, the culture area concept still fit very comfortably with the view that American Indians belonged to the lower races, were remnants of the past, and were not capable of becoming fully civilized (Rydell 1984:58).

These exhibits served as the background for the fair's bas-relief theme of four hundred years of progress, development, and advance of civilization. In the context of this and other world's fairs, however, these exhibits served to exemplify the intimate connections between scientific and political practices. Steeped in unequal power relations, the racial politics of culture was writ large. People exhibited in their "native habitations" served as trophies that bore witness to the triumph of imperial and colonial conquest and domination by late nineteenth-century nation-states (Corbey 1993:338). Simultaneously, people were able to showcase their traditional dances, art, costumes, and languages to the world, in direct opposition to assimilation programs and laws forbidding dancing.

The goal of Putnam and Boas was to make anthropology popular and showcase it as a legitimate and practical science in the eyes of the American public. They were joined by scholars like Mooney, who helped to curate the National Museum's Indian exhibit, and Brinton, who presided over the International Congress of Anthropology, a large conference held in conjunction with the exposition (Wake 1894). In some respects they were each, in different ways, forced to compete with the commercial ethnological exhibits on the midway as well as the ever-popular "Buffalo Bill's Wild West and Congress of Rough Riders of the World," which performed twice daily in an eighteen-thousand-seat stadium just outside the fairground (Kasson 2000:100–101, 110–15). Cody's show was entertainment that claimed to have value as history and ethnology, while Putnam's show was ethnology and archaeology that claimed to have value as entertainment.

The fluidity of science and entertainment at the fair was not lost on some Lakota performers who apparently performed for both Putnam and Cody. An article in the *New York Times* reported that one of the agents Putnam hired to recruit "Sioux, Blackfeet, [and] Crow" never made it to Chicago because some "enterprising competitor" made off with his "stock." The reporter alleged that Cody and his partner John Burke hijacked Putnam's Indians. The reporter continued, "Col. Cody and Mr. Burke assert that 'deed and double deed' they know nothing about it. Mr. Putnam, however, entertains strong suspicions especially since the Wild West combination offers to lend him Indians, out of which gift, it is safe to say, they will take the incidental advertising as a return favor" (NYT, May 22, 1893:9).[14]

In order to compete with Cody, the anthropologists charged with showcasing the relatively young science were each forced to trade on the popularity of shows that included trained animals and wild peoples that had been incorporated within world's fairs since the first U.S. exhibition was organized by Phineas T. Barnum in 1853 (Hinsley 1991:345; Thomson 1996).[15] What could distinguish anthropology from other forms of entertainment? The hope was veracity. Although scripted, choreographed, and selectively edited, both the living and the static exhibits were putatively real, authentic, and in the service of science.[16] The explicit blurring of the lines between entertainment and science and the deliberate offering up of the other for popular consumption was exemplified by one commentator who called the department of ethnology "the great picnic of the nations" (Hawthorne 1893a:70).

Putnam's strategy of dispatching agents to secure individuals and groups to perform authentic renditions of aboriginal ways of life for profit, entertainment, and education was first developed in the mid-1870s by Carl Hagenbeck. Hagenbeck is best known for revolutionizing the modern zoological garden by developing the so-called habitat group, where animals perform within a simulacrum of their native habitat, as opposed to in a circus or a cage. In 1907, he retooled his Hamburg zoo, which still bears his name, Tierpark Hagenbeck, by employing these relatively new concepts. His concept of "native habitat" sprang not from ecology, but from ethnology. His use of elements from people's "native habitat" had been a staple of his popular Völkerschau, or ethnographic show, years before he introduced the philosophy to zoo management. Hagenbeck's company showcased troupes of indigenous people along with their animals, tents, tools, and religious objects throughout Germany and across Europe to amazed audiences (Corbey 1993:345).

In 1874 Hagenbeck hired Johan Adrian Jacobsen as a recruiter and collector, who proved to be very successful for his enterprise (Hinsley

1991:345; Rothfels 2002:110). In 1885, Jacobsen and his brother Fillip recruited nine Salish-speaking Bella Coola from coastal British Columbia for an eleven-month tour, which included "three weeks [of] dancing in Hagenbeck's Hamburg Thierpark" (Hinsley 1991:345). According to Ira Jacknis, the first anthropological employment Boas ever secured was in 1885 when he began organizing artifacts that Johan Jacobsen brought to the Royal Ethnographic Museum of Berlin. The artifacts came from the northwest coast of North America, and Boas painstakingly prepared them for exhibition. Boas admired the aesthetic detail of the objects, and "when Jacobsen brought a troupe of Bella Coola to Berlin in January of 1886," Boas was delighted to have "a chance to meet their creators" (Jacknis 1985:75).

Jacknis identifies Boas's work with Jacobsen's artifacts and his initial introduction to the troupe of Bella Coola as a transformative moment for Boas and his career; it was after all the peoples of the Pacific Northwest "who were henceforth to be[come] the ethnographic focus of his professional life" (Jacknis 1985:91). Douglas Cole echoes Jacknis's analysis and explains that "Boas spent all his free time with" the Bella Coola visitors "during the group's short January and March visits" to Berlin (1999:97).

In Chicago, Boas blended the popular Völkerschau with his vision of museum instruction, which he had outlined in a rather heated debate with Powell and Otis T. Mason in the pages of *Science* six years earlier (Jacknis 1985:75; Baker 1998:104). Boas's Völkerschau created little ontological distinction between the anthropological construction of other and the zoological construction of animal. In fact, the "ethnic arrangement" of artifacts that Boas argued for in the pages of *Science* during the spring of 1887 was predicated upon the tribal arrangements he organized during 1886 in Berlin (Boas and Dahl 1887:587). The way Boas organized people so they could "live in their native habitations" in Chicago was identical to the way Hagenbeck organized the habitat group in his Hamburg zoo (Boas 1893:609).[17]

Boas did not view savages as if they were animals; quite the opposite. Early in his career, Boas demonstrated, through his scholarship and exhibit work, that he wanted to offer the public "examples [that] will show that the mind of the 'savage' is sensible to the beauties of poetry and music, and that it is only the superficial observer to whom he appears stupid and unfeeling" (1887c:385). He did, however, know that the public flocked to Völkerschaus in Germany and to their less didactic counterparts in the

United States. In a sense, he gambled that he could educate visitors with authentic and expressive ethnological exhibits, contribute to science by using the performers as informants and collaborators, and help to salvage and preserve what he considered "good collections." Boas knew full well he was trading on the popularity of sideshows and circuses. When he became frustrated with all of the problems that came with managing his Jackson Park Völkerschau, he sardonically quipped that he would never again "play circus impresario."[18]

Although the ethnological exhibits, performative and static, sought to challenge the unilinear evolution of inventions, they implied that indigenous peoples who performed at the fair were stuck in time and relegated to a particular stage of evolution. Putnam's own understanding that both "past and present" peoples could represent those "who were living on the continent when it was discovered by Columbus" reified a widely shared concept that contemporary peoples who represent a lower "culture grade" were actually some sort of link to a remnant past. Any critique of the comparative method and serious science Boas thought he could muster by helping Putnam to organize the life group displays was seemingly lost on the media and Indian activists alike. Julian Hawthorne, for one, catalogued, "Department M—Ethnology. Isolated Exhibits—Midway Plaisance. Group 176, this I say, I call the 'World as Plaything.' Here are the elements out of which the human part of the planet has been developed; it's all within the compass of a day's stroll. . . . Roughly speaking, you have before you the civilized, the half civilized, and the savage worlds to choose from—or rather, to take one after the other" (Hawthorne 1983b:568–70). Simon Pokagon, a Potawatomi leader and land-rights activist, was a little more sober in his statement to the *Chicago Inter-Ocean*: "The world's people, from what they have so far seen of us on the Midway, will regard us as savages; but they shall yet know that we are human as well as they" (Pokagon 1899:13).

In many respects, controlling Indian bodies after the massacre at Wounded Knee was not as pressing as controlling their image. Would the image be that of the legitimate science of Putnam, Boas, and Mooney depicting authentic, "real" Indians? Would it be that of the captivating entertainment of Buffalo Bill staging dramatic, romantic Indians? Or that of the disciplining education of Pratt showcasing civilized, assimilated Indians? As in the case of African Americans, it would not be an image depicted on Indians' own terms.[19] The clashing and competing images of Indians at the World's Fair would resonate with the clashing and competing ideas about Indians during the congressional hearings on peyote twenty-five years later, and Mooney and Pratt were at the center of both contests.

Although many authors have written about world's fairs of the late nineteenth century and early twentieth and their impact on American society, no other site of cultural production during the late nineteenth century can better demonstrate the conflict and confluence that occurred between educators, entertainers, and ethnologists over the image of the Indian. During the World's Columbian Exposition in Chicago, educators, entertainers, and ethnologists each vied, competed, and colluded with each other. At issue was who had the authority and power to control and indeed market the image of the Indian. As fair managers courted and recruited various contingents to exhibit American Indian culture, history, and progress, these same organizers battled and curtailed respective contingents interested in exhibiting African American culture, history, and progress. The message the managers wanted to send was clear: capitalism and industrial technology fuel an advancing civilization, which ratifies white supremacy and the nobility of imperial expansion. Out-of-the-way, exotic—the more "authentic," the better—Indians and other uncivilized people of the world as well as their antiquities were needed to explicitly exhibit the baseline with which to compare how far Americans had come with regard to technology, arts, and industry.

The venerable Frederick Douglass even used this race-as-indexed-by-culture scheme in his influential speech "Colored American Day." Echoing the way the HFS deployed a perceived temporal distance between the African and Negro on some ladder toward civilization, Douglass juxtaposed the civilizing American Negroes with an extended Fon family from present-day Benin who resided in "the Dahomey Village." Pushing the racial uplift metaphor to an extreme, Douglass implored his rapt audience to "look at the progress the Negro has made in thirty years! We have come up out of Dahomey unto this. Measure the Negro. But not by the standard of the splendid civilization of the Caucasian. Bend down and measure him—measure him from the depths out of which he has risen" (2000:194).

Black men were used explicitly as workers at the fair, but they too were on display. African Americans who were enslaved some three decades earlier emerged in the 1890s as important workers, especially for business interests hostile to labor organizing. Black men were hired exclusively for the 140-person custodial staff. Dispersed throughout the park and within various buildings and guard stations, they were responsible for light cleanup duty during business hours. Issued smart uniforms and assigned highly visible jobs, these men became their own type of exhibit. The black male worker as dapper bellhop, polite porter, and trusted coachman was just the image Chicago business leaders wanted to exhibit. While working hard, these men were also working this particular notion of work. The heavier lifting, dirtier trash removal, and mind-numbing mopping, which occurred in the evening hours, were relegated to whites, presumably recent immigrants. The guides, guards, and the many clerical and administrative workers were also almost exclusively white (Reed 2000:74). The subtle message was that black men had a (and presumably *knew their*) distinct place in modern labor relations. If fair management could produce an image of these men as hardworking, docile laborers, then manufacturers might hire even more blacks in an effort to keep wages down and weaken organized labor. In the years leading up to the fair, African Americans began serving a valuable role in the labor markets of the industrializing North and South because they were increasingly exploited as cheap labor and strike breakers (Kelly 2003). There is little doubt that the image of the trusted custodian of the grounds served to display the availability of a new class of labor.

Two years later at the Cotton States Exhibition in Atlanta, Booker T. Washington echoed in words what the Chicago World's Fair exhibited in its corps of custodians; black American workers could be trusted laborers in menial positions because they were not "of foreign birth and strange tongue and habits" and have been loyal laborers who have "without strikes and labor wars, tilled your fields, cleared your forests, [built] your railroads and cities, and brought forth treasures from the bowels of the earth" (1902:222).

What official representation African Americans were able to muster was the result of well-executed campaigns of protest, organizing, and lobbying, led largely by black women associated with racial uplift and the women's club movement (Reed 2000:21–36; New York Age, October 24, 1891; Sklar and Shaughnessy 1997; Massa 1974: 319–37).

If the 140-member crew of custodians advertised a labor pool of hardworking yet "grinning" black men, Nancy Green did the work of 140 men to advertise a labor pool of hardworking yet "grinning" black women as she gave daylong performances as Aunt Jemima in the exhibit set up by

R. T. Davis Milling Company to advertise its self-rising pancake mix (Manning 1998:60–78; Thomas 2001:58–60). As anthropology traded on the popularity of exotic sideshows to box the Indian into museums, advertising agencies traded on the popularity of minstrelsy to put a slave in a box (Hinsley 1989:170; Manning 1998:60–78).

The limited representation of African Americans in Chicago needs to be juxtaposed with the extravagant representation of indigenous folk throughout the Americas, black folk from other places in the diaspora, and the foreign nationals who performed on the midway (Baker 1998: 54–94). The Chicago World's Fair occurred at the height of the campaign to assimilate the Indian. Land allotments, outing and farm programs, boarding and reservation schools: each worked in conjunction with the other to promote the virtues of Christian civilization to convert them into American citizens (Trennert 1987:203). Thrift, hard work, education, and individualism were the watchwords for Native Americans and white reformers alike, who sought to escort the Indian up from the depths of depravation. In order for the BIA to get its message of assimilation across to the public, it would have to mount an exhibit that would serve as an antidote to the performances directed by both Buffalo Bill and Professor Putnam.

The New and Old Can Be Sharply Contrasted

The commissioner of the BIA at the time was Thomas J. Morgan, who envisioned a fully functioning model boarding school to be his exhibit at the fair. He saw the fair as an opportunity to exemplify, demonstrate, and convince the American people as well as the many foreign visitors why "it has become the settled policy of the Government to break up reservations, destroy tribal relations, settle Indians upon their own homesteads, incorporate them into the national life, and deal with them not as nations or tribes or bands, but as individual citizens" (Morgan 1890:5). Morgan hoped to demonstrate the power and purpose of assimilation by explicitly juxtaposing his school with Putnam's exhibit. Responding to a request to showcase the achievement of Carlisle students at the fair, Morgan denied the request because the commissioner needed complete control over the image of the Indian. Morgan explained the coordinated contrast between the boarding school and the ethnological exhibit:

It is the intention of [my] office to have at Chicago, a specimen Indian boarding school in which delegations of pupils, in turn, from various schools, shall
take possession of the school building erected there for the purpose . . . [of
carrying] on in the building, the studies, recitations, household and mechani-
cal industries, as if they were in their own schools on the reservation and
elsewhere. . . . The Indian exhibit, that is the civilized part of it, is to be this
Indian industrial boarding school, and there is to be no other Indian exhibit,
as such, except that of the uncivilized Indian which is to be prepared by Professor Putnam of Harvard University.

He has charge of the department of ethnology in co-operation with this
bureau, will have families of Indians on the grounds living according to their
primitive methods, manufacturing blankets, pottery, bead work, etc.[20]

As Morgan conceived it, "The new and old can be sharply contrasted."
Although he predicted that "the old may attract popular attention by its
picturesqueness," the school, he hoped, "will impress" upon the public
the value "of extending to the weaker the helpful hand of the stronger
race"(1891:79). Morgan was optimistic that his exhibit, alongside Putnam's, would get attention and demonstrate to the nation and to the rest
of the world that the federal government was successfully engaged in
"the process of evolving United States citizens out of American savages"
(1891:80).

According to Pratt, Morgan initially asked him to "take charge of the
boarding school" exhibit for the duration of the fair. Pratt, however,
fiercely opposed Morgan's scheme to contrast the savage with the civilized. As Pratt recalled, "I urged the Commissioner of Indian Affairs to
eliminate anything like . . . [a] wild west feature. My argument to him was
that Buffalo Bill would be on hand and present his spectacular exaggera-
tion of the aborigine. Mr. Cody had already secured a commanding front
place, and it was plain to me that . . . we [should] illustrate what could be
done in the way of advancing Indian civilization and merging them into
citizenship" (1964:303–4). Pratt was ostensibly still interested in running
the model boarding school, until Morgan explained that a "noted ethnologist" was to head up the general exhibit.

Pratt explained to Morgan that "the ethnologists were the most insidi-
ous and active enemies of Carlisle's purposes" and this scheme would
have "subordinated Carlisle to them" (1964:305). Pratt would not have it
and declined Morgan's offer. Pratt mounted his own exhibit, entitled "Into

Civilization and Citizenship," which he was able to locate in the Liberal
Arts and Education Building among "the many exhibits from schools all
over America and from other nations" (1964:303). In notably gendered
terms, Pratt underscored the mission of his exhibit:

> Carlisle's exhibit showed how the Indian could learn to march in line with
> America as a very part of it, head up, eyes front, where he could see his glo-
> rious future of manly competition in citizenship and be on an equality [sic]
> as an individual. The exhibit contrived by the two government bureaus was
> calculated to keep the nation's attention and the Indian's energies fixed upon
> his valueless past, through the spectacular aboriginal housing, dressing, and
> curio employments it instituted. The illustrative Indian boarding school in
> their exposition camps said to the Indians: "You may have some of our edu-
> cation, but not enough to enable you to become one of us. You are to remain
> a separate and peculiar people, and continue under our Bureau supervision."
> (1964:303)

According to the historian Robert A. Trennert Jr., Pratt's exhibit "fell
flat" and "seemed uninspired" because Pratt simply displayed "samples of
school work—writing, drawing, math papers, compositions and industrial and homemaking skills." Despite the fact that Carlisle had a teacher
or student present to explain and promote the mission of the school, fairgoers were neither impressed nor interested (Trennert 1987:211).

Like Pratt's exhibit, Trennert explains, the model government school
received little press and scant attention at the fair. He concludes that "the
comparative theme seemingly worked in reverse; instead of impressing
the public with the superiority of the assimilation program, it stimulated
interest in traditional life. The 1893 Exposition actually helped make Indian lifeways more interesting to the public" (1987:212). Joy S. Kasson offers a similar assessment about the popularity of Buffalo Bill's Wild West
and Congress of Rough Riders of the World. It was during Buffalo Bill's
Chicago season that the show solidified its dominance in a new form of
American entertainment "that was not a circus, not a burlesque, not a
freak show; [and] like Vaudeville, it called on a variety of resources from
high and low culture. It claimed 'serious' historical significance and at the
same time energetically deployed melodramatic conventions. . . . It used
music, colorful costumes, and display of 'exotic' peoples" (2000:121).

Kasson attributes the show's popularity in part to its alliance with the
rise of antimodernism during the progressive era, but she also notes

how subversive possibilities arose from the exhibits mounted by both Putnam and Cody. Kasson suggests that "the 'celebratory' flavor of these displays threatened to undermine cultural hierarchies and overthrow the very power relations they asserted." Kasson is careful to note, however, that there was nothing in the Wild West that contradicted "the imperialistic, hierarchical assumptions woven so deeply into contemporaneous ethnographic displays" (2000:218). Kasson echoes Philip Deloria's argument about the unique role Indians played in white folk's yearning for authenticity as antimodernist desires mounted during the progressive era (Deloria 1998:94). She distinguishes Indian performances from "minstrel shows and vaudeville acts representing African-Americans and other ethnic groups as objects of low comedy" and cautiously asserts that "the Indians were special favorites with audiences." With the help of an often-sympathetic press, Kasson argues, these various performances achieved a popularity that "complicated the racial stereotypes and hierarchies" (2000:219).

Despite the suggestive possibilities of antimodernism with regard to the image and popularity of American Indians, the exhibits of Pratt, Cody, and Putnam, Elizabeth Cook-Lynn explains, actually articulate anti-Indianism in modern America. In many respects, these exhibits parallel the many "fantasy stories about Indians (produced mostly by the white, male American writer) [and] while they are often harmless·articulations about hope and deeply held personal convictions, [the narratives] become divisive and damaging works when they keep in the foreground false and damaging images of how it is that American Indians make history and live their lives" (2001:20).[21]

Cody, Pratt, Putnam, and Boas each traded upon the hidden and not-so-hidden desires of the American public. Science, education, popular culture, and public policy during the decades that straddled the beginning of the twentieth century were not always in alignment. This was a turbulent, unstable period of growth and development, disfranchisement, and genocide. Of course, each constituency distrusted and questioned the others' efforts while maintaining a deeply held commitment that what they were doing was in the best interest of American Indians. American Indians also allied themselves within and between these various positions, and Cody, Pratt, and Putnam each claimed considerable indigenous support while attracting vociferous detractors of their respective positions and initiatives.

The high-stakes clash of commitments during the World Columbian Exposition erupted into a very public drama that laid bare the stakes involved in the racial politics of culture. Emma Sickels, took on both Mooney and Putnam in one of the many battles of these culture wars that would serve to define the limits of well-meaning enterprises that too often turned on the lose-lose goal of either preserving or assimilating American Indian cultural practices.[22]

The Exhibit Is to Educate, Not Mislead the People

Mooney began his fieldwork for *Ghost Dance Religion* during the winter of 1890 and conducted intensive ethnographic fieldwork with the Arapaho, Cheyenne, Kiowa, Comanche, Apache, Caddo, and Wichita, who were all living in close proximity to each other in the western part of the Oklahoma Territory. His fieldwork began at the very moment the Ghost Dance began to wane at the very place where the revivified peyote meetings began to wax.

In April of 1891, Mooney had completed his first field season in Oklahoma and returned to Washington, where he was "commissioned to make an ethnological collection for the World's Columbian Exposition." He chose "the Kiowa for that purpose as a representative prairie tribe" (Mooney 1896:653). Mooney simultaneously researched material for his *Ghost Dance Religion* while he acquired material for the Smithsonian's exhibit at the upcoming World's Fair. He conducted years of research with the Kiowa, whom he deemed to be the least assimilated of those who inhabited the plains. Mooney explained that "after having seen a great many tribes" he chose to study the Kiowa because he considered them to be "the best study tribe upon the plains, and the most conservative." Mooney described the Kiowa as "the most Indian" (Hinsley 1981:221).

Mooney developed trust and lifelong friendship with many Kiowa, and it was the Kiowa people who helped Mooney produce some of his most impressive ethnography (Mooney 1897, 1898). He never won the same level of trust or support from the Lakota. Citing the Lakotas' distrust of all white people in the wake of the massacre at Wounded Knee, Mooney tried to explain: "I found the Sioux very difficult to approach on the subject of the Ghost dance. This was natural, in view of the trouble that had resulted to them in consequence of it. To my questions the answer almost invariably was, 'The dance was our religion, but the government sent soldiers to kill us on account of it. We will not talk any more about it'" (1896:1059–60). Although he tried the same tactics he had employed to elicit the sacred formulas of the Cherokee, he was unsuccessful. For the section in his book entitled "The Ghost Dance among the Sioux," he was forced to rely on a narrative "written originally in the Teton Dakota dialect by George Sword, an Oglala Sioux Indian," translated by "Miss Emma C. Sickels and published by her courtesy." Mooney reprinted the translated document in toto, and it served as the sole description of the Ghost Dance among victims of the massacre (Mooney 1896:797; also see Sickels 1892). George Sword (c. 1847–1919) remains a noted literary figure among many Lakota, and his writings are still popular among those who are interested in indigenous spirituality.[23] Less is known about Sickels, who began serving as the superintendent of the Indian Industrial Boarding School at Pine Ridge during 1884. Although she left the school under a cloud of controversy, the agency called her back to help the federal government in its efforts to gather intelligence and negotiate with Lakota leadership in the wake of the murder of Sitting Bull.[24]

Just days after Sitting Bull was shot, Sickels headed to the Dakotas. After securing "the necessary authority" from both the War and Interior departments, she departed on December 22, 1890, but made a stop in "Chicago to receive instructions from Gen. Miles" (Colby 1892:185). Her goal was to negotiate with Little Wound and his constituents and broker a peaceful resolution. According to a published report from years later, "Word was sent to Little Wound that Miss Sickels was a spy and that he should beware of her. On her next visit to the camp [of Little Wound] she was met by Indians armed with knives and guns ready to kill her on the least provocation. She was unprepared for this greeting as she did not know of the report sent out about her. She managed to quiet them, promising to publish their grievances in the paper. She also arranged for a meeting between Little Wound and the government officials at Pine Ridge agency" (Bishop 1911:376). Apparently she was successful because the *New York Times* heralded her as the "heroine of Pine Ridge," and reported on her efforts to help the Oglala Lakota leader Chief Little Wound negotiate a peaceful resolution with officials of the agency and the army in the aftermath of the Wounded Knee massacre (*NYT*, April 21, 1893:12).

Sickels stayed on at Pine Ridge for several months and came back to New York to help organize Indian exhibits for the New York Press Club and the Chicago World's Fair. Sickels firmly believed that "if the better side of the Indian character were brought to the notice of prominent and influential persons, it would result in a better understanding of the Indian question and an improvement in the condition of the red men" (*NYT*, April 21, 1893:12).

Cut from the same cloth as Pratt, Sickels secured a political appointment from Congressman Davis, who assigned her to Putnam during the planning stages of the fair. Putnam objected to the appointment, and Sickels immediately began to challenge, critique, and question Putnam's focus on archaeology and his emphasis on "degrading phases of Indian life" (*NYT*, May 22, 1893:9; Dexter 1966:327). Putnam fired her on May 1, 1893, and Davis signed off on the dismissal—months before the fair even opened. Sickels "was employed as an assistant," Putnam reported, "from October 15, 1891, until February 29, 1892, when I dispensed with her services as the work she wished to do and persisted in doing was not of an ethnological character" (Dexter 1966:327). Not to be dismayed, she secured an appointment working for the Board of Lady Managers.

The Chicago World's Fair was a watershed for women's movements. The powerful Board of Lady Managers, led by Bertha M. H. Palmer, debated but eventually embraced a "separate but equal" strategy and began planning for their own Woman's Building (di Leonardo 1998:8). As they launched a worldwide women-only competition for an architect, the managers explained that this one building must be designed to house "not only a general and retrospective display of woman's work . . . but space must be provided for the exhibits of charitable and reformatory organizations, for a library, an assembly-room, for parlors, committee rooms, and administration and other purposes. All this must be accomplished in a space 400 feet long by half that width, adjacent to the Midway plaisance and the Horticultural hall" (Bancroft 1894:257). A graduate of the Massachusetts Institute of Technology, Sophia G. Hayden, won the bid, and her building quickly sustained "a daily gathering of women, who . . . expressed their ideas regarding the social, business and political affairs of humankind and all that pertains to making a greater future for the human race" (Eagle 1894:6). Virtually overnight the Woman's Building became the hub for debating the spheres, rights, and duties of women as well as for organizing and recruiting for such causes as temperance, settlement house work, education, suffrage, business, politics, and women's clubs. Steeped in ideas of domesticity, Victorian virtues, and progress,

the women followed their male counterparts with an extravagant display
of Native North America while excluding African American women from
exhibiting their progress (Massa 1974:319–37). The exhibits organized by
the Woman's Department embraced the theme of progress by demonstrating the evolution of women's industrial arts and domestic technologies. The stated goal of the exhibits was "to dispel the prejudices and mis-
conceptions, to remove the vexatious restrictions and limitations which
for centuries have held enthralled the sex" (Bancroft 1894:267).

Spinning Douglass's metaphor to "bend down and measure him,"
Palmer and her Board of Lady Managers demonstrated that women had
always been leading industrialists until men "pushed [them] aside." To
emphasize women's role in the development of industry and technology,
the managers outlined the rationale for the display of "primitive peoples"
in their exhibit prospectus:

> It will be shown that women, among all the primitive peoples, were the origi-
> nators of most of the industrial arts, and that it was not until these became
> lucrative that they were appropriated by men, and women pushed aside.
> While man, the protector, was engaged in fighting or the chase, woman con-
> structed the rude semblance of a home. She dressed and cooked the game,
> and later ground the grain between the stones, and prepared it for bread. She
> cured and dressed the skins of animals, and fashioned them awkwardly into
> garments. Impelled by the necessity for its use, she invented the needle, and
> twisted the fibers of plants into thread. She invented the shuttle, and used it
> in weaving textile fabrics, in which were often mingled feathers, wool, and
> down which contributed to the beauty and warmth of the fabric. . . . Especial
> attention will be called to these early inventions of women by means of an
> ethnological display to be made in the Woman's building, which will supple-
> ment the race exhibit to be made in the department of Ethnology. (Bancroft
> 1894:268–69)

In many respects, this was exactly the evolution of things that still inspired Mason of the Smithsonian's National Museum, who eagerly pitched
in with his support by contributing and organizing eighty exhibits entitled
"Women's Work in Savagery" (Mason 1894:212; Visweswaran 1998b:103).
To punctuate the theme, the managers mounted a performance of their
own savage at work: "In one of the landings on the southwestern stair-
case" there was a "loom manipulated by a Navajo woman of Colorado"
(Bancroft 1894:271).

Mooney was also called upon to assist, and Sickels was delighted with the prospect of showcasing the progress of both women and Indians (Moses 2002:80). According to a report in the *Chicago Inter-Ocean*, Mooney was charged with "modeling and dressing" all of the "Indian figures in the exhibit" for the Woman's Building. Sickels also played a curatorial role, and she was charged with shaping the overall message of the exhibit "to show the gradual evolution of women's industries by means of life-sized figures representing all types of women from the earliest times." According to the reporter, "the lady manager [Sickels] suggested to Mr. Mooney that he could put the historic dress which had been secured upon a figure representing a woman of another tribe. To her eye there was no physical difference. 'No, madame,' said the young ethnologist. 'The hands and arms of that figure never belonged to the tribe that wore this blanket. The exhibit is to educate, not mislead the people'" (McCabe 1893).

Sickels wanted to dress the mannequins in calico and gingham and did not want to argue over the provenance of a particular piece of clothing (Moses 2002:80). Mooney's commitment to science, authenticity, and the display of specific traditional cultural practices was at odds with Sickels, who was keenly aware of the stakes involved in the racial politics of culture. She wanted to show the world that American Indians were like other Americans who could and should become part of the melting pot and not be relegated to their own crucible of race.

The insistence of Mooney and Putnam upon veracity and provenance, according to Sickels, amounted to depraved indifference. They were reproducing seemingly negative images that demonstrated that Indians were unlike most Americans, which prevented her from executing her stated agenda to foster "a better understanding of the Indian" in order to improve the dire conditions she witnessed at Pine Ridge. Mooney was not only challenging a particular representation of race, but also curtailing a representation of gender that the Board of Lady Managers was trying to develop within the confines of their building at the gateway to the midway. Kamala Visweswaran calls the representation of gender at the fair an example of "expository feminism":

> This "show-and-tell" stage of Victorian feminism was due, in part, to the successes of the first generation of professional and social reform women. The exhibitions and fairgrounds of the nineteenth century provided avenues for

the leisured middle classes to view the hierarchically ranked achievements of women such that the progress from savagery to civilization was confirmed. While some historians suggest that the world's fairs moved away from a conception of culture as the function of time, and toward a notion of culture as a function of place through the display of ethnological villages, I would argue that the latter actually consolidated an evolutionist, "time centered" view of culture that was itself deeply gendered. (1998b:103)

After being fired by Davis and Putnam and then censored by Mooney, Sickels began procuring money, political capital, and volunteers from the many women at the fair who were involved in cognate causes. Sickels's two-count indictment of the fair managers mirrored charges leveled by Wells and Douglass in their pamphlet. First and foremost, Wells and Douglass were infuriated that blacks were not allowed to demonstrate that "the Afro-American has made some progress in education, in the professions, in the accumulation of wealth, and literature" (1999:44). And second, they were outraged that the fair managers wanted to "shame the Negro," by bringing "the Dahomians [*sic*] . . . here to exhibit the Negro as a repulsive savage" (1999:13). Likewise, Sickels was furious that the educated or "self-civilized" Indians could not demonstrate their own progress and appalled that the exhibit of Indian life at the fair was "an exhibit of savagery in its most lowest specimens" and only showcased "those noted for bloodthirsty deeds" (*NYT*, October 8, 1893:19). Wells, Douglass, and Sickels were each very adept advocates who understood how best to make their case to the larger public. Although no one doubted their sincerity, it is difficult to know whether Douglass and Wells really thought the West Africans at the fair were "repulsive savages" and whether Sickels really believed that the Kwakiutl outside the Anthropological Building participated in any "bloodthirsty deeds." Sickels, Douglass, and Wells were each effective progressive-era activists who knew how to craft a message in a way that would resonate with particular segments of a reform-minded public, and it is easy to understand why they developed the second indictment as a way to underscore the first, which was ultimately their main concern. Despite the celebrity and popularity bestowed upon the ethnological exhibits by the public, these skilled reformers understood the ideological and interpretive work the indigenous performers were engaged in as they staged a form of ethnographic minstrelsy under the direction of Boas and Putnam, who were left looking a little flat-footed as they attempted to popularize anthropology (*NYT*, May 22, 1893:9; Dexter 1966:315–32).

Sickels waited for Chicago Day, when locals flocked to the fair, to score what turned out to be nothing short of a public relations coup. Using her political connections, she was able to convince the mayor of Chicago, Carter Henry Harrison Sr., to invite Pokagon to give a welcoming address and ring the "liberty bell" to open the day's festivities. Pokagon's lawyer and publicist would later explain that this was fitting because Pokagon "was the great master link between She-gog-ong as an Indian village and Chicago as one of the greatest commercial cities of the world. His father, for forty-two years the leading chief of the Pottawattamies, had owned the city site, including the Exposition grounds. His son Pokagon, the present chief, when a boy, had lived in Chicago, was there when it was transferred to the United States, and had camped many times with his father on the very grounds where stood the 'White City'" (Pokagon 1899:13–14). Sickels held a tea for Pokagon in the Woman's Building, where she formally invited him to give the Chicago Day address. Pokagon thanked the "ladies friendly to his race" for ensuring that "the educated people of my race take part in the great celebration," and he promised that his speech would serve not only his race but "the dominant race" and be a much better representation "than war-whoops and battle-dances, such as I today witnessed on Midway Plaisance" (1899:12).

Pokagon had been lobbying the federal government for years to secure the money promised to his father, who had made several treaties with Andrew Jackson as part of the Indian removal policies. Simon Pokagon, the author of "The Red Man's Greeting," was a true self-promoter. Together with his lawyer, publicists, and publisher, C. H. Engle, he welcomed the opportunity to promote their book and their cause (Clifton 1987; Pokagon 1898:254–56; Pokagon 1897:698–709). Chicago Day was October 9, 1893. True to Sickels's plan, she, Pokagon, and Mayor Harrison stood together in front of a replica of the Liberty Bell to welcome the crowd. The *Chicago Inter-Ocean* reported, "Miss Emma Sickles [*sic*], the red man's friend, introduced Chief Pokagon. . . . After Miss Sickles had spoken of the contract which gave to the civilized world the location of Chicago, Pokagon seized the rope and swung the ponderous bell until the entire exposition grounds rang with its notes" (Pokagon 1899:25).

In his address, Pokagon, the self-styled Potawatomi poet, struck a much more conciliatory tone than he did in his book, preaching that "we must teach our children to give up the bow and arrow that is in their hearts; and, in place of the gun, we must take the plow, and live as white men do" (1899:21).

While Sickels succeeded in getting the mayor to invite Pokagon to address the fair to represent the so-called civilized Indians, she simultaneously succeeded in getting the editor of the *New York Times* to run an article that headlined "Miss Sickels Makes Charges," which featured a story about her allegations that "the World's Fair is being used to further one of the darkest conspiracies ever conceived against the Indian race." The article ran on October 8, 1893, one day before Chicago Day, which meant that any copies that arrived in Chicago by overnight rail would be read on the very day Pokagon rang the Liberty Bell. Sickels identified the coconspirators as "Prof. F. W. Putnam of Harvard University, who had charge of the Indian exhibit, Mr. Thomas J. Morgan, then Indian Commissioner," and the so-called "gigantic land rings which have been doing their utmost to show the Indians to be incapable of self-government and unfit to hold land." Sickels charged that, together, these men agreed "to exclude from the fair all but savages and school children." Sickels's major concern was the fact that "every means was used to keep the self-civilized Indians out of the fair, such as the Cherokees, the Choctaws, and others of the civilized tribes in the Southwest. The Indian agents and their backers knew well that if the civilized Indians got a representation in the fair the public would wake up to the capabilities of the Indians for self-government and realize that all they needed was to be left alone" (*NYT*, October 8, 1893:19). Sickels argued that "if the thousands of prosperous Indian farmers could have made a display at the fair, these land rings would have been utterly discredited" (1893:19). She was disappointed that the "Indian Congress had been put aside and not held," and she observed that "every effort has been put forth . . . to make the Indian exhibit mislead the American people. It has been used to work up sentiment against the Indian by showing that he is either savage or can be educated only by Government agencies" (1893:19).

The *Times* implied that her allegations might be sour grapes on the count that "she was dismissed by Prof. Putnam" and that her "interest in the civilized Indians made her obnoxious" to him. The paper also allowed Morgan to deny that "he belonged to a ring, organization, or combination of any kind which sought to gain control of Indian lands or bonds" (*NYT*, October 8, 1893:19). Nevertheless, the *Times* took her charges seriously and painted Putnam as an evil scientist who conspired with land rings and the government to destroy Indian autonomy. The article made an explicit connection regarding anthropology's fabrication of an image of the Indian in a way that justified both boarding schools and seizures of land. The *Times* actually pointed out what Robert Rydell would later argue: ethnology, evolutionary theory, and entertainment interlocked at the fair to become "active agents and bulwarks of hegemonic assertions of ruling-class authority" (1984:62).

Mooney continued to get in trouble with both reformers and performers. For example, he oversaw the Indian exhibit at the Trans-Mississippi International Exhibit held in Omaha, Nebraska, during the summer of 1898. Science and entertainment colluded to such an extent at this exhibit that the putatively ethnological display developed into a full-fledged Wild West show (Moses 1991:221; Mooney 1899:126–49; Shaw 1898:836–53). There was also the incident of the Sun Dance, which almost ended his career. During the summer of 1903, the superintendent of the Cantonment Indian Training School accused Mooney of paying a Cheyenne sun dancer fifteen dollars to attach the head of a freshly slaughtered steer to his back by means of a lariat and skewers. Although Mooney did witness the incident, took several pictures of the ritual, and paid his "informant," he was exonerated of any wrongdoing, but not before Pratt and other reformers fueled rumors and fanned allegations in the press about Mooney's efforts in promoting torture and paying for savagery (Moses 2002:149–51; *NYT*, August 26, 1903:8).

As the nineteenth century ended, Mooney, Boas, Putnam, and BIA ethnologists like WJ McGee and Frank Hamilton Cushing continued to focus almost exclusively on Native Americans and fabricate dynamic displays at fairs and static displays in museums. Simultaneously, these same men began professionalizing anthropology by means of institutionalizing the AAA, training graduate students, and developing departments of instruction in colleges, which slowly (but never surely) moved anthropology out of the museums and world's fairs and into the universities (Baker 1998:53; Darnell 1971:83–103).

Ethnologists helped to curb the powerful government-backed campaign of assimilation, and the museum processes helped to underscore the value of cultural preservation and traditional practices. Nevertheless, anthropologists reified the exotic and put a rather large premium on those Indians they called conservative. This was precisely the type of view that led Mooney to believe that Zitkala-Ša was perpetrating a fraud and Alfred Kroeber to believe in 1911 that he had found the last wild or real Indian when he reportedly found Ishi in northern California (Starn 2004:7–36). Anthropologists, of course, were not alone in this endeavor; Wild West promoters, tourism boosters, Camp Fire Girls, art collectors, novelists, and the like were all pieces of the puzzle that cobbled together a racial politics of culture that is still being worked out today (Sturm 2002:137).

As anthropology became a discipline of academic professionals, it played an important role in legitimating one side of the Janus-faced racial reform that many industrialists sought to achieve. The Peabody Education Fund, John F. Slater Fund, and General Education Board helped to underwrite what Donald Spivey calls "schooling for the new slavery" (1978), and these organizations never contributed much to what David Adams calls "education for extinction" (1995), leaving the federal and state governments and missionaries to pick up the tab for educating American Indians. Yet many of the same people who were on the boards of these Negro education funds helped to institutionalize a fabricated authenticity for the American Indian through the museum process (Science 1905:29). Using what Eric Anderson and Alfred Moss call "dangerous donations" (1999), philanthropists funded natural history museums to curate Indian bones and brains, artifacts and languages while they funded normal and industrial schools to educate Negro minds by disciplining their bodies and behavior. For example, Andrew Carnegie and Mary T. Hemenway each supported the professionalization of anthropology by funding research on Native Americans, while they simultaneously paid for teachers and reformers to educate African Americans in the South. These philanthropic efforts, of course, formed an elaborate backdrop to the promotion of "high culture" among elite whites when Carnegie endowed his hall in New York the same year John D. Rockefeller endowed the University of Chicago.

Morris K. Jesup best exemplified this trend. He was the president of the American Museum of Natural History and the Chamber of Commerce of New York City. The patron to the famous Jesup North Pacific Expedition to the Northwest Coast and Eastern Siberia (1897–1902), at the same time he contributed to the General Education Board, the Metropolitan Museum of Art, Williams College, and the Rockport Public Library (Jacknis 2002:75–11; Hoxie 1992:969–96; Dennis 1998:142–56).

The symbolism and materiality of this discourse were stunning and best exemplified by Rockefeller's monuments to some of his favorite causes, which included the Laura Spelman Rockefeller Memorial Hall at Spelman College (1918), the Laura Spelman Rockefeller Memorial Carillon given to Riverside Church in upper Manhattan (1930), and the massive Laura Spelman Rockefeller Memorial Carillon given to the University of Chicago (1932). Spelman College, Riverside Church, and the University of Chicago were all gracious beneficiaries of Rockefeller's wealth (along with Colonial Williamsburg, the Israel Museum in Jerusalem, and the International Institute of African Languages and Cultures). The Baptist Church, the work of missionaries, medical research and health care, education, and racial uplift were the supposed noble virtues Rockefeller actively supported through his philanthropy. These virtues were chiseled and embodied in the stone statues of the many noble men and women who make up the impressive chancel screen at Riverside Church. Across the street from Grant's Tomb, where Harlem meets the Hudson, the one-hundred-foot-high Gothic-inspired cathedral sits atop Morningside Heights and towers over Manhattan's Upper West Side. Amid the ninety notable artists, educators, and physicians carved as lifelike figures within the screen, three are prominently placed at the right hand of Jesus in something like the holy trinity of racial uplift: Abraham Lincoln, Booker T. Washington, and Samuel Chapman Armstrong (*NYT*, March 3, 1931:19).

Although the Rockefeller Foundation supported social anthropology in Britain and Australia and physical anthropology in the United States, it notoriously funded sociology over cultural anthropology in the United States (Fisher 1986:6). Perhaps American cultural anthropology never achieved the status within the organization of a "field of concentration" because George Edgar Vincent, a sociologist at the University of Chicago, took over the presidency of the Rockefeller Foundation in 1917. Nevertheless, other philanthropists supported early anthropology and helped to support both original research and museums exhibits. Morris K. Jesup, Andrew Carnegie, George Peabody, Mary T. Hemenway, and Seth Low, together with the emerging disciplines of anthropology and sociology, institutionalized two very different concepts of what soon would be called culture. Putative conservative Indians and others outside the cities of the modernizing United States had it, while so-called progressive Indians, east European immigrants, Negroes, and people within the orbit of the modern urban environs did not, or were in the process of freeing themselves from the shackles of tradition through acculturation. Although there are exceptions, in the broadest terms Boas and anthropology at Columbia University helped to articulate the former, while Park and sociology at the University of Chicago helped to extend the latter. Commissioner of Indian Affairs John Collier and Chief Justice Earl Warren provide instructive examples of how this division of labor within the social sciences became law and an indelible part of American society. Collier used anthropology and its concept of culture as outlined in Lewis Meriam's report *The Problem of Indian Administration* (1928) to underpin the Indian Reorganization Act (1934), while Warren turned to sociology and its concept of culture in Gunnar Myrdal's *An American Dilemma* (1944) as the basis for his unanimous decision in *Brown v. Board of Education* (1954).

Mooney, Boas, Putnam, and other well-meaning anthropologists who wanted to do the right thing were agents in these multivalent processes, and each worked to advance the science of authenticity by choreographing the minstrelsy of the real. Other well-intentioned agents like Pratt, Zitkala-Ša, Sickels, and even anthropologists like La Flesche and Fletcher hotly contested turn-of-the-twentieth-century anthropology with its style of redface minstrelsy and fought anthropologists who wanted to exhibit the conservative Indians while they promoted the progressives. Although just as sincere, their view was just as narrow and just as limiting.

Mooney, Putnam, and Boas were trying to understand, preserve, and document Native North American cultural practices and ultimately were actors in a pernicious pattern of racism that was circumscribed by Chinese exclusion in the West, Jim Crow segregation and disfranchisement in the South, the genocide of Indians in the Midwest and Southwest, and the white man's burden in the Pacific.

Under the aegis of science, anthropologists of the era cemented a very narrow image of an authentic Indian by staging, fabricating, authenticating, and editing what was and was not Indian. While this scientific intervention fueled the antimodern desires of those who played Indian, yearned for an exotic authenticity, and appreciated the aesthetic value of an Indian head on a nickel or an Edward Curtis portrait, it also policed and precluded any variation, culture change, or diversity within traditional American Indian practices and worldviews. In the end, this kind of anthropology complemented the vanishing policies. By documenting and salvaging lost languages, religious and spiritual practices, kinship and tribal organization, or phenotypic diacritics, anthropologists weighed in with science to help ratify the idea that a genuine Indian identity could be constituted only through the race, language, and culture of specific tribal populations, and anyone who fell out of bounds of these narrow demarcations was simply not a real Indian.

(3)

Race, Relevance, and
Daniel G. Brinton's Ill-Fated
Bid for Prominence

"What is relevant about anthropology?" Fashioned as a bright blue com-
puter graphic, this question was stamped across each issue of *Anthropology News* during the final year of the twentieth century. The question
served as the annual theme for the discipline's most widely read publication; a century earlier, the architects of the field had grappled with the
identical question as they institutionalized the A A A (Brinton and Powell
1892: McGee 1903; Boas 1899). In 1999, members of the A A A were still debating not only what was relevant about anthropology but also how one
makes anthropology relevant. During the previous year, the newsletter's
theme asked, "Is it race?" and articles and commentaries over the course
of that year debated and addressed this question. Race and relevance have
served as mutually reinforcing themes of anthropology for many years.
In the United States, a peculiarly enigmatic relationship has formed between race and the relevance of anthropology on one hand and anthropology and the relevance of race on the other (Baker 1998; Harrison 1995;
Smedley 1993; Stocking 1968; B. Williams 1989).

Although anthropologists have routinely engaged contemporary social
issues that impact the broader public, there is an eerie permanence about
the fact that anthropology has always addressed issues pertaining to race
and that the U.S. public has always grappled with racial issues. Com-
pounded by the fact that anthropology in the United States has never
been as eminent as economics or psychology, anthropologists have routinely justified the relevance of their discipline as the science of race. Race
and the relevance of anthropology were entwined during the antebellum

period with the emergence of the first American school of anthropology, and the relationship took on increased importance as the institutional foundations of American anthropology were forming after Reconstruction and at the beginning of the industrial revolution. Although most nineteenth-century ethnology was concerned with describing and recording American Indian languages and customs, those descriptions were always already nestled in a discourse of white supremacy, evolution, and racial hierarchy. Moreover, race and culture were often seen as being one and the same. The evolution of languages, agricultural implements, and kinship systems was integrated within a rubric used to explain the so-called evolution of the races, which meant the anthropology of brains and bodies often spilled over into the ethnology of languages and customs. As well, anthropometry, anatomy, somatology, and even phrenology were routinely claimed as important fields that encompassed the rather unwieldy science of humans, as scholars like John W. Powell, Otis T. Mason, and Daniel Garrison Brinton tried to outline the limits and define the nomenclature to professionalize the field (Darnell 2003:32–33). Even when Boas began to sunder race from culture, he kept the then-distinctive modalities in conversation and in close proximity, as evidenced by his arrangement of the anthropological building at the Columbian Exposition of 1893 and his early efforts to decouple race from civilizations (Boas 1895; Boas 1911a; Boas 1911b).

In this chapter, I shift the focus of my analysis from the racial politics of culture to the cultural politics of race. I argue that by the late nineteenth century, the public was more interested in the brains and bodies of the many in-the-way races than in the languages and customs of out-of-the-way peoples. Unlike the preeminence it had in the study of American Indians, anthropology did not hold sway over the discourse on race, which was a much more crowded field. Yet race remained highly relevant to anthropology, and anthropology remained relevant to the study of race. In the waning years of the nineteenth century, Brinton leveraged anthropology and its relevance to the study of race to make a bid to become a prominent public intellectual. He also invested time and money in institutionalizing anthropology by organizing and helping to establish professional journals for the consolidating discipline. Despite the fact that he was nominally considered the first university professor of anthropology, he never practiced anthropology within a department of instruction, which was emerging as the new seat for anthropological production.

Although his timing was impeccable when it came to addressing the hot topic of race, he failed to see how the institutional apparatus for knowledge production was shifting under his feet. In short, he bet on the right horse but ran it in the wrong race.

Brinton used the science of race to bolster the relevance of anthropology during a distinguished career that began with antiquarian research in the 1880s and concluded with research that addressed relevant social issues and public problems in the 1890s. In this chapter, I will map the trajectory of Brinton's career activities and piece together his segmented biography to shed light on how he articulated a popular anthropology of race that insisted upon a neo-Lamarckianism that emphasized evolution. I also sketch how Brinton's popular racialist anthropology was eventually replaced by Boas's unpopular anthropology of race, which insisted upon an environmentalism that emphasized plasticity.

Additionally, I use Brinton's complicated biography to highlight what I consider to be a very critical moment in the history of anthropology. As the arena for the production of knowledge and civic discourse moved from the lyceum and museum to the college and university, anthropology in the United States became a less reliable narrator in the narrative of white supremacy by deflecting the powerful trajectory of the American School of Anthropology while building upon Americanist anthropology within the ivory tower (Bender 1993:33; Hinsley 2003:18–19; Darnell 2003:22; Conn 2004:193). Brinton's considerable influence, much of it predicated upon his appealing racialist science, was never sustained because he never fully understood that in the United States, the university was emerging as the premier venue where academics produced the best scholarship and most trusted science (Brinton 1892a). On the other hand, Boas's unpopular research on race was sustained precisely because he was viewed as a disinterested scientist who conducted research as a university professor. More importantly, Boas had students to help develop his research programs, while Brinton didn't. Finally, I will offer some historical perspective on that almost Faustian deal between the science of race and the relevance of anthropology by plotting Brinton's success on the road to obscurity.

Although I focus on Boas in this transition, Frederic Ward Putnam and his visionary leadership should get much of the credit for situating anthropology within colleges and universities (Browman 2002:510–11). Although departments of instruction and university graduate schools came with their own demands and challenges, it was Putnam more than any other anthropologist in the late nineteenth century who enabled anthropology to escape the demands of patrons in the parlor and congressmen on the Hill (Darnell 2003:22; Hinsley 2003:19; Baker 2002:8; Browman 2002; Conn 2004:192).

The transition of anthropology from the museum into the university was not seamless, and there was considerable resistance both inside and outside of the academy to Boas's early research and writings on race. It took time for Boas to solidify his academic standing in the United States, and it happened only after he and anthropology were securely ensconced within departments of instruction on college campuses. Even with the support of Putnam, Boas had a bumpy ride until he found a permanent faculty appointment, which he used to consolidate enough influence to eclipse scholars like Brinton and Powell. To exemplify this point, I describe the troubles Boas had when he tried to measure schoolchildren's heads while serving as a docent at Clark University in Worcester, Massachusetts.

Race and the relevance of anthropology have had a long and enduring relationship in the United States. When the institutional home of the field made the transition from the museum to the classroom, the anthropological discourse of race became increasingly less congruent with, and more critical of, the prevailing views and laws of the broader society. In the early twentieth century, departments of instruction, graduate students, and new doctorates of anthropology began to proliferate within institutions of higher education, while the influential cohort of ethnologists who worked in museums and at the BAE simply died. Subsequently, activists and intellectuals regarded this new, more critical, science of race and culture as reliable and normal and began using it to erode and chip away at the legislative and institutional apparatus that reproduced racial inequality and the idea of racial superiority and inferiority (Baker 1998: 127–42).

The professional infrastructure of anthropology in the United States was established, in large measure, by the leadership of Brinton at the University of Pennsylvania, Putnam at Harvard University, and Powell at the Smithsonian Institution. All of these luminaries produced volumes of research, touted the practical and public significance of anthropology, provided leadership in various anthropology societies, and, following in the steps of Lewis Henry Morgan, were elected president of the AAAS.

Of these founding fathers of American anthropology, Brinton is per-haps the least well known, but it is his storied past that best illuminates how scholars used the study of race to make anthropology—or, in this case, one's anthropological research—more relevant. Although the rela-tionship between racial determinism and nineteenth-century anthropol-ogy is well-tilled soil, by focusing explicitly on Brinton I can offer new per-spectives on the roles of patrons and publics, physicians and ethnologists, in the production of anthropology in late nineteenth-century Philadel-phia (Baker 1998; Degler 1991; Frederickson 1965; Hinsley 1981; Smedley 1993; Stocking 1968). The history of anthropological activity in Philadel-phia is often neglected in favor of the histories of anthropology that focus on Cambridge, Washington, and New York (Conn 2003:166). Actually, the reasons for the retrospective insignificance of anthropology in Phila-delphia are yoked in part to Brinton's inability to securely establish the field at a university in the Delaware Valley.

Mounds and Medicine

With Brinton's appointment at Penn in 1886, he became the first profes-sor of anthropology at an American university and served as dean of the Philadelphia axis of the emerging academic discipline. He represents an important bridge-figure in the history of anthropology because he helped to steer it through distinct phases of its development, beginning with his participation in local antiquarian clubs. He then helped to validate an-thropology as a natural science in prominent academies and museums and worked to establish the *JAF* and the new series of the *American An-thropologist*, both of which were specialized journals that helped to ce-ment anthropology as a distinctive discipline in the United States.

Brinton was born on May 13, 1837, on his family's farm in Chester County, Pennsylvania. He died on October 27, 1899, at the age of sixty-two. Brinton's lifelong interest in Native American antiquities was piqued as a boy by his explorations of artifacts of Delaware Indians and his con-stant reading of research by antiquarians. His affluent Quaker family hired a tutor, in lieu of formal schooling, to prepare him for Yale College, where he majored in literature. In 1856 Brinton went to Florida for a respite from ill health and the winters of New Haven, and he took that opportunity to pursue his interest in antiquities. The result was his first book (written at the age of twenty-two), *Notes on the Floridian Peninsula, Its Literary History, Indian Tribes and Antiquities* (1859). It was to be the first of more than twenty books and well over a hundred articles and pamphlets documenting Native American history, literature, and linguistics (Smyth 1900: 18–20).

Brinton graduated from Yale in 1858 and returned to the Philadelphia area to enroll in Jefferson Medical College, where he received an MD degree in 1861. He immediately pursued further training in Paris and Heidelberg, but he came back to the United States when the War between the States intensified. In 1862 he volunteered for the Union Army and was quickly promoted to surgeon-in-chief of the Second Division, Eleventh Corps of the Army of the Potomac. Brinton's war record was impressive, and he served in combat at such pivotal battles as Chancellorsville and Gettysburg (Chamberlain 1899:216–17).

The battle of Gettysburg was his last, and he was transferred to Illinois, where he served as surgeon-in-charge of the U.S. Army hospital in Quincy. In 1865 he was discharged from the army and married Sarah Tillson. He left Illinois to return to Philadelphia's Main Line to practice medicine, but medicine was not his sole pursuit. He again began to write about Native Americans, producing, among other articles, "The Shawnees and Their Migrations" (1866a), "Artificial Shell Depositions in the United States" (1866b), and "The Mound-Builders of the Mississippi Valley" (1866c). His article on mound building was one of the first studies to assert that indigenous peoples had erected those structures.

In addition to developing his medical practice, Brinton began to edit and publish the weekly *Medical and Surgical Reporter*, the quarterly *Compendium of Medical Science*, and *Napheys' Modern Therapeutics*. From the beginning of his career, he engaged in public outreach by offering public lectures on health and hygiene and writing for popular magazines.[1] As he practiced and published in the medical field, he developed a commitment to scientific rigor, professionalism, and the standardization of terminology, which remain his lasting contribution to the field of anthropology (e.g., Brinton and Powell 1892; Darnell 1988:7). By 1874, he had quit practicing medicine to focus on the management and editing of his journals, but he never curbed his growing interest in American languages. He wrote three books and eleven articles concerning American grammar, linguistics, and folklore. During this period of his career, his audience was composed of mostly armchair enthusiasts and amateur antiquarians. Unlike other American physicians who contributed to anthropological inquiry before the Civil War, Brinton never felt compelled to combine his interests in ethnology and medicine (Haller 1971a:40–68; Smedley 1993:231–54).

In 1887, at the age of fifty, he relinquished his management of the medical publications to devote himself strictly to science, which he considered a considerable financial sacrifice. Brinton explained, "I deliberately left a profitable business that I might, on a modest competence, pursue my life as an observer, a thinker and an unpaid writer." He shared the philosophy behind his decision in a letter to Sara Y. Stevenson, the influential director and chief fundraiser at Pennsylvania's University Museum who had just asked Brinton for a financial contribution (Hinsley 2003:13): "In some respects, I thoroughly believe in the philosophy of Comte. He taught that society should be divided into two great classes—first, those men and women who are willing to pass their time in the study of science, and for that object, renounce the ambitions of practical life; and second, the money-makers, the producers, the workers in applied science; and from the latter should come the support of the former. It is the duty of the rich, the prosperous, the practical citizens of Phila. to support our institution. Surely were I one of them, I should aid."[2] Although Brinton's personal commitment to science evidently changed over the course of his life, his evocation of Auguste Comte provides a useful reference point to help identify how he viewed himself as a scientist working in the public's interest, how he viewed the folks he studied, and how he employed a neo-Lamarckian social theory to inform his writings.[3]

Brinton established three patterns within his scholarship that remained constant for the balance of his life. These are articulated even in his first book, *Notes on the Floridian Peninsula* (1859), published the same year as Charles Darwin's *On the Origin of Species by Means of Natural Selection*. First, Brinton's method of research included critiquing and synthesizing other peoples' writings on a given subject, then drawing conclusions from all the work he read. He did not produce original scholarship per se, and fieldwork to him was literally reading everything in the field—as in the field of philology. Actually going into the field to talk to indigenous people would have required that he go outside, and at least in Florida he simply could not bear "the incredible swarms of mosquitoes" (1859:167). Second, Brinton established himself as a meticulous scholar. He had a penchant for source citation and was scrupulous with regard to his footnotes, which were often peppered with German, Spanish, and French works. He fussed about the lack of academic rigor at a time when much of the material written about indigenous peoples was travelogues and missionaries' accounts. He even bemoaned the fact that he was so dependent on the information provided by the superficial notices of military explorers, who held no interest in anything other "than the political relations of the nations they were destroying" (1859:111). Finally, he adopted a unique blend of theories to explain both the unity of, and differences between, the so-called races of mankind. Brinton combined Lamarck's idea of acquired characteristics and Spencer's racialist hierarchies to form a theory that maintained both a determinant view of the environment and a notion of psychic unity.[4]

George W. Stocking Jr. notes that Brinton shared this latter-day doctrine about the inheritance of acquired characteristics with "the three most outspoken and influential Lamarckians," Powell, Lester Frank Ward, and G. Stanley Hall (1962:242). These Lamarckians of the *fin de siècle* combined the social theory of Comte, Morgan, and Spencer with new methods of research to advance notions about social evolution that turned on the idea that the "transmission of culture" through the inheritance of acquired characteristics was a crucial factor in biological evolution, especially the evolution of the mind (Stocking 1962:243; Greene 1959). These scholars articulated evolutionary ideas just as those ideas were winning wide acceptance owing to their proliferation in nearly every division of scholarship and their popularization through new forms of media (Loewenberg 1941:341).

From Brinton's perspective, everyone had a common psychic heritage, but the constant effects of living in one's environment allowed certain races to become superior to others—mentally as well as physically.[5] He consistently maintained that "certain mental traits and faculties are broadly correlated to these physical features, and no amount of sentimentality about the equality of all men can do away with this undeniable truth" (1898:273). Brinton used this theoretical orientation for three decades as he helped to usher anthropology from an avocation of collectors to a professional academic discipline.

Brinton was a principal steward of institutionalizing the field, but it was not because of his scrupulous scholarship. He knew that if the study of the "primitive races of mankind" was to compete with geology and physics, compelling ideas were not enough; he needed the support of scientific organizations and control over specialized journals (Flagg 1897; Stocking 1968:22). Even before Brinton abandoned his business ventures, he began volunteering for positions in scientific societies that governed publications and public education. This allowed him access to various venues that enabled him to make the case that anthropology was not only relevant but necessary as a science that could help identify social problems.

Brinton was a member of many organizations, but the five most important were the American Philosophical Society (APS), the University of Pennsylvania Museum of Archaeology and Anthropology, the AFLS, the Academy of Natural Sciences of Philadelphia (ANSP), and the AAAS.

Americanist-in-Residence

In 1869 Brinton was elected to the APS and became one its most active members and prolific writers (Wissler 1942:189–202). He contributed forty-eight articles to its *Proceedings*, chaired its publications committee, participated in its council, and served as secretary. For years he played an integral role in selecting speakers for the society's meetings and submissions to its *Proceedings*, often inviting anthropologists to deliver papers and publish in its organ. The speeches anthropologists gave at APS and the articles they published in its organ gave the aspiring discipline both credibility and validation. Brinton methodically rose to power within the society by working diligently, and in 1896 he was tapped for its vice presidency. In being appointed to the position he beat out William Pepper, the former provost of the University of Pennsylvania. Pepper, who was better known, was not elected because he had "presented but one scientific contribution to its publications" and never "manifested any interest in its aims or welfare."[6]

Brinton published twice as much in the society's *Proceedings* as he did in any other serial, and most of these articles were papers he had presented to the society (Darnell 1988:11–12). His overall publication record shifted away from linguistics and grammar, but his contributions to the society remained focused. He did not write about theories of the evolution of races or European racial stratification, as he did for the ANSP; nor did he write about problems of anthropological theory and nomenclature, as he did for *American Anthropologist*.[7]

Since the days of Thomas Jefferson, the APS has promoted "useful knowledge" about Native American language, culture, and history (Conn 2004:87–88; Carter 1993). Brinton proudly upheld its century-long tradition by advancing scholarly research on the Americas—which may explain his rationale for routinely using its *Proceedings* as an outlet for his linguistic research. Given the society's long tradition of studying American Indians, it may seem obvious why Brinton maintained his identity as an Americanist at the APS. However, there is another compelling reason. By upholding its tradition, he received attention and respect from some of the most distinguished scholars in the country. Brinton never won the same scholarly recognition within anthropological circles, especially from members of the bureau and the AFLS. William W. Newell, founder of the AFLS, even noted, "He is somewhat sensitive, never having received as much attention from this part of the country [Boston] as he deems himself entitled to."[8]

Like other linguists and philologists, Brinton did not find broad support for his research, so he used his considerable influence over the society's *Proceedings* to publish it. This lack of interest seemed particularly glaring in 1887, when he described for Boas, then an editor at *Science*, the fate of *Brinton's Library of Aboriginal American Literature*: "The encouragement extended to my series of publications in the aboriginal languages has been so little that after printing the seventh volume, now in press, I think I shall give up in despair. . . . When in this country of fifty million shall we find five hundred willing to support with their means the study of the greatest of all sciences—that of man?"[9] Brinton initially found support for his research at the University of Pennsylvania, but that too quickly faded.

Pennsylvania's Indian Man

In 1881 Pepper became provost of the University of Pennsylvania and immediately began transforming the institution from a "small sleepy place" to an "institution of national and international renown" (Kuklick 1996:27). On the day of his inauguration, he announced Joseph Wharton's gift for the new business school, and he never stopped building, erecting the library and more than a dozen departments and schools during his eleven-year tenure (Cheyney 1940:285–324). Among Pepper's many interests were archaeology and ethnology, and he imagined adding a great museum to his expanding university. In 1886 he appointed three new faculty members to facilitate the process, including Hermann Hilprecht, a Babylonian archaeologist, and Morris Jastrow, a specialist in Near Eastern philology. The third was Brinton, whom he appointed as professor of American archaeology and linguistics.

Brinton shared with Pepper more than APS membership and an interest in anthropology: he shared Pepper's vision of an extensive anthropological museum that was "a vast means of instruction in anthropology and not a mere collection of curiosities" (Darnell 1970:81). In 1889 Pepper convened influential business leaders, scholars, and noted antiquity collectors to form the University Archaeological Association; Brinton became its president the following year.

The provost and trustees charged the association with raising funds, sponsoring expeditions, and securing a new building for a financially independent museum. In 1891 Pepper formally established the Department of Archaeology and Paleontology and its Free Museum of Science and Art, now called the University of Pennsylvania Museum of Archaeology and Anthropology (Cheyney 1940:351; Culin 1900:199). Brinton chaired the department's American Section between 1892 and 1894 and quickly established a public lecture series. The series was greeted warmly by Pepper, who regarded it "as a movement of the first importance, not only in the interest of the Museum, but of the entire subject of Archaeology in this community." Pepper pushed the trustees to ratify the series by passing a resolution: "That a course of lectures be organized by the chairman of the committee of the American Section of the Museum of the University, illustrative of the objects in that department of the Museum, said lectures to begin in November next, to be delivered either at the Museum or elsewhere as may appear most favorable for interesting the public in the Museum and for the instruction of the students of the University. The course [is] to be free."[10] Brinton could not wait until November, so he chose the auspicious occasion of Columbus Day in 1892—the four hundredth anniversary of the New World's "discovery"—to give the first lecture.

Brinton began this address by highlighting Columbus's "infinite courage and unswerving faith" but quickly turned his attention to the aboriginal race: "Wherever you find its representatives, you see the same peculiar hair, color, eyes, and other physical signs of racial unity; and wherever you trace their history, you find the same forms of religious and social life, the same lines of culture-development, and that same ineradicable love of liberty which seems to be inhaled with the air of this New World, and to become a part of the nature of men of whatever race who settled upon its soil . . . ever urging them to wider horizons and a higher evolution" (1892b:4).

Brinton often gave these "Indian appreciation" lectures to the public. Like Morgan, his predecessor in Americanist anthropology, Brinton spoke in romantic terms about Native Americans and the unity of races—but never about racial equality (Deloria 1998:71–94; Conn 2004:113). Brinton viewed racial differences in terms of inferiority and superiority: "Beyond all other criteria of race," he assumed, a scientist first "must rank its mental endowments. These are what decide irrevocably its place in history and its destiny in time. . . . Thus appraised, the American race certainly stands higher than the Australian, the Polynesian or the African, but does not equal the Asian" (1891:42).

Although Brinton demonstrated measured success at the museum in terms of public instruction and directing the American Section, he soon tangled with Stevenson over the museum's direction. Stevenson stitched together an influential network of support within the museum, the university, and the local philanthropic communities. With the help of her close friend Provost Pepper she parlayed her network into a powerful position of leadership (Danien and King 2003:40–45; Hinsley 2003:16). She had a special interest in classical archaeology and made it a priority to curate the museum's Babylonian, Mediterranean, and Egyptian sections. Stevenson knew firsthand "the gravity of the responsibility assumed in agreeing to erect and maintain a Museum Building, without expense to the City, or to the university funds."[11] Quite appropriately, she developed the direction of the museum to ensure solid funding, which was not aimed toward Americanist anthropology. Frankly, she and the patrons of the museum were interested in the dramatic antiquities of the Near East, not in the pottery shards and arrowheads of Native Americans. Philadelphia's well-heeled Protestants underwrote explorations into the Holy Land and envisioned more of an art museum than a natural history museum. In response to the demands of the museum's patrons and her own interest, Stevenson prioritized a classical archaeology and Egyptology that emphasized biblical history and Near East civilizations, while neglecting anthropological archaeology, with its emphasis on science and ethnology (Conn 1998:75–114; Kuklick 1996:11–78; Hinsley 2003:4; Danien and King 2003:40). The museum's budget also reflected these priorities. In 1893, for example, the Egyptian, Mediterranean, and Babylonian sections received $8,000, whereas the American and Prehistoric Section received $331 (Conn 1998:93).

Stevenson's and Pepper's emphasis on Egypt and the Mediterranean created a wedge between the classicists and the ethnologists. Charles Abbott, Stewart Culin, Brinton, and the board member C. Howard Colket each challenged the scope and direction Stevenson and Pepper envisioned. Colket actually resigned because he could not agree with the provost and the trustees that "the Department should be given the broadest scope—as broad, in fact, as the British Museum. This brings the Department in direct competition with two well established Museums in this city, and I do not see the necessity of establishing the third."[12] Abbott resigned after a bitter dispute, and in 1903 Culin filed a defamation of character suit against Stevenson and the museum (Conn 2004:148; Meltzer 2003:48–87; Darnell 1970:82–83). His dismissal followed. Brinton eventually distanced himself from the museum, and in July 1894 he severed all ties. He explained to Stevenson that he was a "valueless auxiliary" because he had "no money to give, and no capacity for raising any." Brinton was also incensed about provisions placed on certain collections and the overall direction of the museum: "I learn for instance, that a large collection of Peruvian pottery is to be installed there, under a prohibition forbidding the officers of the Museum from copying or describing specimens in it. In my own department, I am not allowed to study for publication objects placed there? . . . A University-museum, it seems to me, has two main purposes—the one, of investigation, the other of didactic instruction. That it should be made an attractive show room, or a sales room for those with collections to dispose of, is to me unwelcome."[13] Brinton finally remarked, "I have no thought of 'resigning,' but I do not contemplate a reappointment in connection with the Museum."[14] Artifacts from the Nile River valley were simply more popular than artifacts from the Ohio River valley, but Brinton clung to his academic integrity and refused to bow to the pressure of the public and the influence of the patrons. Although he distanced himself from the museum, he never gave up his title as professor of anthropology at Philadelphia's most prestigious university.

Pepper's appointment of Brinton in 1886 made him, at least nominally, the first university professor of anthropology in the United States, even though he neither taught students nor received a salary (Darnell 1970: 81–85). Brinton used his title at every opportunity. It gave him credentials few other anthropologists possessed: an academic platform from which to advance the field and the authority to assume the role of a purveyor of science to the Philadelphia public—even though, technically, it was only an affiliation.[15]

Steven Conn explains that "the infighting at the Penn museum reflected the larger struggles over the public attention archaeologists working in the American field could command, the support—institutional and financial—they could generate, and the prestige that work could garner in the increasingly professionalized world of university-based research" (2004:149). Although financial support and academic interest in the artifacts, languages, and customs of American Indians may have begun to wane in the final years of the 1890s, interest in race waxed as Jim Crow became the law of the land, lynching of black men became routine, and populations of black and not-quite-white people began to migrate and immigrate into Philadelphia, New York, and Boston. While Brinton was rejecting the public's interest in artifacts from the Holy Land at the University Museum, he was pandering to the public's interest in race at the ANSP.

The institution where Brinton proved most successful was the ANSP. He did not succeed at curating the American Section at the University Museum and could not find support for *Brinton's Library of Aboriginal American Literature*; one can understand why he tried something different when lecturing at the ANSP.

The Academy's Public Intellectual

As Brinton was struggling to define his role as an academic and curator at Penn, he was playing the role of public educator with aplomb across the Schuylkill River at the ANSP. In 1884 he was appointed professor of ethnology and archaeology at the academy, and he immediately embarked upon organizing both regular and popular courses in ethnology for its program of public instruction. Brinton outlined the importance of his lectures in his first prospectus to the committee on instruction: "Few people understand what ethnology is, or why it should be studied—surprisingly few. They must first be taught this. . . . I [will] deliver eight lectures, two a week, *free to the public*, on the general principles of the science. If at their termination there is enough interest in it to get together a class for study, I will form . . . sort of weekly ethnological conferences."[16] Delivering the lectures was a pleasure for Brinton, and he enjoyed educating the public about the value of ethnology.[17] His lectures were not subjected to departmental politics as they were at Penn or held to rigorous academic standards as they were at the APS. The titles of some of his popular courses were "Modern Methods in the Study of Man," "The Success and Failure of the Races," "Man's First Home," and "Rock Inscriptions and Other Interpretations."[18] He viewed all the lectures as "semi-scientific" and described the audience as "a cultivated one. . . . Not large (125 about) largely made up of teachers and persons already familiar with the principles of science."[19]

If the formation of the AAAS and the AFLS can be viewed as the constitution of a community without locality, the academy was an intellectual community tethered to the local—the city of Philadelphia. Philadelphia and its Main Line served as the center of a locally based intellectual life that was inhabited through face-to-face interaction, public education, and fundraisers. That, of course, was a contrast to intellectual communities fostered within the professions, where community life was inhabited through printed texts, higher education, and conferences (Bender 1993:4–5).

Thomas Bender has explored the roles, relationships, and dynamics among scholars who addressed academic audiences and scholars who addressed civic audiences during the nineteenth century. He argues that lyceums and museums—urban cultural centers like the ANSP—were the sites of intellectual life during the nineteenth century: "Only later would one of these institutions, the college converted into the university, achieve hegemony in intellectual life and transform the urban-based world of learning into university scholarship" (1993:33).

The ideas Brinton articulated at the academy were situated within a particular social matrix that constituted his most civic audience. Better than other institutions with which he was affiliated, this one provided him with an engaged audience that was motivated to learn. And, following Bender, Brinton's audience would have afforded him legitimacy, concepts, motives, and key questions that shaped his public education at the academy in a way that fostered shared meanings and intellectual purposes (Bender 1993:3–4).

Unlike Brinton's all-male audience at the APS, his audiences at the academy were mostly women. Most of his lectures were free and open to the public, and there was no record of attendance. The academy did keep records of the classes, for which it charged a one- or two-dollar fee.

For example, there were a dozen members in both Brinton's second and third "Course in Archaeology and Ethnology," taught in 1885 and 1886, but only one man attended. For his class "Popular Course: Friday Evening Lectures, January 25, 1889," seventy-seven attended, of whom more than fifty were women.[20]

Brinton's constituents were Philadelphia society ladies. He was often supportive of women who wanted to pursue science not as an avocation but as a career, even though many men thought it was exclusively their domain. Yet Brinton never hesitated to share the scientific details of their alleged reproductive shortcomings and ethnographic descriptions of their "savage sisters." For example, in a lecture to the ANSP given in 1896 entitled "The Relations of Race and Culture to Degenerations of the Reproductive Organs and Functions in Woman" he painted a sweeping organic analogy between the reproductive functions of women and animals. Quoting Spencer, Brinton described the "maxim that the increased mental and moral development of women in modern times necessarily leads to degeneration of her reproductive powers" (1896a:2). To describe the disparity between birthrates of "Aryans" living in the cities of Europe and America and the "savage woman" in the hinterlands, Brinton simply remarked, "The same contrast is seen in the lower animals. . . . The highbred Silesian ewes of Saxony can scarcely drop their lambs without artificial assistance; 'pedigree' cows, bitches, and mares are always greater sufferers in natural labor than the lower and wild varieties" (1896a:3).

What Brinton called "the perfectly developed modern white women," he argued, had a larger pelvis than other women, and that was "the criterion and the necessary condition of racial progress of the evolution of the human species." According to Brinton, the pelvis was the only physical advantage the "Aryan American woman" had over her "savage" sisters because the Aryans, having a "high moral and intellectual education," suffered postponed "appearance of menses," "an impairment in the function of lactation," and an "underdeveloped and adherent clitoris." Brinton noted, however, that "the clitoris is well developed in most anthropoid apes and also in the negro race" (1896a:4–5). He elaborated at length upon the "passionless" girls from New England and the oversexed and amoral savages. This lecture, like many of his popular lectures, was widely circulated in print, published as a feature article in Philadelphia's *Medical News.*

Brinton's interest in brains and reproductive organs was not unique. Nineteenth-century investigators routinely deemed those corporeal locations the most definitive in their pursuit of ranking and ordering the races of humankind while analogically wedding white women to the supposedly lower races (Wiegman 1995:43–78). Although Brinton noted the putative moral and intellectual prowess of white women, he did not hold out the possibility of their participation in duties of citizenship. The duty of woman, he underscored, was that of advancing racial progress by means of her reproductive organs. In the later part of the nineteenth century, natural history ceded its epistemological framework to biology in the life sciences and to anthropology in the social sciences. Each became a site for identifying natural gender-specific functions and structures, temperaments, and abilities that scholars and laymen alike recruited for the legitimation of women's subordination and explanation of women's exclusion in the public sphere of citizenship (Laslett et al. 1996:1–3). Like his work on racial difference, Brinton's work on gender difference was at the forefront of science because it synthesized old ideas in new ways. What made him unique in the history of anthropology was his ability to recruit different sciences into the burgeoning field of anthropology while introducing anthropology to those fields from which he recruited—again, trying to make the science of anthropology relevant.

Racial Inferiority: The Key to Brinton's Success

Two of Brinton's most influential books, *Races and Peoples* (1890a) and *The American Race* (1891), grew out of public lectures delivered at the ANSP. His lectures at the academy mark a shift away from antiquarian and academic focus on Native American linguistics and grammar to a broader, more popular focus on racial classification and ethnography. As well, they denote his shift from a local intellectual to an international scientist, and they appear to have been the key to his success in scientific societies. The irony is that his careful linguistic classification, analysis of grammar, and detailed transcription of folklore were far more rigorous and original than his synthetic overview of racial hierarchies.

On the heels of publishing *Races and Peoples*, his most extensive exegesis on racial hierarchies, Brinton became president of the AFLS (1890), president of the International Congress of Americanists (1893), president of the AAAS (1894), and vice president of the APS (1896). The lectures that inspired *Races and Peoples* were originally billed as "Outlines of Ethnology: The Study of Race, Peoples, and Nation." Convening in the library of the Academy of Natural Sciences, Brinton was to hold forth for ten consecutive Monday evenings beginning in January of 1890.[21]

He had addressed many of these topics in previous regular courses, but evidently he retooled them to be delivered as this popular course. In the introduction to *Races and Peoples*, he stated that he was writing a compendium of the "latest and most accurate researches on the subjects treated," and he did not depart from his technique of culling and critiquing all of the available material (1890a:5).

Although Brinton's definition of ethnology is evident in the title of his lecture series in 1890, his methodology—ethnography—was not exactly what one would consider ethnography today. For Brinton, the aim of ethnography was to "study the differences, physical and mental, between men *in masses*, and ascertain which of these differences are least variable and hence of most value in classifying the human species into its several natural varieties or types" (1890a:18), or what he also called races and subspecies (1890b:100). More like geography, ethnography for Brinton involved mapping, recording, and classifying races and peoples.

In the first chapter of *Races and Peoples*, "Lectures on Ethnography," Brinton began with a survey of the "physical elements of ethnography," detailing the range of features used to classify and rank races. His "physical criteria of racial superiority" included cranial capacity, color, muscular structure, stature, ethnic relations of the sexes, vital powers, and sexual preference. He concluded the chapter by writing, "We are accustomed familiarly to speak of 'higher' and 'lower' races, and we are justified in this even from merely physical considerations. These indeed bear intimate relations to mental capacity.... Measured by these criteria, the European or white race stands at the head of the list, the African or negro at its foot" (1890a:47–48).

With prose resembling a how-to guide, Brinton linked his physical elements of ethnography to supposed social and psychological elements of ethnography. He assumed that the only successful way to rank-order the races was to consider mental and physical differences equally because "the mental differences of races and nations are real and profound. Some of them are just as valuable for ethnic classification as any of the physical elements" (1890a:51). These mental criteria for racial superiority included another array of factors, such as social instincts, dispersive elements, arts of life, migratory instincts, and combative instincts. The first section of the book, "Elements of Ethnography," mirrored chemistry's periodic table of the elements; Brinton essentially produced a table of the elements one should use in classifying and ranking races.

In chapter 3, "The Beginnings and Subdivisions of Races," Brinton discussed evolution, but he simply recycled the same Lamarckian view he held when he wrote *Notes on the Floridian Peninsula* thirty years earlier. He did develop an elaborate discussion of the various origins and variations within the white race, which was "the leading race in all history" (1890a:103).[22] Challenging the prevailing view that Aryans, Teutons, and Caucasians originated in Europe or Asia, Brinton argued that these white races originated on the great Libyan Plateau, which he called Eurafrica. He sustained this argument by carefully distilling extant paleontology, philology, geology, and ethnography to present what one reviewer called "formidable opposition" to the then-orthodox view that west European groups originated in Europe or Asia but definitely not in Africa. Like his initial work on the mound builders of the Mississippi Valley, some of his findings presaged later and more rigorous findings. At the time, however, this finding flew in the face of contemporary science, which was based on common sense and grounded in racist assumptions (i.e., Native Americans could not have erected the mounds, and Aryans could not have come from Africa).

When Brinton described the various stocks and groups of black people, he merely restated widespread racial stereotypes and validated them as scientific facts. Some were long-standing and quite blatant: he suggested, for example, that "the true negroes are passionately fond of music, singing and dancing" (1890a:192). Others were simply caustic, placing the "African negro midway between the Orang-utang and the European white," based on what he saw as the Negroes' exaggerated prognathism, in which the jaws project beyond the upper face; after all, "the African black . . . presents many peculiarities which are termed 'pithecoid' or apelike" (1890a:25; Brinton and Farrard 1902:133).

Brinton wove the authority of science into the tapestry of contemptuous images dispersed through magazines, lithographs, and minstrelsy, but the themes he recast as ethnology in the 1890s were already routinized in

American popular culture, helping to sell everything from maple syrup to sheet music. His scheme mirrored other schemes that positioned each race on a rung of the ladder to civilization.

Brinton's style of ethnography was heartily embraced, and *Races and Peoples* received positive reviews on both sides of the Atlantic. The noted natural historian Agnes Crane, for example, raved to her middlebrow English readers that "no popular work of this scientific character has appeared since the publication of M. A[rmand] de Quatrefages's 'L'espece humaine' in 1877. . . . But twelve years are an epoch in ethnography—no science advances with more rapid strides—and every epoch needs its special chroniclers. If M. de Quatrefages is now somewhat behind the age, Dr. Brinton may be said to be a little ahead of it, for he is an advanced evolutionist, *au courant* of the times and prodigal of original speculations."[23] Boas also gave the book a judicious, qualified yet positive review, both as an anonymous reviewer for *Science* and as an associate editor of the *JAF*. In identical opening sentences he gingerly approved of Brinton's work: "Dr. Brinton has undertaken the difficult task of presenting the whole vast field of anthropological science in a concise and readable form, and he has admirably succeeded in giving us a book that is attractive, and in all its parts suggestive" (Science 1890:276; Boas 1891b:87). In *Science*, Boas commented on the didactic value of *Races and Peoples* for the greater public. "Therefore not only will it prove useful in making the public acquainted with the facts and some theories of ethnological science," Boas explained, "but it will also incite the painstaking student to more thorough investigation of mooted questions, and open new vistas in many fields of research" (Science 1890:276).

The way Brinton compared Africans to apes did give Boas pause, and he voiced this concern in a comment in the anonymous review in *Science*, stating that "too much is made of the peculiarities of the 'lower' races, which in some respects might be called rather exaggerated human types than simian in character" (Science 1890:276). Boas basically gave Brinton a pass on the primate parallels and chose instead to focus his attention on the way Brinton conflated linguistic groups with racial groups. The review in the *JAF* was much shorter and provided only a cursory outline of the book. Each review concluded by stating that Brinton emphasized "justly the close relations between ethnography and historical and political science. This work will undoubtedly greatly contribute to making this close connection better known and more thoroughly understood" (Science 1890:277; Boas 1891b:88).[24]

Boas in the Bull Pen

Boas is generally recognized for debunking such racialist research in anthropology, but his critique did not find firm footing until he was established in a university department. Moreover, his critique was not fully sustained until 1911, when he published *The Mind of Primitive Man* (Boas 1911b; Stocking 1968:161–94; Williams 1996:4–36). Though many scholars recognize Boas as a crusader against racial formalism and for racial justice, his biographers demonstrate that this role emerged slowly. Julie Liss, for example, points to his identity formation as a way of explaining that "Boas's early attempts to establish a secure scientific position for himself were frustrated, at least in part because his vision of an unformed scientific field awaiting the fructifying genius of Germanic science was not appropriate to the realities of the American scientific scene" (1996:181–82). George W. Stocking Jr., on the other hand, suggests that Boas's tepid rise as a leading opponent of racial formalism was slow to gain steam because of "the current state of biological knowledge." "Furthermore," Stocking explains, "he carried with him a residue of polygenist and evolutionary assumption which was the baggage of physical anthropology generally" (1968:169–70).

Both lines of inquiry offer insights into Boas's shift toward a more critical view of the science that maintained racial hierarchies in the United States. At least at the beginning of his career, however, the alacrity with which he tackled scholars and scholarship articulating ideas about racial inferiority marched in lockstep to his incremental institutional security within the AAA and Columbia University.

When Brinton severed his ties with the University Museum in 1894, he was president of the AAAS and recognized internationally as a leading figure in the emerging field. At the same time Boas was struggling desperately to secure a regular appointment and expand his research program beyond the languages, texts, and folklore of the peoples of the Pacific Northwest. After publishing *Races and Peoples* (1890), Brinton was able to bask in the glow of an admiring public and revel in the accolades bestowed upon him by learned scholars. Simultaneously, Boas was hammered by an angry public, only selectively supported within the academic community, and not given a regular rank faculty position at a university.

Boas's unpopular research on race was reproduced and began to flourish only after he was established within a university department. But that is only part of the story. Other factors included his ability to skillfully navigate through the AFLS and the AAA and to buttress his shifting paradigm with his students, several of whom founded departments of anthropology at leading institutions of higher education and many of whom went on to contribute to the field in enduring ways.

Being part of a university in itself did not guarantee academic freedom or offer protection from an engaged public and the popular press. When Boas first attempted to develop his research on race and human development at Clark University, he had a very difficult time. This story highlights the sharp contrast between Boas's early struggles and Brinton's later-day successes as anthropology moved out of the museum hall and onto the college campus by the early twentieth century. During the 1890s the field was transitional, and it got treacherous for the young German scientist.

In 1889 G. Stanley Hall hired the inaugural faculty of Clark University in Worcester, Massachusetts. Boas was hired as one of a cluster of stellar scientists and researchers; Hall was explicitly trying to compete with Johns Hopkins as the nation's leading research university. Serving as a docent and teaching twice as much as his colleagues on the regular faculty, Boas launched an aggressive program for researching growth and racial plasticity to complement his ongoing research in ethnography and folklore (Cole 1999:137–39).

After a decade and a half of experiments, measurements, and careful documentation that took him to Oakland and Toronto, Boas began challenging some basic assumptions of physical anthropology while advancing biostatistics in the United States (Camic and Xie 1994). These efforts culminated in a major study Boas conducted between 1908 and 1910 for the U.S. Immigration Commission, published as *Changes in Bodily Form of Descendants of Immigrants* (1912). In it, he demonstrated that the environment played a significant role in determining physical attributes like head size, which were so often used to demarcate racial difference (Stocking 1974:189–90).[25] The method and preliminary findings for this important study were worked on at Clark in 1891, and the entire study was almost terminated by a petulant anti-elitist newspaper editor who targeted Boas to challenge the powerful elite associated with the new university.

When Boas arrived in Worcester to begin his teaching career, the city had a population of just under eighty thousand. From its bucolic dairy and produce farms to its bustling business district and factories, the city was a major hub of the industrial revolution. Inhabited by New England blue bloods, it was rapidly being populated by immigrants from Europe and Canada—Boas arrived during a tumultuous period in Worcester's history. The city's industrial might centered around a wire- and machine-manufacturing industry that opened the way for other industries and services to produce, among other things, thousands of miles of barbed wire to be shipped west for fencing (Southwick 1998:37–42). Although the metal and machine trades prevailed, no single industry dominated, and many independent industries made Worcester their home—textiles, boots and shoes, and paper products, to name a few. "In the U.S. Census of Manufacturers, the category 'other' perennially led the list of Worcester's top industries" (Rosenzweig 1983:12).

As factories belched black smoke from hundreds of stacks across the city, workers poured into the city to fill the need for labor. In subsequent waves of immigration, beginning with French and English Canadians in 1860, the population of Worcester grew sixfold between the 1840s and 1890s. By the mid-1890s, one-third of the population was foreign born. Most of the immigrants were from Ireland, Sweden, and Canada, but there were sizeable communities of Armenians, Poles, Lithuanians, Syrians, Finns, Norwegians, Assyrians, Germans, Danes, Russians, Ukrainians, Greeks, Italians, and Albanians (Southwick 1998:38).

Although Worcester's ethnic and religious diversity was unmatched by any inland city of its size, the gulf between factory workers and the educated, moneyed elite was typical of many industrializing cities of the 1890s (Gutman 1973:571–85). Yet as a result of (or perhaps as a cause of) Worcester's diversified industries, the gulf between ethnic groups within the working class was atypical of such cities. Segregated by language, occupation, leisure activities, and religion, each ethnic group worked, worshiped, and lived together, rarely reaching across ethnic lines or bridging language barriers. This self-segregation limited union activity, and the Knights of Labor were thwarted in their efforts to organize effectively. The historian Roy Rosenzweig has outlined these dynamics: "On the one hand, ethnic divisions militated against class-wide mobilization of workers in trade unions or political parties. . . . Consequently, the insularity and separatism of the immigrant communities limited immigrant working-class influence over economic or political issues. On the other hand, these ethnic enclaves . . . provided a refuge and resource for those who confronted the unemployment, poverty, disease, and accidents that accompanied life and work in industrializing America" (1983:31).

Worcester's factory owners fostered and manipulated this segregation by favoritism, paternalism, and ruthless labor practices. Town boosters even used the city's great "number of nationalities" as a pitch to attract new business. An advertisement sponsored by the local board of trade, for example, explained that Worcester was a great place to locate a new factory because "these nationalities do not affiliate, [and] concerted efforts for promoting strikes, labor unions, and similar movements among the working class become impossible" (Rosenzweig 1983:24). Along with this diversity came bitter political contests, aggressive assertion of ethnic interests, and a bevy of well-disciplined and politically savvy social and civic clubs, temperance societies, and parish churches, each organized along ethnic lines. Among poor and working-class Yankees, however, a long tradition of anti-Catholic and anti-immigrant hatred found an institutional home first in the Know-Nothing Party and later in the American Protective Association and the Ku Klux Klan (Southwick 1998:58; Meagher 2001:138, 309).

With such an array of immigrants and a public school system that counted half of its student body as foreign born or children of immigrants, Boas had at his disposal an ideal laboratory in which to gather data on patterns of growth from people with a wide range of backgrounds (Southwick 1998:38). Proposing to study patterns of children's growth, Boas quietly secured the permission of the Worcester school committee to set up a small station in each school for "measuring" children. Although members of the school committee had some initial questions, the board member Fallon prevailed upon them that "the committee should put no obstacle in the way of the advance of science" (Worcester Daily Spy, March 4, 1891:1). As a public service, Boas also proposed testing the hearing and eyesight of each child from whom he took head, girth, and height measurements (Worcester Daily Telegram [hereafter WDT], March 4, 1891). Although he had ideal subjects to measure, the ability to measure them proved less than ideal.

Boas's modest program, modeled after the studies conducted by Henry P. Bowditch in Boston's public schools (1877), alarmed some parents because they did not understand exactly what he was going to measure and why. To assuage any "misapprehension [that] exists regarding measurements," Boas printed a circular to be distributed to the parents detailing the purpose of the measurements, which had the "object of getting data regarding growth of the head, growth of the brain, [and] growth of the bodies with questions as to nationality, occupation of parents, numbers of brothers and sisters, etc." He carefully explained to a reporter from the *Worcester Daily Telegram*, "I do not desire to measure any child against its own wish or the will of his parents" (*WDT*, March 7, 1891).

This initial study of schoolchildren, which served as a foundation for his seminal work in physical anthropology, was almost derailed by Austin P. Cristy, the acerbic publisher of the *WDT*, Worcester's most popular daily (Rice 1889: 94). "Franz Boas, the man who has received from the school board the open sesame to the anatomies of the public school children of the city," the *Telegram* reported, "must have been a scrapper from way back." The paper described that "he has scars on his face and head that would make a jailbird turn green with envy. His scalp is seared with saber cuts, and slashes over his eyes, on his nose, and on one cheek from mouth to ear, [which] give his countenance and appearance which is not generally considered au fait, outside the criminal class" (*WDT*, March 3, 1891). Cristy sarcastically asked parents how they would "enjoy the hero of German duels feeling their sons' and daughters' heads and bodies over, just as he did those of the Eskimaux" (*WDT*, March 3, 1891). On a more sanguine note, Cristy reported, "The chances are if Franz Boas, PH.D. Kiel, should enter one of the schools, the boys—as soon as they recognize his battle scarred visage—will draw their pea-shooters with one accord and annihilate him with a volley" (*WDT*, March 7, 1891).

It is unclear exactly what motivated Cristy's attack (Tennenbaum 2003:10). Did he want to protect children? Was he concerned about what Boas might discover? Did he know about other anthropologists' findings and thought that Boas would reproduce racial hierarchies within the immigrant population? What is known is that Cristy routinely exploited several crosscutting tensions within the city in order to fuel the circulation of his paper, and he held nothing but contempt for Clark.

Editorially, Cristy's newspaper was affiliated with the Republican Party and hostile to immigrants and labor, but the paper also had an anti-elitist bent (Rice 1889:94). His target audience was native-born working-class white men and women who voted Republican. Working-class Yankees who voted Republican usually identified with the elite, seeking social mobility through the fraternal organizations and Protestant churches their bosses and employers frequented (Rosenzweig 1983:86). As part of his bid to increase circulation and articulate his anti-elitist position, however, Cristy's reporters often covered developments important to Worcester's ethnic and working-class communities (Rosenzweig 1983:291).

This was not the first time Cristy targeted the faculty at Clark University to articulate his agendas. In 1890, the *Telegram* had launched a graphic antivivisectionist campaign that detailed laboratory experiments conducted on animals at the university. The paper was sending a clear message that the new university was not welcome (Koelsch 1987:34). At the time of the controversy surrounding Boas's experiments, there was a power struggle going on within the school committee that pitted the superintendent, Albert Marble, who was sympathetic to the interests of the Irish and Catholics, against "loyalist republicans" who organized to oust him (Meagher 2001:223). Whatever the motivation of the paper, it now targeted Boas and his proposal to measure the thighs of the town's schoolgirls (Cole 1999:142). Although the editor caused a stir, the majority of school committee members continued to support Boas. After all, this was the age of science, and they were not going to let a provincial publisher get in the way of progress. The committee members stood by their decision to provide Boas the opportunity and facility with which to measure students' bodies, and they spoke out against Cristy's efforts to derail scientific progress.

The committee's major concerns included the fact that the *Telegram* did "not give them an opportunity to demonstrate the wisdom and value" of the research, did not reflect the views of the "large majority of the best people of the city who approve of the action of the school committee," and, finally, did "not fairly reflect the prevailing public sentiment in opposing the measurements" (*WDT*, April 15, 1891). Cristy railed against each charge, noting that his paper printed the written "opinions or letters of those with whom it differs," and "not a line attempting to demonstrate the wisdom or value of the proposed measure has been offered to the *Telegram* for publication." "As for 'correctly reflecting public sentiment,'" Cristy lamented, "the *Telegram* don't [*sic*] pretend to try to; it reflects its own 'sentiment' to a hair and that is all the 'sentiment' it ever pretends to 'reflect.'" Cristy was particularly upset with the charge that he should report the views of "the majority of the best people in the city [who] supported the school committee." He clarified that "the *Telegram* is not very well posted as to 'best people'; it don't take much stock in 'best people,' anyway" (*wDT*, April 15, 1891). Although Cristy was explicit that "the *Telegram* does not believe that anything like a majority . . . approve" of the board's action, he decided to give the committee "a chance to demonstrate the *Telegram* is mistaken" by giving "'public opinion' a chance to 'reflect' itself" (*wDT*, April 15, 1891).

In an article headlined "*Telegram* Offers All a Chance to Vote on Boas Measurements," Cristy averred that "the only known way to get anything like the sentiment of a community is by voting. Therefore, vote and find out how Worcester stands":

> There is but one way to get the facts; if the measurers and their friends have got the public sentiment they boast of, let them say so in votes. If the opponents of the scheme are the more numerous or sufficiently numerous to be entitled to immunity from having any such outside enterprise thrust upon the school system—let them say so in votes. . . . The votes, "yes," or "no," must be written upon a ballot printed in the *Telegram* and sent by mail, or brought to the *Telegram* office. Everybody buys the paper anyway. . . . The *Telegram* has always advocated female suffrage, and mothers as well as fathers and all teachers and all school pupils and all others can vote during this expression of the sentiment of all the people. School committeemen and docents can vote, also. Prepare your ballots! (*wDT*, April 15, 1891)

Cristy's timing could not have been better, and Boas's timing could not have been worse. After several fits and starts, Boas went forward with his plan to measure eighth and ninth graders in the Woodland Street School, April 16, 1891, the day after Cristy printed the ballots and called for the vote. The *Worcester Daily Spy* (hereafter *wDS*), a competing paper, called Boas's and the school committee's effort to move forward in the name of science a "rebuke to sensationalism," and it reported that this finally ended "the most puerile and at the same time the most indecent and disreputable newspaper hoax that has ever been perpetrated upon the long suffering public in Worcester" (*wDS*, April 17, 1891:4). Unfortunately for Boas, Cristy was just getting started.

Cristy shouldered the press's responsibility as community watchdog and dispatched one of his reporters to the school to write "a detailed description of the way they do it." The *Telegram* reported, "Docent Boas and his two assistants, Docent G. M. West and Mr. A. F. Chamberlain of Clark University . . . arrived before 8:30 o'clock." The reporter detailed how the scientists used their "paraphernalia," which included calipers, sheet lead, paper, a square box, a "machine for measuring the strength of the eyes," and a "chart used for detecting astigmatism of the eyes." While the reporter detailed what Boas measured, he was more concerned with how he measured the children—especially the girls.

The reporter watched carefully as Boas and his assistant weighed and measured the students. The *Telegram* reported the entire process, which began with the student answering questions about nationality, age, color of eyes, etc. "Next the docent took a small strip of sheet lead, a quarter of an inch in thickness, and, telling the subject to shut the eyes, leaving the impression [of the nose] in the soft lead" (*wDT*, April 17, 1891). The paper painted Boas as a lecherous foreigner who pawed at the bodies of innocent girls with "a hand that fooled around the topknots of medicine men and toyed with the war paint of bloodthirsty Indians" (*wDT*, March 5, 1891):

> "Please remove the shoes," was the next request. This did not trouble the boys, but when there were two girls and one boy together with Docent West and a [*Telegram*] reporter in the little room . . . the reporter noticed the girls, young ladies, rather, of 15 or 16 years, glance from one to the other hesitatingly before removing the shoes and appearing in stockings. There was more removing, too. The young ladies who had long hair braided and knotted on the back part of the head had to take it down, and hair-pins and ribbon had to be removed. Then the subjects were ready for Docent Boas and his calipers. . . . Those calipers of Docent Boas's are triple-jointed affairs, made of cold steel. One end of the cold steel Docent Boas put in amongst the young lady's back hair till it rested on the extreme point of the occiput. Then he closed them together over the top of the head till the other end rested on the middle of the forehead. (*wDT*, April 17, 1891)

The votes and editorials began to pour into the offices of the *Telegram*. After the first day of voting, there were 870 No votes and only 11 votes in favor of Boas's research. Quickly deemed the "caliper question," editorials proposed "giving Mr. Boaz a new suit of clothes made of tar and feathers, and a free ride on a rail . . . to the wharf where he can get a nice whiff of sea air as he returns to the land of his nativity" (*WDT*, April 17, 1891).

Although Boas was "fed up with the whole thing," he was unmoved by the popular sentiment reflected in the paper and continued to measure children for whom he had received written permission slips.[26] Apparently, Boas and his measurements were more popular than Cristy and his paper would have had the public believe. As the weeks wore on, 80 percent of the permission slips given to the schoolchildren were returned with the signatures of their parents (Cole 1999: 143; cf. *WDT*, April 23, 1891). However, the support of the parents and enthusiasm of the students did not square with overwhelming opposition for the measurements voiced by the public. On May 12, 1891, Cristy reported the final tally on the caliper question, "Shall Docent Boas and 'his assistants' measure the public school pupils of Worcester?" It stood at 15,116 No and 345 Yes. Yet Boas was nonetheless able to measure hundreds of children with their parents' consent. Cristy's grand scheme to derail Boas's research ultimately backfired, but not without a thorough investigation by his newspaper's reporters.

Cristy sent out reporters to investigate the disconnect between public opinion as measured by his poll and the success of Boas's data collection. For the teenagers of Worcester, being measured by an exotic man with unusual instruments while raising the ire of parents and the press alike became fashionable and irresistible. In an article headlined "Parents Send 'No' Votes But Sign Permission Blanks," the paper explained that "a great number" of children "beg their parents' permission to have the measurements made. . . . 'My boy teased me so much to let Docent Boas measure him,' said a parent yesterday, 'that I signed the blank presented for the purpose, although I am opposed to the measurements and have voted 'no' in the *Telegram*'s vote contest' " (*WDT*, April 23, 1891). "When a reporter asked" some boys from a local baseball team "if they had been measured, they said they had and that they liked it first rate. 'I've voted, too,' said one of them. 'So has pa and ma.' 'What did you vote?' queried the reporter. 'I voted 'no' and so did all of us. But we like to get measured all the same because it is such fun." The reporter concluded:

> The pupils of the lowest grades are having even more fun out of Docent Boas than those of the higher grades. The youngsters haven't the slightest idea whether they are being sized up according to the requirements of the

Shamanistic rites with which Docent Boas is conversant, or to furnish statistics for gumdrop manufacturers. They wink and blink at the shining calipers
and cabalistic measuring beam, and step on the scales as if they were going
to receive a stick of candy at the conclusion of the examination. All the while
they keep up a huge expression of merriment and, the thought of studies and
recitation never enters their heads. (*WDT*, April 23, 1891)

Thanks in large measure to the indiscretion of Worcester teens, Boas was
able to circumvent the "power of the press" and the putative "will of the
people" to conduct a pilot study that laid a solid foundation for his efforts
to challenge the science of the body in the late nineteenth century. The
real significance of this victory, however, was the fact that a progressive
school board supported science conducted under the auspices of university research and refused to bow to popular opinion. Unlike Emma Sickels
and Richard Pratt, however, Cristy did not have an explicit reason for
campaigning against anthropology; nevertheless one can begin to discern
that throughout the 1890s anthropology came under withering attack
from very different quarters within the public sphere. For Boas, this was
the first in a long line of public assaults on his research and writings on
race and culture. Anthropology was buffeted by public outrage ginned
up by reformers and racists, but Boas was able to find some protection
in the lee of the university that provided the field with both legitimacy
and scientific authority. First, however, he had to establish the scientific
authority of his research, and to do that he had to go through Brinton,
whose legitimacy was earned more by currying public appreciation than
by commanding scientific authority.

Brinton v. Boas and *Plessy v. Ferguson*

When Boas wrote the reviews of Brinton's *Races and Peoples* in 1890, he
was a thirty-two-year-old Jewish immigrant without steady employment;
it was not until the following year that Hall hired him at Clark and he
first started his long-term research project ultimately entitled *Changes
in Bodily Forms of Descendants of Immigrants* (1912) that was almost derailed by Cristy. The data collected in Worcester would eventually provide
evidence to bolster his later challenges to Brinton's style of ethnology. In
1890, Boas had neither the data nor the power to launch a direct, public

assault on Brinton, who was so well ensconced in the type of institutional framework Boas needed to secure his scientific authority and advance himself and his vision of anthropology.

Brinton was president of the AFLS when *Races and Peoples* was published, and Boas chaired both the editorial committee and the council of the society. Boas's committee members included Putnam, Brinton, and Mason of the National Museum at the Smithsonian, who was elected president of the AFLS the following year (Boas et al. 1891:5). Newell, a staunch ally of Boas, understood the stakes involved if Boas were to give Brinton's book a negative review. However, Newell was the journal's editor, and he also understood the stakes involved in allowing only a cursory review of the president's magnum opus. In a letter to Boas about his rather curt review of *Races and Peoples*, Newell proposed a compromise: "As Dr. Brinton is our president, and the notice [of *Races and Peoples*] is perhaps rather brief, and as you, of course, have not been able to enter at length into any of the theoretical questions of which Brinton treats, I should like, if you have no objection, to add to your notice the words here enclosed, or some equivalent, if you prefer it, which merely state the fact, that we have not space to enter on a general discussion in our reviews."[27] Newell did add a rather cryptic line at the end of the review section of that issue, stating, "Want of space forbids us to extract further" (Newell 1891:93).

Regna Darnell has discussed in detail the cordial, polite, but somewhat tense relationship between Brinton and Boas during the early 1890s (1988:64–81). It is not clear, however, whether Boas was tempering his animosity toward the senior ethnologist in order to ensure his upward mobility within the organizations in which Brinton held sway or actually supported Brinton's findings. Vernon J. Williams Jr., in *Rethinking Race: Franz Boas and His Contemporaries*, offers a compelling argument that Boas granted Brinton's views. I initially questioned Williams's claims in support of Boas's concerns over his self-advancement (Baker 1996:909; Williams 1996:10), but, after closely examining the text and context of Boas's "Human Faculty as Determined by Race" (1895), his first antiracist address to a scientific society, I concluded that he was being careful not to challenge Brinton directly *and* accepted some of his findings.

In 1894 Boas served as vice president of Section H of the AAAS (anthropology), and he delivered his address to the section at the meetings in August. During that month, he was also mourning the death of his young son, avoiding his creditors, and facing unemployment (Herskovits 1953:16; Williams 1996:8). Without citing names, he addressed "observers" and "recent writers" who have "claimed that the white race represents a higher type than all others" (Boas 1895:301). He focused on how proponents of evolutionary hierarchies always "interpret as racial character what is only an effect of social surroundings" (1895:326).

Boas explained how various civilizations developed independently and through cultural diffusion, emphasizing that they arose in various parts of the world regardless of the inhabitants' race. Even though this contradicted the prevailing notions of race, Boas deferred to (or conceded) much of Brinton's ethnology. He challenged Brinton's notion about the relationship between Negroes and apes in his anonymous review of *Races and Peoples* in *Science*, but in this public address he evidently concurred with Brinton that Negroes expressed a certain primate-like morphology: "The alveolar arch is pushed forward [in Negroes] and thus gains an appearance which reminds us of the higher apes. There is no denying that this feature is a most constant character of the black races and that it represents a type slightly nearer the animal than the European" (1895:311). Boas also conceded the discourse that linked head size and brain weight to so-called cultural achievement: "It would seem that the greater the central nervous system, the greater the faculty of the race and the greater its aptitude to mental achievements. Let us review the known facts. . . . There are . . . sufficient data available to establish beyond a doubt the fact that the brain-weight of the whites is larger than that of most other races, particularly larger than that of the negroes. In interpreting these facts we must ask, does the increase in the size of the brain prove an increase in faculty? This would seem highly probable and facts may be adduced which speak in favor of this assumption" (1895:314).

It is difficult to discern in this address whether Boas accepted or just interpreted extant findings. The broader conclusions he drew from the data, however, were in stark contrast to Brinton's conclusions. Boas argued that there was considerable overlap of racial characteristics and underscored the fact that nothing "has been found yet which would prove beyond a doubt that it will be impossible for certain races to attain a higher civilization" (1895:317). In a direct challenge to Brinton's ethnography, Boas declared that the main reason for African American inequality was not retarded faculties, arguing instead that "the old race-feeling of the inferiority of the colored race is as potent as ever and is a formidable obstacle to its advance and progress." He suggested that scientists should investigate how much Negroes have "accomplished in a short period against heavy odds" because "it is hardly possible to say what would become of the negro if he were able to live with the whites on absolutely equal terms" (1895:307). Boas was adamant that "historical events appear to have been much more potent in leading races to civilization than their faculty, and it follows that achievements of races do not warrant us to assume that one race is more highly gifted than the other" (1895:308). Although Boas was careful, he essentially issued a challenge to Brinton while erecting the scaffolding for his sustained critique of scientific notions of racial inferiority (Baker 1994; Hyatt 1985; Stocking 1968; Williams 1996). Brinton accepted Boas's challenge the following year and delivered "The Aims of Anthropology" (1896b) as the presidential address to the AAAS. Brinton took that opportunity to upstage Boas's vice presidential address to the section, and to put young Boas in his place.

Brinton saw industrialization as the only road to civilization: "The progress of man is his progress of gaining independence from nature, of making her forces his slaves and not leaving them his masters" (1898:276). His view of inevitable progress and his notions of racial hierarchies were commensurate with *fin de siècle* ideas of laissez-faire fitness that curbed regulatory reform, emboldened monopolies, and structured racial segregation (Brinton 1898:276; Hofstadter 1955:45; Wiecek 1992:492–93). Brinton presented these notions with force and candor in his address to the AAAS. Calling anthropology "a natural science" that sought to test and explain "organic laws," he declared that "the black, the brown and the red races differ anatomically so much from the white . . . that even with equal cerebral capacity they never could rival its results by equal efforts" (1896b:67–68). Although Brinton employed the same ideas about racial inferiority he had posited in his early book, the address had more scientific authority coming from the president of the AAAS, and it had a much wider audience because it was published in *Popular Science Monthly*.

The president of the AAAS advanced anthropology along the lines he had developed as a public intellectual at the ANSP—not along the lines he continued to practice at the APS. Brinton was adamant that anthropology's future rested on producing "very direct or visible practical applications" with a "concern with the daily affairs of life" (1896b:59). To make anthropology more relevant, he turned to race. He was trying to navigate the growing tension between the expectations of institutions and industries that employed scientists and experts to analyze problems and offer practical solutions and benefactors and philanthropists who used scientists and pundits to reinforce their ideologies and sway public opinion.

One of the most salient concerns in the daily affairs of people in the United States during the 1890s was the Negro problem, and Brinton argued that anthropology could address this issue in practical ways. Anthropological research, he concluded, "offers a positive basis for legislation, politics, and education as applied to a given ethnic group" (1896b:69; see also Haller 1971b:722). As president of the AAAS, he issued a popular call for legislation that conformed to putative organic laws—ratifying and naturalizing white supremacy. Although there is no evidence the U.S. Supreme Court took any judicial notice of Brinton's address, these ideas were so widespread that the Court unwittingly answered his call and ruled on *Plessy v. Ferguson* (1896) the following year.[28] *Plessy* made the ideas of racial inferiority constitutional law, forcing African Americans into inferior schools, bathrooms, accommodations, and Jim Crow train cars.

Plessy was one of many examples of laissez-faire constitutionalism, a form of jurisprudence that assumes the U.S. Constitution simply reinforces the laws of nature and the rules of common law. Natural market forces, the inferiority of certain races, and the inequality of women were so natural or organic that any constitutional tinkering was tantamount to slapping the hand of God.[29] Brinton's presidential address in 1895 exemplifies how his vision of anthropology fit neatly within these ideas of the Gilded Age, dovetailing with elaborate rationales used to underwrite legislation that sustained oppression along racial and gender lines and prevented legislation that regulated commerce and working conditions. Although laissez-faire constitutionalism held sway in the Supreme Court well into the twentieth century, during the late nineteenth century state legislatures and Congress began to heed the demands of journalists and reformers, scientists and experts for regulatory laws that curbed monopolies and regulated maximum hours and minimum wages. These reforms impugned tooth-and-claw notions of the survival of the fittest, marking the waning of the Gilded Age and the waxing of the progressive era (McCormick 1993:319). From this perspective, Brinton's retrospective insignificance can be understood from a unique register: he engaged in discursive practices that slowly became eclipsed by the reform-minded intellectuals of the progressive era. It is not that racism or stereotypes abated during the progressive era; the eugenics movement, for example, blossomed during this period. The science of race, however, slowly veered from a natural science to a social science with the aim of solving, rather than simply identifying, problems. In the wake of child labor, unsafe working conditions, monopolies, overcrowded tenements, and a myriad of public-health concerns, intellectuals proposed new theories, and legislators imposed new regulations. Whereas most Americans still had an unwavering faith in progress, it was not inevitable; progress had to be managed. In this context, university professors, credentialed scientists, and budding graduate students emerged as a powerful class of intellectuals.

Brinton: Radical or Reactionary?

Although there is little direct evidence that Brinton's shift away from Indian linguistics and grammar caused his ascension to positions of leadership in science, his positions on race and gender mirrored popular stereotypes, public opinion, and legislative statutes and no doubt facilitated an increase in his popularity. I cannot draw a conclusion from the historical record as to whether Brinton had a mission to advance anthropology in the public's interest and simply chose the best way to do so or just abandoned whatever failed and chose a path to ensure his own popularity. What *should* be clear from the record is that Brinton won accolade after accolade from prestigious institutions of science during the tumultuous 1890s and that he validated ideas of white supremacy, which were consumed as "popular science" in lectures, magazines, and books. Brinton's scholarship simply crystallized, in vivid relief, many prevailing views, even among people who were considered open-minded or even radical.

At the same time Brinton began to write scientific essays that seemingly promoted racial and gender inferiority, he appears to have become more politically radical, to have adopted certain socialist values, and to have been embraced by people who were committed to socialism and anarchist communism. Horace L. Traubel, editor of the *Conservator*, a radical Philadelphia journal inspired by Walt Whitman's legacy, noted, "At one period Brinton was a bigoted antagonist of industrial [socialist] revolution. I had encounters with him when the brute power of his prejudice astonished me. But in his mellower final years all such rudimentary quality seems to have gone out of his composition" (1899:131). The following year the same paper explained how "there was a latterday Brinton who seemed to some of us as much more valuable to the community. . . . It was only in his later life that in the domain of economics, of property, of government, his views were collaterally liberalized and seemed to some of his alarmed orthodox associates on the border line of the dangerous if not actually reaching into the territory of the hallucination" (The Conservator 1900:189). "During Dr. Brinton's later years," Helen Abbott Michael noted, "it was known in a small circle of comrades" that he "believed that a duty devolved upon scholars with socialistic views to carry the force of scholasticism to their own social class as well as to bring whatever aid it might to the masses" (1899:103, 102). In a letter to Stewart Culin, she noted even that "Doctor Brinton always stood as the advocate of women and he has always been fair to her in her efforts towards intellectual freedom."[30] Brinton's reputation as an insurgent voice in his final years even reached across the Atlantic. An obituary in London's *Freedom: A Journal of Anarchist Communism* suggested "it would be straining a point to call [Brinton] a comrade," but "we are doing no injustice to his memory when we say he was nearer to us than to any of the various schools of thought which deal with the social problem; and had he begun the study of this question earlier in life he would have been a worker for Anarchist Communism" (Freedom 1899:74).

Virtually nothing in Brinton's published works and professional correspondence documents his political views of the government or the economy.[31] Although his Quaker background and these obituaries raise some intriguing questions, they demonstrate how deeply ingrained notions of white supremacy were even among radical scholars and activists, how accepted notions of racial evolutionism were among the intelligentsia regardless of political orientation, and how integral notions of racial hierarchies were to anarchist ideology during the last decade of the nineteenth century (Traubel 1996:112). They also reflect Brinton's ability to contribute and operate within various circles and institutions that pursued diverse goals and agendas.

Although I could not determine exactly how Brinton "mellowed" in his final years, his last book, *The Basis of Social Relations* (1902), demonstrates that on the issues of race and sex as they relate to black people in the United States he was as acerbic as ever: "I fail to see any difference from a physical standpoint," he observed, "between the sexual furor of the negro and that which prevails among the lower animals . . . namely, that the *furor sexualis* in the negro resembles similar sexual attacks in the bull

and elephant." He noted even that these attacks have "been especially frequent among the negroes in States cursed by carpetbag statesmanship"
(1902:160–61).

I do not think it helps one understand the checkered past of anthropology any better to indict Brinton as a racist, for he conducted his research
during a period marked by some of the most virulent racism ever experienced in American history. After all, he was quite innocuous compared
with such legislative lapdogs of white supremacy as Benjamin Tilman and
John Sharp Williams, and he was not even in the same league with such
hucksters of scientific racism as Madison Grant and Nathaniel S. Shaler.
Moreover, if one wanted to measure the influence Brinton had on articulating notions of racialized evolution, he would pale in comparison
with someone like Booker T. Washington, whose countless speeches, addresses, and pamphlets promoted racial uplift, imbued with similar neo-
Lamarckian ideas. Brinton's career trajectory does help one understand,
however, how the cultural politics of race in the United States helped
to forge that enduring relationship between race and the relevance of
anthropology.

Brinton's Retrospective Insignificance

I began this narrative with a discussion of race and relevance, but part of
the story is why Brinton became irrelevant in historical narratives of the
field. As an actor in the production of late nineteenth-century anthropology, Brinton played a starring role. He was an actor who lived and worked
in this period, an agent who exercised power within specific structures,
and a subject who chose with purpose and candor different voices and
was aware of his own vocality (Trouillot 1995:22).

As Stocking, Darnell, Bronner, and others have explained, Brinton was
integral to the movement to professionalize the field and make anthropology a relevant discipline at the close of the nineteenth century, and it
was this movement that established the institutional apparatus anthropologists are using to advance their discipline in the twenty-first century
(Bronner 1986; Darnell 1971; Stocking 1960).[32] So why is so little known—
and even less written—about this venerable father of anthropology? The
easy answers for this lack of significance include the fact that he did not
leave a legacy in terms of students and scholarship and that he never

found a university home where he could successfully and securely articulate his vision of anthropology. Brinton worked during a period when institutional change was rapid and significant. Although he contributed to nascent national organizations, his attempts to address and respond to various audiences at different institutions in Philadelphia suggest that there was no single type of institution where he could effectively anchor anthropology in the Delaware Valley. Even within these institutions, Brinton held tenuous positions. He was neither a conventional professor nor independently wealthy. He also was not a charismatic orator.

As a heuristic device, compare briefly the retrospective significance of Brinton and Boas. Although the significance of Boas to the history of anthropology has oscillated from decade to decade, Leslie White aptly noted that Boas's "reputation grew like a rolling snowball" (1947:373), and Regna Darnell explains how Boas's stature reached legendary proportions (1971:90). An easy explanation for this disparity is the fact that Boas has an enduring legacy in terms of scholarship and students and that he had a position at a university from which he could securely and successfully articulate a vision for anthropology. These dynamics can also go a long way toward explaining Putnam's retrospective significance. Morgan and Powell, however, did not have graduate students or a university home. However, their retrospective significance can be linked to efforts by scholars to resuscitate their research and revive their writing in an effort to identify the historical roots and routes of contemporary theoretical and political concerns (e.g., Leacock 1979; Roscoe and Larkin 1995; Worster 2001).

There is a further distinction. Both Brinton and Boas worked to professionalize and institutionalize the field, in an effort to make it a less "dilettante occupation, suited to persons of elegant leisure and retired old gentlemen" (Brinton 1896b:59). Brinton advanced his vision that the professional anthropologist would identify and explain problems and address the "daily affairs of life," whereas Boas eventually developed his vision that the professional anthropologist would conduct fieldwork and teach in a university. The critical success factor was the security and insularity of a university department. Although Boas engaged in dramatic battles with university administrations, the structure of a department enabled him to produce basic research and instruct students and only then to engage in public affairs. Although somewhat dependent on philanthropists such as Morris K. Jesup, Boas was able to advance his anthropology through university instruction, the *JAF*, and organizational leadership. His strategy was not sutured to the needs of Congress, like Powell's was; to the wishes of museum patrons, like Stevenson's; or to the appetites of the public, like Brinton's.[33] Brinton's late nineteenth-century model led to a dead end; Boas's model was sustained throughout the twentieth century, despite widespread criticism of the research programs he conducted that forever changed the science that buttressed white supremacy.

At one level Brinton successfully straddled institutions—introducing anthropology to other fields and other fields to anthropology (Brown 2005:642). This was a particularly successful strategy in the late nineteenth century, when so-called vernacular science of a more popular nature flourished in lyceums, museums, and public lecture halls (Bender 1993:26). Although he succeeded at this type of science at the ANSP, his success was contingent to a certain extent upon a market in which people's demands and desires supported particular content—like the University Museum's privileging of Near Eastern over American archaeology. Thomas Bender poses the argument that the vagaries of the market steered academics into more esoteric research, and he explains that "intellectuals turned to academic culture as a hedge against the market—whether to insist upon the superiority of honor to market values, or for a sanctuary from intellectual chaos and competitiveness, or to purify and clarify discourse, even at the risk of social irrelevance" (1993:xv). Brinton, of course, did not hedge. Quite the contrary, he participated in that market to make anthropology as relevant as possible by using it to address one of the most pressing and popular issues of his day: the Negro problem. And although professional science of a more esoteric nature became increasingly isolated, the anthropologists who eventually took that tack (after several attempts to popularize anthropology at world's fairs and museums) are more relevant today, as is their anthropology. The way it turned out, the vagaries of history and historiography contributed to Brinton's seeming irrelevance in the annals of anthropological history. Yet obscurity does not mean irrelevance, and Brinton's career and record of publication are salient as anthropologists look toward the past to grapple with those enduring, albeit changing, themes of race and the relevance of anthropology.

(4)

The Cult of Franz Boas

and His "Conspiracy" to

Destroy the White Race

In August 1997 *American Renaissance*, a magazine that bills itself as the leading journal of race-realist thinking, published rank-ordered lists of Americans who have advanced and damaged white interests (Taylor 1997:9) (see table on page 157). Reasonably well argued and free of the glaring racial epithets and jarring anti-Semitism that pepper much of white pride literature, *American Renaissance* is a favorite among the tweed-jacket-and-sherry set of the white pride movement. The magazine's editor, Jared Taylor, published this list along with others in an article that reported the findings of an extensive survey he conducted about the views, beliefs, and interests of his readership.

After one crosses off presidents, recent presidential candidates, Supreme Court justices, first ladies, and Civil War heroes, the list becomes interesting as it relates to the history of anthropology. On the side that documents those who have damaged white interests, there are two names left—Franz Boas and Martin Luther King Jr. The people remaining on the other side include an interesting mix of scientists, pundits, organizers of white supremacist organizations, and one of the most celebrated heroes of the white pride movement, the American aviator turned Nazi sympathizer Charles Lindbergh. The survey was wide ranging, and Taylor dutifully enumerated the number of children, handguns, and years of education each of his readers had. At first glance the survey seems to be of little significance, save for the sentiments of the 391 loyal respondents who deemed the magazine's editor the most important "American who has advanced white interests" (Taylor 1997:9).

TABLE. Lists Printed in *American Renaissance* Magazine, 1997

Americans Who Have Damaged White Interests	Americans Who Have Advanced White Interests
1. Lyndon Johnson	1. Jared Taylor
2. Franklin Roosevelt	2. Patrick Buchanan
3. William Clinton	3. David Duke
4. Abraham Lincoln	4. Thomas Jefferson
5. Theodore Kennedy [sic]	5. Samuel Francis
6. Earl Warren	6. Robert E. Lee
7. Martin Luther King Jr.	7. George Washington
8. John Kennedy	8. Wilmont Robertson
9. Jesse Jackson	9. Nathan B. For[r]est
10. Richard Nixon	10. Arthur Jensen
11. James Carter	11. William Pierce
12. Franz Boas	12. Teddy Roosevelt
13. Dwight Eisenhower	13. Charles Lindburgh [sic]
14. Eleanor Roosevelt	14. Charles Murray
15. Harry Truman	15. George L. Rockwell
16. Woodrow Wilson	16. William Shockley
17. Robert Kennedy	17. Andrew Jackson

Source: Jared Taylor, "Who Reads American Renaissance?,"
American Renaissance 8(7&8) (1997):10.

Why was Franz Boas even considered alongside such historic figures as King, Earl Warren, and Lyndon B. Johnson—people easily identifiable with the civil rights movement? Within the diverse communities that advocate such things as white pride, Holocaust denial, white supremacy, immigration restriction, and a cornucopia of racisms, Boas is singled out as the one scholar whom white supremacists and anti-Semites love to hate.

Deemed the "Godfather of the Multicult Nightmare" and the fabricator of the "equalitarian dogma," Boas is often portrayed within these circles as the man who somehow single-handedly perpetuated the myth that all races have an equal potential for achieving intelligence and developing civilizations as well as the idea that cultures cannot be evaluated against the standard of Western civilization. From the late 1940s through the

mid-1960s, scholars, politicians, and pundits who were fearful of desegregation and threatened by the specter of racial amalgamation sort of in-
vented or reinvented a Franz Boas as the evil Jew who attracted a cult following responsible for spreading vicious propaganda about racial equality
and cultural relativism. As one pundit opined, the idea that there are no
pure races was a "hoax contrived by Franz Boas, a twisted little Jew, who
popped into the United States, [and] was, for undisclosed reasons, made
Professor of Anthropology in Columbia University, and founded a school
of fiction-writing called 'social anthropology'" (Oliver 2003:24–25).

The fact that Boas was a Jewish immigrant and often viewed as the scientist responsible for toppling racial determinism and promoting cultural
relativism somehow continues to push all the right buttons of members
of these types of communities. In addition, many of Boas's students (only
some of whom were Jewish) were influential in reshaping academic anthropology in the United States in a way that forever changed the social
sciences (Frank 1997:731). And it *was* this new social science that Chief
Justice Warren cited as his justification for hobbling Jim Crow segregation when he wrote his opinion for *Brown v. Board of Education* (1954).
Taken together, all of the elements of an old-fashioned Jewish conspiracy
converge.

The so-called Boas conspiracy, however, has been circulating around
anti-Semitic and white supremacist networks in one form or another for
some sixty years (Winston 2001:2). Boas's influence over American anthropology, his public efforts to challenge ideas about racial purity, his
assertions that whites were not necessarily biologically or culturally superior, and his belief that amalgamation might actually solve the problems
created by racism, all came together in the minds of some to metastasize
into one more conspiracy theory for the paranoid, anxiety-ridden per-
petuators of the unfortunately all-too-popular myth that Jews control the
banks, the media, the legal system, and so on.

By the late 1950s, anthropology had become an unreliable narrator in
the story of white supremacy, and Boas was to blame; he subsequently
emerged as the likely lightning rod to spark one more version of this incendiary myth: Jews now controlled science! The staying power and wide
circulation of this well-traveled lore explain why Boas catapults to the top
of the list of people who have "damaged white interests." Ferreting out
the provenance and mapping the circulation of this narrative are compli-

cated and difficult, although most intellectual historians correctly point to Carleton Putnam's *Race and Reason: A Yankee View* (1961) as the agent that catalyzed the most virulent, conspiratorial, and indeed folkloric renditions of the Boas conspiracy (Winston 2001; Tucker 1994:159; Jackson 2001:255).

As I demonstrated in the last chapter, however, Boas had been embroiled in controversies that made him the object of public scrutiny and the target of salacious allegations since 1891, when he was lambasted in the press by Austin Cristy. Mapping these controversies offers a unique way to understand an extradisciplinary history of anthropology by identifying how agents of specific racial projects interpreted, consumed, and used anthropology to reach specific partisan ends. An examination of these controversies also highlights some of the stakes involved in the racial politics of culture and the cultural politics of race, which have always swirled around the science of race and culture.

Since 2002, the conspiracy theory has found new footing in the aftermath of Corey Sparks's and Richard Jantz's report in the *Proceedings of the National Academy of Sciences* that suggested Boas published erroneous conclusions in his pivotal work *Changes in Bodily Form of Descendants of Immigrants* (1910), the landmark study that proved to be critical in undermining the idea of racial typologies and rigid racial categories (Brand 2003). The two authors reanalyzed Boas's statistical findings, generated from measurements taken from a sample population of nearly eighteen thousand immigrants and their children in New York City, thus explicitly challenging the empirical foundation of Boas's influential study (Sparks and Jantz 2002). *Changes in Bodily Form* was the first authoritative text to document biological plasticity. It has been routinely cited as evidence that the environment plays an integral role in cranial plasticity and the morphology of so-called racial types (Gravlee et al. 2003:25). Sparks and Jantz concluded that "reanalysis of Boas's data not only fails to support his contention that cranial plasticity is a primary source of cranial variation but rather supports what morphologists and morphometricians have known for a long time: most of the variation is genetic variation" (2002:14637). The same day the National Academy reported Sparks's and Jantz's findings, Nicholas Wade of the *New York Times* ran an article entitled "A New Look at Old Data May Discredit a Theory on Race" (Wade 2002:F3), which prompted a flurry of e-mail, discussion, and commentary from a range of divergent perspectives (R. Holloway 2002; Francis 2002).

Sam Francis, the former *Washington Times* columnist turned ultra-right-wing pundit, seized this opportunity to tether the results of Sparks and Jantz to Derek Freeman's widely publicized allegations that Margaret Mead engaged in fraudulent research practices in Samoa (Freeman 1983, 1999). Taken together, Francis argued, this was proof positive that anthropologists in general and Franz Boas in particular orchestrated a vast left-wing conspiracy to destroy the idea that whites were racially superior to blacks and to impose a moral and cultural relativism that has forever crippled American civilization, and he did it with fraudulent data. Francis asserted his case: "As Dr. Jantz told the [*New York*] *Times*, Boas 'was intent on showing that the scientific racism of the day had no basis, but he did have to shade his data some to make it come out that way.' In other words, Boas decided what his conclusions would be before he finished the research and then 'shaded'—i.e., cheated on—the data to make them support the conclusion he wanted. This is not science; it's fraud—and modern liberalism is founded on it" (Francis 2002).

Francis did not note, however, that Clarence C. Gravlee, H. Russell Bernard, and William R. Leonard also reanalyzed Boas's data on immigrant bodies. Reporting their independent findings in *American Anthropologist*, Gravlee and his colleagues concluded that "on the whole, Boas was right, despite the limited analytical tools at his disposal" (2003:125). The Associated Press quickly syndicated a story about the dissimilar findings, and *Science* magazine ran an article aptly titled "Going Head-to-Head Over Boas's Data." Balanced reporting did not sway the conspiracy theorists; these proponents only saw Sparks's and Jantz's work confirming their *X-Files* mantra—"The truth is out there" (Bergstrom 2002; Holden 2002).

Debating Boas's research and writing and his role in early American anthropology is nothing new. Regna Darnell has observed that "virtually continuously since his death in 1942, North American anthropologists have been obsessed with the role of Franz Boas. Although none have denied his disciplinary hegemony for most of the past century, assessments have ranged from anti-theoretical villain to beloved teacher beyond criticism to institutional and intellectual founder of the contemporary four-field discipline. Boas's scholarship is highly intertextual; anthropologists who are not disciplinary historians follow it avidly" (2000:896). Darnell's perceptive observation that Boas's scholarship "is highly intertextual" extends beyond his academic scholarship to include academic and public discourse about Boas. Commentary, discussion, and news about Boas and his research have never been anchored exclusively to academic genres. The relationship between text and context outside the academy has far-reaching implications, but it is rarely addressed in the scholarship about Boas. Much of the history of anthropological theory documents debates within the field or within the academy. More attention needs to be paid, however, to the way in which the public has consumed anthropology, often championing its virtues or punishing it in pillory (cf. di Leonardo 1998).

In the United States, the anthropological imaginary and notions of race and culture continue to captivate Americans' ideological investments in identity. The professional purview of anthropology includes descriptions of the other and assessments of race and culture, so it is not surprising that partisan critics set up anthropologists and the research they conduct in a way that provides rhetorical purchase for arguments that bolster ideological agendas. Cultural anthropology in the United States also deals with the narrative stuff—race, gender, sexuality, culture, and class—that has undergone dramatic changes since the Second World War. These aspects of anthropology don't work alone to foster and bolster the conspiracy, because the conspiracy is fueled by shifts in the economy in which downsizing, globalization, outsourcing, and flexible accumulation have made the once economically stable, heteronormative white working-class, home-owning family seem like an elusive ideal. Car manufacturers, steel mills, and factory work in general are no longer reliable sources of lifelong income, retirement pensions, and health-care benefits for white men and their families. At the same time immigrant families have been willing to take the least attractive jobs, which has put downward pressure on working-class wages. As a result, white men are feeling victimized and are searching for answers. Researchers have tied the demise of these white "losers" to the rise or recycling of a complicated matrix of common-sense strategies used to combat a newfound perception that the white man is now the victim (Hartigan 1999:25).

It is impossible to know with certainty, but most of these people deploy fairly benign strategies such as finding Jesus and becoming a promise keeper, listening to popular talk-radio hosts, or asserting that gay rights, women's liberation, and affirmative action are a triumvirate of culprits that have triggered the downward spiral of American civilization and white working-class stability (Kusz 2001:391–92; Knight 2001:40). However, there are people who deploy more extreme strategies within this matrix. For example, they might join one of the many militias, believe in Christian Identity, or enlist in the various white pride hate groups such as the Ku Klux Klan, the National Alliance, the World Church of the Creator, the American Nazi Party, or the National Socialist White People's Party. There are also less viperous groups to join or participate in, such as the Council of Conservative Citizens, the Federation for American Immigration Control, or the Order of Saint Andrew. One reason it is impossible to determine the extent of people's involvement within this loose constellation of semiorganized groups is that a member's participation is often anonymous and may be limited to occasionally lurking in Web site chat rooms. What is possible to determine, however, is the extent to which these groups saturate the Internet with texts, statistics, graphics, and streaming media to form a massive archive of material that is often cross-referenced, copied, and linked to other groups.

Whether outlining the details of a conspiracy, proving the superiority of the Nordic race, or denying the Holocaust, the writers and archivists of these groups often use copious documentation, citations, and cross-references to bolster their positions, discussions, and tracts. An almost obsessive desire for proof, not truth, has led to an uninterrupted electronic historical record that is routinely deployed as alleged evidence. The electronic archive is complemented by a range of popular books written by such authors as Jared Taylor, Kevin MacDonald, J. Philippe Rushton, Arthur Jensen, and David Duke.

Often painstakingly transcribed into hypertext markup language (HTML) from the primary source materials, this selective historical record is routinely deployed as source material by writers who produce analytical texts for such outlets as *American Renaissance, Mankind Quarterly*, Historical Review Press, and Noontide Press. Together, the historical documents and contemporary analyses propagate a dizzying network of Web sites, blogs, and online commentary dedicated to an alliance of issues ranging from twin studies and evolutionary psychology to Holocaust denial and immigration restriction. Linked by search engines and keywords, gigabytes of information are at the fingertips of anyone interested in finding sources, citations, history, and articulated rationales for a bevy of rather diverse issues that both soothe and explain the anxieties experienced by a rather large swath of Americans in the wake of the civil rights movement and deindustrialization.

Although groups that espouse hate, extremism, anti-immigrant sentiments, anti-Semitism, and downright racism have inhabited the margins of American history since the founding of the United States, the difference in the evolution of these new mainstream-resistant species is that they flourish in a forest of anonymity as the result of the Internet and in a context of a conspiracy culture in which Oliver Stone's movies and the ever-popular television show *The X-Files* reinforce the idea that the truth (the truth that reinforces our group's understanding of the world) is out there! It is a truth, however, that is deeply suspicious of elitism, the media, and the so-called powers that be, which have allowed a modicum of diversity to emerge as a heartfelt but ultimately not foundational value within a wide range of institutions in Western democracies at the moment that wealth is rapidly concentrating and consolidating in the offshore accounts of the very wealthiest global elite.

The proof *is* out there. People can selectively click on information that intuitively reinforces common-sense ideas that help explain the problems they face or the beliefs they hold to help make sense of their daily lives. Personally, I am astonished by the amount of attention that Boas and other anthropologists receive from these loosely associated and incredibly diverse nodes within a network of hate and insecurity.

In this chapter, I use this so-called Boas conspiracy as a framing device to sketch outlines for broader questions about how anthropology is appropriated outside of the academy in an effort to attain a better context for understanding the role anthropology has played in the overall history of ideas. I also revisit how the AAA resisted a well-funded campaign to bring the fight for white supremacy in the South into the arena of science during the early movement for civil rights.

Although the idea that Boas was a public intellectual is widely embraced, nothing has been written that specifically addresses the way in which his public discourse on race, racism, nationalism, and war—the issues for which he used anthropology in public arenas—was appropriated to serve as a foil for those bitterly opposed to ideas of racial equality, desegregation, immigration, and, above all, amalgamation.

Investigating the history of this conspiracy is difficult because it lies in the shadows between myth and science, history and folklore. I am not a folklorist, but I believe it is important for anthropologists and historians of science to be aware of how people read, use, and appropriate anthropology and other behavioral sciences to extend particular projects and ideological agendas. I think it is also instructive to see how the leadership of the AAA was pulled into the political debate during the battles to maintain Jim Crow segregation in the South and how they ultimately pushed back. Although the organization was reactive, as opposed to proactive, its statement on race in 1961 and Sherwood L. Washburn's presidential address in 1962 provided a scientific bulwark during the turbulent years between the *Brown v. Board of Education* decision of 1954 and the Civil Rights Act of 1964.

Some of the published renditions of the Boas conspiracy are troubling because of their anti-Semitism and repugnant racism, but many academics at prestigious universities and numerous mainstream sources of print media were among the first to legitimate many of these allegations. The myth that Boas was engaged in an elaborate hoax to get his cult of disciples to hoodwink America into believing that the races are equal and cultures were relative was born of a scientific debate regarding heredity in the 1960s, well after Boas was dead and gone. As the elements of this so-called conspiracy emerged, however, a subsequent crescendo of anti-Semitism was incorporated into the narrative. The scientific debates, led by the psychologist Henry E. Garrett of Columbia University and the anthropologist Carleton Coon of the University of Pennsylvania, gave legitimate cover for people like the former executive of Delta Airlines Carleton Putnam to popularize the Boas conspiracy. Extremists like George Lincoln Rockwell then eagerly appropriated and retrofitted the supposed collusion by adding even more drama and intrigue to the narrative so that it would square with and adhere to other Jewish conspiracy theories.

In this chapter, I first map the complicated history and genealogy of this explicitly anti-Semitic and racist conspiracy, which was actually incubated in the academy, while highlighting how the AAA responded to it. Second, I document a crucial episode in which Boas and his work were initially pulled into the public debates that presaged—but ultimately were linked to—the development of the conspiracy theory. Finally, I briefly describe aspects of Boas's work as a public intellectual to offer some context or perspective on the virulent critique of Boas and his work.

I am not concerned with the theory of conspiracy per se. I view conspiracies simply as one type of public discourse regarding anthropology (Stewart and Harding 1999). If one analyzes this conspiracy together with the HFS, the writers of the Harlem Renaissance interpretation of anthropology, and anthropology's impact on federal policies governing African Americans, American Indians, and immigrants, a pattern emerges. Anthropology has played a small, complicated, yet important role in the racial politics of culture in the United States. The way particular constituencies have appropriated and manipulated anthropology to serve particular ends means that the discipline has its own social history, which has served as both an ally and a bogeyman for various popular movements (Patterson 2001). It is a social history that transects the fear, anxiety, and anger that many indigenous people share regarding the intrusive and exploitative practices of anthropologists, which in turn have sparked perennial rumors and stories of mysterious poisonings and allegations of grave robbing along with tangible frustration stemming from the desecration of human remains in the name of science (Harjo 2003; Tierney 2000:5).

The 1960s version of the Boasian conspiracy continues to swirl in the United States in what Peter Knight calls a "conspiracy culture" (2001) and Michael Barkun a "culture of conspiracy" (2003). The fact that Boas is so routinely gainsaid by racists and white supremacists evinces his impact on the history of ideas.

In some respects I agree with Kamela Visweswaran, who argues that "the attempt to expunge race from social science by assigning it to biology, as Boas and his students did, helped to legitimate the scientific study of race, thereby fueling the machine of scientific racism" (1998a:70). I also somewhat agree with Herbert Lewis in his "defense of Boas" when he vehemently stands up for Boas, despite the fact his work helped to essentialize notions of culture. Lewis argues that an unrepentant defense of Boas is warranted because he "both professed and acted upon the finest and highest ideals of his (and our) culture and time" (2001:462). Although the critiquing and defending of Boas and early American anthropology have their place, I am more interested in providing context to better understand the connections and genealogies of people and ideas, while describing the rich social and political history of the field.

By exploring how explicitly racist people used and interpreted Boas's work outside of the discipline, one comes away with an understanding that perhaps anthropology *was* more important and did have a larger impact and audience outside of the academy than scholars have realized, especially as it concerns concepts of race and culture. For example, when the white supremacist David Duke preaches about the evils of anthropology and rails against Gelya Frank, a professor of anthropology at the University of Southern California, for writing an article in *American Anthropologist* that discusses anthropology's "agenda for activism," she is contributing to a very different public discourse than, I suspect, she intended (Duke 1998:279). As a result, Frank emerges as a different type of public intellectual from one normally associates with the term.

Public intellectuals are usually academics who go beyond the academy to influence public policy, public opinion, or popular science and culture. The notions of a public and influence are not stable in the fast-paced, populist world of the Internet. Beyond questioning what constitutes a public, I want to raise several open-ended questions: Can academics become public intellectuals as a result of vociferous detractors? What can one learn about the impact of Boas's scholarship by exploring the public discourse that continues to deride it?

Since the late nineteenth century, popular science and public intellectuals have played an important role in reform movements and popular culture in the United States. Anthropologists have routinely contributed to these movements, playing often ambivalent roles in the history of ideas and in the public's understanding of both race and culture (Baker 1998; Barkan 1988; Beardsley 1973; Hyatt 1990; Stocking 1960; Williams 1996; Lewis 2001). Although Boas is recognized widely as a public intellectual, he did not rise to prominence as such because he wrote for popular audiences or because he was a compelling orator. Prior to 1905, he produced only research and texts for colleagues at scholarly institutions. Although Boas did not venture beyond academic circles early in his career, this did not preclude his participation in public arenas, as we saw in the Worcester case. The case I describe here, from 1905, involves William B. Smith and is directly related to Boas's moniker, the "Godfather of the Multicult Nightmare" (McCain 2001).

"All This Equality Garbage Was Started by a Jew Anthropologist Named Franz Boas"

Perhaps the high-water mark of the conspiracy theory was articulated by Rockwell when a young Alex Haley published his interview with the "self-appointed führer of the American Nazi Party and self-styled messiah of white supremacy and intransigent anti-Sem[ite]" in *Playboy Magazine* in April 1966 (Haley 1966:71). A charismatic publicity-seeking extremist, Rockwell was a frequent speaker on college campuses. He galvanized some support for his unimaginative yet invective white power movement among young men disaffected by the war in Vietnam, urban riots, the civil rights movement, and white flight to the suburbs they could not afford (Schmaltz 1999:271).

In 1966, Rockwell and his American Nazi Party (ANP) were a "motley and minuscule" crew that began opening up regional headquarters and working closely with the Ku Klux Klan (Haley 1966:72). Rockwell and members of his party successfully disrupted the nonviolent demonstrations of the Southern Christian Leadership Conference, followed and antagonized the Freedom Riders in their "hate bus," physically assaulted King in Birmingham, publicly ridiculed the Mississippi Freedom Democratic Party, and staged a counterdemonstration at the march on Washington in 1963, where King delivered his famous "I Have a Dream" speech (Schmaltz 1999:167–237). Although the editors at *Playboy* knew the interview might generate even more support for the ANP, they justified it by aiming to paint a "revealing portrait of both rampant racism and the pathology of fascism" (Haley 1966:72).

Haley, who later wrote the blockbuster novel *Roots: The Saga of an American Family* (1976), conducted four interviews with Rockwell over the course of the year 1965. During that time Haley was completing a work he coauthored, *The Autobiography of Malcolm X* (1965), which was inspired by the *Playboy* interview he conducted with Malcolm X in 1963. In the introduction to the interview with Rockwell, Haley describes the setting of his initial meeting:

> About a dozen Nazis stared icily as the guards walked me past them up the stairs to Rockwell's door, where a side-armed storm trooper frisked me. . . . Finding me "clean," the guard ceremoniously opened the door, stepped inside, saluted, said, "*Sieg heil*"—echoed brusquely from within—then stood aside and nodded permission for me to come ahead. I did. As if for dramatic effect, Rockwell was standing across the room, corncob pipe in hand, beneath a portrait of Adolf Hitler. Warned about my Negritude, he registered no surprise. . . . [Then] he took out a pearl-handled revolver, placed it pointedly on the arm of his chair, sat back and spoke for the first time: "I'm ready if you are."

Haley's skills as an informed journalist and a seasoned interviewer erected a stage on which Rockwell gave a command performance. True to the editors' goals, readers of *Playboy* got a bird's-eye view of both rampant racism and the pathology of fascism. Rockwell begins by asserting, "I don't mix with your kind, and we call your race 'niggers.'" Showing his wry cynicism and unflappability, Haley cleverly responded, "I've been called 'nigger' many times, Commander, but this is the first time I'm being *paid* for it. So you go right ahead. What have you got against 'niggers'?" (1966:74). Haley's gambit was perfect: Rockwell went off, spewing the invective rhetoric that earned him his nickname, "the Barnum of the bigots." Rockwell explained that civil rights really "boils down" to "race mixing" and evoked Senator Theodore Bilbo's back-to-Africa scheme by suggesting he is "speaking for the majority of whites," who believe "we should take the billions of dollars now being wasted on foreign aid to Communist countries which hate us and give that money to our own niggers to build their own civilized nation in Africa" (1966:74).

Waxing nostalgic, Rockwell deployed a familiar trope, one that Theodore Roosevelt liked to use when he lamented the loss of "barbarian virtues" among the most civilized whites (Jacobson 2001:4). "The white man is getting too soft," Rockwell bellowed, explaining how desk work, electric lawn mowers, and fur-lined toilet seats had made the white man "soft and squishy." White women, Rockwell asserted, were also to blame for the perversion of white youth. "Some of our white women," he continued, "especially in the crazy leftist environment on our college campuses, get carried away by Jewish propaganda into betraying their own instincts by choosing a healthy black buck. . . . I have to admit that a healthy nigger garbage man is certainly superior physically and sexually to a pasty-faced skinny white peace creep" (1966:74).

Haley used this opening to escort Rockwell into a discussion of other areas in which Negroes might be superior to whites, but Rockwell balked. Rockwell asserted that the average hardworking white American male is basically the most superior being in the world. He then discussed the great civilizations whites have built, while Haley countered with the great civilizations Africans have built, but Rockwell quickly turned his argument about the superiority of white blood into a discussion of evolution and the pathological impact of "mongrelization." Haley pointed out that "the words superior and inferior have no meaning to geneticists . . . neither does mongrelization. Every authority in the field has attested that the world's racial groups are genetically indistinguishable from [one] another. All men . . . are created equal." At this point in the interview, Rockwell's adversarial tone came to a palpable halt.

Dripping with sarcasm and with a hint of paternalism, Rockwell evoked the Boas conspiracy as if he were going to present exculpatory evidence that would cinch the case that all men are not created equal:

> You're bringing tears to my eyes. Don't you know that all this equality gar-bage was started by a Jew anthropologist named Franz Boas from Colum-bia University? Boas was followed by another Jew from Columbia named Gene Weltfish. And our present Jew expert preaching equality is another Jew named Ashley Montagu. Any anthropologist who dares to preach the facts known by any farmer in the barnyard—that breeds differ in quality—is simply not allowed to survive in the university or in publishing, because he can't earn a living. You never hear from that side. But Carleton Putnam has written a wonderful book called *Race and Reason*, showing that there is plenty of scholarly evidence to back up my contention that the nigger race is inherently inferior to the white race intellectually. (1966:76)

After Haley challenged several of his assertions, Rockwell retorted, "I don't feel like quibbling. What I am saying is that I believe the Jews have consciously *perverted* the study of anthropology and biology and human genetics in order to reach this phony conclusion—and thus destroy the great white race" (1966:76). Rockwell then explicitly linked the work of Boas, Weltfish, and Montagu to a larger Jewish conspiracy to destroy the white race. Haley asked, "You said the Jews are behind this plot. Since they are whites themselves, how would they benefit from their own destruc-tion?" "They won't be mingling like the rest of us," Rockwell responded, "they believe they're the chosen people—chosen to rule the world. But the only world they could rule would be a world of inferior beings. And as long as the white man is pure, they cannot succeed. But when the white man permits himself to be mixed with black men, then the Jews can mas-ter him" (1966:76). Rockwell went on and on, describing even more far-fetched plots about how a cabal of Jewish conspirators instigated the riots in Watts, Rochester, and Harlem. He also provided disquieting descrip-tions of Jewish control over "Martin Luther Coon," the Communist Party, and the media and sarcastically quipped that the real God for the Jew is money. To complete his jeremiad, Rockwell put forth a long-winded but unconvincing denial that "there is any valid proof that innocent Jews were systematically murdered by the Nazis" (1966:78).

As evidenced by the letters to the editor responding to the interview, most people agreed that "defeating by ignoring" was not the best approach and that *Playboy* had provided an educational service in exposing the "the mentalities, the motives, and the modus operandi of an animal pack that is discounted by the aged maxim that 'it can't happen here'"(Serling 1966:7). As a result of the *Playboy* interview, Rockwell's notoriety increased, and he was in even greater demand on the lecture circuit. However, his detractors, most notably the Jewish War Veterans and the Anti-Defamation League (ADL), found new support for their vigilance against people many considered just marginal extremists, but whom these organizations took very seriously.

Although many Americans had never heard of Rockwell before the much-publicized interview, the Federal Bureau of Investigation perhaps made a decent assessment in an internal memorandum that called him a "professional bigot, a 'con' man, a malcontent, and a chronic failure, who will stop at nothing to gain notoriety." They warned their agents (several of whom infiltrated Rockwell's barracks through the infamous Counter Intelligence Program) that "though small in numbers and influence, the ANP is a dangerous organization of misfits who are psychologically and physically capable of perpetrating acts of violence. . . . Hitler, like Rockwell, was ridiculed and scorned. . . . We would do well to heed the American Nazi Party and to remember that history is replete with incidents where a nucleus of an organization and the 'right' conditions merged to shake the foundations of the world" (Schmaltz 1999:153).

Shortly after the *Playboy* interview was published, Rockwell fine-tuned the propaganda machine of his party and launched the *National Socialist World* to appeal to a supposedly more sophisticated audience than that of his other two publications, the *Rockwell Report* and *Stormtrooper*. Rockwell envisioned targeting the full class spectrum, as he notes: "We have designed some great products to appeal to specific customers: the 'hawg-jowl' *Stormtrooper*, the 'Delmonico steak' *Rockwell Report*—and now the 'Cherries Jubilee' which you hold in your hand, the *National Socialist World*" (Rockwell 1966:12). In the inaugural issue, Rockwell outlined this all-inclusive strategy of spreading propaganda in an aptly titled article: "From Ivory Tower to Privy Wall: The Art of Propaganda." Here again he hammers on the Boas conspiracy, this time citing Putnam's *Race and Reason* (1961) explicitly in footnote 3, which was noted at the end of the following passage:

The whole of Jewry pitched in to boost their boy. Boas was praised in every Jewish-owned newspaper and periodical and given every academic prize they could promote. Little by little, Boas gained such "stature" by this Jewish mutual-admiration society technique that he became an "acknowledged authority" in social anthropology and ethnology. His students and colleagues at Columbia—Herskovits, Klineberg, Ashley Montagu, Weltfish—as unsavory a collection of left-wing Jews as one might hope for—spread his doctrines far and wide, deliberately poisoning the minds of two generations of American students at many of our largest universities. (1966:10)

The *National Socialist World* was not sustained and did not receive wide circulation; today collectors fetch over two hundred dollars for an original copy. The Boas conspiracy could have run its course as the wistful musings of a cantankerous separatist and died along with Rockwell when he was gunned down in the summer of 1967 by one of his lieutenants at a laundromat in Virginia (Schmaltz 1999:323). Rockwell and subsequently his writings, however, sustain an avid following among white supremacist and anti-Semitic groups today. He is lionized as a result of his (for lack of a better word) ecumenical approach toward racism and anti-Semitism. Considered the father of the white power movement, Rockwell believed that to contribute one need only be white and not Jewish (Ridgeway 1998:85). He thus eliminated the criterion that members must be Protestant Nordic or Aryan.

This one article, "The Art of Propaganda," is reproduced on the Web sites of the ANP, the National Socialist Movement, the First Amendment Exercise Machine, and Don Black's infamous Stormfront, also known as the White Nationalist Resource Page, which advocates "White Pride—World Wide" and boasts seven thousand hits a day. The ADL explains that Stormfront is one of the oldest, most popular, and most comprehensive of these sites (Anti-Defamation League 2000). Moreover, the Boas conspiracy shows up in chat rooms, commentaries, and myriad online articles in a narrative form that differs little from the way Rockwell outlined it some forty years ago.

Perhaps the most disconcerting rendition of the Boas conspiracy is found on a site called "Martin Luther King, Jr.: A True Historical Examination," which is located at www.martinlutherking.org. The home page rather innocuously details the life and history of King. It looks very professional and very legitimate. During April 2008, Google's popular search engine page-ranked this site at number 4, when the term "Martin Luther King" was searched. It was preceded by a Wikipedia entry, a brief biography of King posted on the Nobel Foundation's Web site detailing his peace prize in 1964, and the "The Official Website of the King Center in Atlanta Georgia." Once an unsuspecting reader or student begins clicking through the links, he or she is served rather noxious white supremacist revisions of King's legacy. Many of the articles are written by people on that *American Renaissance* list of people who have "advanced white interests" (see table on page 157). By clicking the link titled "The King Holiday: Bring the Dream to Life," for example, an article by Samuel Francis loads into the browser. In this article, the author recounts how he and former Senator Jesse Helms of North Carolina lobbied against the establishing of the national holiday commemorating King's life and legacy. Printed directly below the byline, as if to validate it, is a line noting that the article is reprinted from *American Renaissance*. By clicking the link "Bring the Dream to School," a menu of seemingly innocent flyers with a picture of King loads; the tag line reads, "Learn exciting new facts about Martin Luther King, Jr." and gives the Web address for this revisionist Web site. The site was actually created and is hosted by Don Black's Stormfront organization. Explicitly targeting schoolchildren who are asked to write reports on King, the creators of the site instruct students to "print out these flyers and pass them around your school."[1]

When one clicks on the link "Jews & Civil Rights: Who Led the Civil Rights Movement," what appears is a copy of chapter 18 of David Duke's autobiography *My Awakening: A Path to Racial Understanding* (1998). The editors of the Web site introduce him as a "European American civil rights activist" but fail to mention he was the former national director of the Knights of the Ku Klux Klan. After selectively recounting the stories of several spies, namely Alger Hiss and Julius and Ethel Rosenberg, Duke expounds upon what he perceives to be a link between every Jewish person, communist ideology, and the idea about the equality of the races, and then he moves awkwardly to the second section, called "The Racial Egalitarian Dogma."

Duke begins this section by describing the influence Boas had on "the modern egalitarian school of anthropology." He then laments the good old days of anthropology when "physical anthropologists were truly race scientists" (1998:277). After providing a fairly accurate, although slightly exaggerated assessment of Boas and his family's political background (cf.

Stocking 1992:95), Duke says, "Boas began to advance the quack idea that there are really no such things as individual human races." He goes on to list the names of all the women, Negroes, and Jews who became his "disciples," conveniently leaving out the names of Alfred Kroeber and Robert Lowie, two of Boas's most prominent students. In a very conspiratorial tone, Duke continues to report on this Web site aimed at students who are looking for information on King that

> Boas and his entire cadre of disciples had extensive Communist connections. . . . Whenever egalitarians achieved positions of influence or power, they aided their comrades to rise in the teaching departments they administered. They could count on fellow Jews who held influential positions to assist their co-religionists, as well as Gentile egalitarians, in getting professorships and research appointments and promotions. Similar collusion took place in the ranks and on the boards of anthropological associations and journals. However, the coup de grace was the massive support given the egalitarian dogma by the media establishment, which was overwhelmingly in Jewish hands. (1998:278)

This is simply a fabrication; historians of anthropology have documented that Boas was only nominally Jewish and had limited ties to Jewish organizations. Moreover, historians have documented the struggle that most of Boas's students had in attaining funding for research and positions in the academy (Caffrey 1989:259–80; Gershenhorn 2004:123–69; Stocking 1992:92–113; Harrison and Harrison 1999:1–36; Glick 1982:555; Liss 1996). Conspiracies offer both a balm and a solution to often complex problems that are perceived in terms of good and evil. They are also almost impossible to fully refute. In this case, like that of Rockwell, however, Duke reveals who helped shape his ideas.

The premise of Duke's autobiography is embedded in the title, *My Awakening*. In what he calls "a thesis in autobiographical form," Duke maps out how he came to learn the supposed truth about the inferiority and superiority of the races. He begins by describing his idyllic childhood and his love of books and nature in Jim Crow Louisiana. As the civil rights movement waxed, the young Duke read voraciously and believed that "racial differences in poverty, illegitimacy, crime rates," and the like were "caused purely by environmental differences among the races" (1998:27). Duke explained that after reading Ashley Montagu's *Man's Most Dangerous Myth: The Fallacy of Race* (1952), the subject interested him enough that he read *Black Like Me* (Griffin 1961) and *To Kill a Mockingbird* (Lee 1960). He summarized his state of ignorance, before his awakening, by stating, "I sympathized with the plight of the Negro" (1998:30).

Written as a classic bildungsroman, the book relates that Duke's education was the key to his coming of age and making it as his own man. The critical lesson, he explains, was a school assignment in which he had to argue the case against school desegregation, which made him question his early inclinations. After wandering into the office of the White Citizens' Council, an organization of local groups organized largely to oppose desegregation, he was surprised to find "an opposing viewpoint on racial integration that was literate, reasoned and intelligent—even supported by famous Americans—not simply the ranting of backwoods White supremacists" (1998:32). Duke recounts, with inescapable drama, a transformative event: "I didn't have much money—it was 1963 and I was 13 years old—so I asked the lady at the desk which book she would recommend. She picked up a copy of *Race and Reason: A Yankee View* by Carleton Putnam and put it in a bag for me with a hand written receipt" (1998:32). As Duke recalls, "I had no inkling, when I walked out of the drab little office on Carondolet Street that I was about to read a book that would change my life" (1998:33). The next chapter of Duke's *Awakening*, quite literally a new chapter in his life, is called "Race and Reason," and he gushes in praise of Putnam's science, his boldness, and the novelty of his arguments. The balance of this seven-hundred-page book details how Duke fused Putnam's ideas about race with various forms of anti-Semitism to come to power as a local politician and eventually run for president of the United States of America. His presidential candidacy gave him the platform to become one of the best-known leaders in the white pride movement or, as he sees it, a leader of those "racially conscious White men and women who are dedicated to the survival and evolutionary development of our people" (1998:645).

Indivisible, with Liberty and Justice for All

Carleton Putnam (1901–98) was educated at Princeton and earned a law degree from Columbia in 1932. A Yankee's Yankee blessed with two last names, Putnam had a lineage that stemmed from some of the most established families in New England. After law school, he went to California to start an airline between Los Angeles and San Francisco, eventually securing a lucrative government contract to fly mail from Chicago to New Orleans. His company successfully expanded during the Second World War until his Chicago and Southern Airlines merged with Delta in 1953 to form Delta C&S Airlines. Putnam served as chairman of the board but soon began focusing his time and energy on writing a biography of Theodore Roosevelt. Putnam planned to write a four-volume work, and the first volume was published in 1958 to critical acclaim; the other three, however, never materialized because his passion for history waned as his penchant for activism waxed. From the late 1950s through the turbulent 1960s, Putnam emerged as a well-heeled stalwart of the White Citizens' Councils. Leveraging his New England heritage, Putnam served as an unimpeachable public intellectual who helped stem the tide of desegregation in an effort to preserve white civilization (Jackson 2001:250; Thomas 1998:B7; Tucker 1994:158, Tucker 2002:103; Putnam 1958).

As Putnam recounts, it was not the Supreme Court's decision in *Brown v. Board of Education* that motivated him to take action, but the order issued by the Supreme Court in *Cooper v. John Aaron* (1958), which affirmed the ruling of the U.S. Court of Appeals for the Eighth Circuit that Central High School in Little Rock, Arkansas, must remain integrated, despite the fiasco surrounding the school board's efforts to desegregate the school in September of 1957 (Putnam 1961:5). Although the court in *Brown* had mandated that school districts implement plans for desegregation with "all deliberate speed," Southern school systems were slow to dismantle the technologies and bureaucracies of white supremacy. Seeing little moral leadership from President Dwight D. Eisenhower, many people, including Putnam, never quite believed that the "law of the land" had jurisdiction in the South, and if it did, no one ever imagined the president would deploy the 101st Airborne Division of the U.S. Army to enforce it.

These assumptions changed in late summer of 1957 when the entire nation focused on Little Rock, watching and waiting in anticipation for the inevitable showdown between states' rights and federal mandates, between Governor Orval Faubus and President Eisenhower, and between nine brave high school students and hundreds of angry, scared, and hysterical opponents of integration. A constitutional crisis hung in the balance.

The Little Rock school board developed a comprehensive plan to integrate Central High School beginning the first day of school, September 3,

1957—a full three years after *Brown*. However, Governor Faubus bowed to many of his working-class white constituents and ignored court orders and federal injunctions to desegregate Central. Deploying troops from the Army and Air National Guard, the governor ordered his commanders to defy the court's order and "place off limits to colored students those schools heretofore operated . . . for white students" (Brownell 1957:24).

Daisy Bates, the president of the Arkansas branch of the NAACP, was the fearless leader of the movement to desegregate the schools of Little Rock. Emboldened by an order issued by a federal district judge compelling the school board to integrate "forthwith," Bates, along with local pastors and a phalanx of media reporters, escorted the nine black students to the doors of the school on September 4, the second day of school, but the National Guard turned them away. As Melba Pattillo Beals, one of the entering students, recalls, "Mother and I got separated from the others. The two of us narrowly escaped a rope-carrying lynch mob of men and women shouting they'd kill us rather than see me go to school with their children" (1994:1).

President Eisenhower gave Faubus every opportunity to comply with the law—court orders, injunctions, face-to-face meetings, even a presidential proclamation—but the recalcitrant Faubus was heartened by the will of his many loyal constituents who were panic-stricken by their fear of integration and the erosion of states' rights. Faubus, vowing to fight the desegregation order in the courts, finally yielded to an injunction but only after issuing a defiant statement to the press stating that the "Governor of the State of Arkansas cannot and will not concede that the U.S. Government . . . can question his judgement and discretion acting as the chief executive officer of the sovereign State of Arkansas" (Harper 1957:191). Once the troops were withdrawn, the security of the students and the management of the ever-vigilant crowd of parents, concerned citizens, and "hard-core anti-integrationists" fell onto the shoulders of the mayor of Little Rock, Woodrow Wilson Mann (*NYT*, September 22, 1957:191).

On September 23, there were approximately one thousand people milling around outside the school waiting and wondering if indeed the nine students would dare to come to school; classes started on time with no Negro students in attendance. Vice Principal Elizabeth Huckaby poignantly observed, "As we started [to say] the words," 'I pledge allegiance to the flag of the United States of America,' I heard clapping, and I looked from the flag to the mob, there they [the mob] stood, applauding as if they were at a parade. The irony nearly overcame me, and I choked out the final words, 'indivisible, with liberty and justice for all'" (National Parks Service 2005:3).

With the help of the local and state police, the students were quietly ushered into the school through a door on the side of the building shortly after classes had begun. Once it was known that the Negro teens were inside the building, a panic went through the anxious crowd. Several white students walked out of the building, so the teachers locked the doors; then several students jumped out of windows, and the teachers locked the windows. Parents started rushing the police barricades in an attempt to rescue their children from the dangerous "contamination" they would supposedly suffer from being in close proximity with Negro children (Fine 1957:1). Once the black students were inside the school, there was little disruption of the normal routine, but the crowd outside the school became restless. The act of integrating Central High School carried a powerful symbolic load. The nine entering students, who became known as the Little Rock Nine, represented a dangerous pollution that threatened social order in Arkansas's capital city (Douglas 1966:3). "They won't let the white kids out. My daughter is in there with those niggers. Oh, my God, oh, God," shouted a frantic Mrs. Clyde Thomason, the recording secretary of the Mothers' League, who had led the legal fight to keep Central High all white and worked closely with the Capital Citizens' Council (Godfrey 2003:46).

While some of the white students and parents feared ritual contagion and symbolic pollution inside the school, the black students feared physical violence and hostile retribution outside the school. As Beals recounts, "[we] maneuvered our way past an angry mob to enter the side door of Central High. But by eleven that morning, hundreds of people outside were running wild, crashing through police barriers to get us out of school. Some of the police sent to control the mob threw down their badges and joined the rampage. But a few other brave members of the Little Rock police force saved our lives by spiriting us past the mob to safety" (1995:2). Observing that the local police could not control the crowd, Mayor Mann sent a telegram to President Eisenhower asking for assistance.

The next day Eisenhower reluctantly signed an executive order federalizing the Army National Guard and sending twelve hundred members of the 101st Airborne Division from Fort Campbell, Kentucky, to Little Rock to ensure that the court orders were executed. The president addressed the nation from the White House on the eve of this historic event: "I could have spoken from Rhode Island. . . . But I felt that, in speaking from the house of Lincoln, of Jackson and of Wilson, my words would better convey both the sadness I feel in the action I was compelled today to make, and the firmness with which I intend to pursue this course until the orders of the Federal Court at Little Rock can be executed without unlawful interference." Couched in the strict terms of court orders and obstruction of justice, the speech warned Americans about the Cold War implications of the events in Little Rock and the need to demonstrate "to the world that we are a nation in which laws, not men, are supreme. I regret to say that this truth—the cornerstone of our liberties—was not observed in this instance" (1957:14).

The nine students arrived at the school early the following morning, September 25, and their military escorts walked them to the building without incident. Governor Faubus was furious and asked for broadcast time on the television networks so he too could address the nation. Whereas Eisenhower raised the deep-seated fear of the Cold War, Faubus raised the long-simmering anxieties of the Civil War. "We are now an occupied territory," roared Faubus. "Evidence of the naked force of the Federal Government is here apparent in these unsheathed bayonets in the backs of schoolgirls, in the backs of students, and in the bloody face of this rail road worker." Contrasting Eisenhower's emphasis on the rule of law, Faubus used the "will of the majority" to make his case that "the basic principles of democracy are destroyed. And we no longer have a union of states under a republican form of government" (1957:10).

The Little Rock Nine bravely finished that difficult school year under a shroud of terror accompanied by constant threats, intimidation, harassment, and fear for their lives. Instead of complying with the court order, the next year Faubus simply closed down the high schools. The world watched, for the first time on television, as the dramatic events of the civil rights movement began to unfold.

The Ghost of Boas Sat on the Supreme Court

Lines were drawn and alliances were made for the pitched struggle over the future of the United States. The often bloody battles were waged within a variety of theaters—buses, lunch counters, performance halls, courthouses, schools and colleges, voting booths, churches, and the streets and bridges. The halls of science and the pages of anthropological journals were also important theaters. The question of equality or equality before the law was salient for the many people who were desperately trying to shore up the technologies and bureaucracies of segregation, disfranchisement, and white supremacy.

The fear and anxiety caused by a shifting racial order brought on by *Brown* and by a shifting world order brought on by the Cold War emboldened leaders like Faubus, the Commissioner of Public Safety T. Eugene "Bull" Connor in Birmingham, Alabama, and Governor Ross Barnett of Mississippi to use violence and intimidation to restore not law, but order. Exploiting complex crosscurrents of race, class, and gender, elected leaders utilized the rhetoric of fear to foment racial tensions that buttressed their popularity and claims to power.

Anthropologists, psychologists, sociologists, and, later, geneticists were routinely called upon to justify desegregation in scientific terms, while others were called upon to prove the natural inferiority of the Negro, physically and morally, in an effort to provide scientific justification for the separate-but-equal doctrine. Anthropologists decidedly backed the desegregation cause. For example, during its annual meeting in 1959, the AAA held a press conference to address the crisis in Little Rock. Mead held forth, explaining that Northerners had to do more and focus on de facto segregation and prejudice against Negroes in the North and West. She argued that there was "not one community in the nation that is free of the stigma" of racial prejudice, and she suggested that "racial segregation must not be handled as a regional problem but rather considered as part of an international moral responsibility for the welfare of the children of the world" (*NYT*, November 21, 1958:19).

The South's social and political structures of racial segregation had long been buttressed by an implicit, yet anxious belief in the inherent inferiority of blacks and the superiority of whites. The fear and anxieties about "mongrelization" and the routine violence perpetrated against those who did not "know their place" were born from a prescient understanding that the racial hierarchy was tenuous. Nevertheless, the idea of white supremacy was so embedded in the hearts and minds of the many people vested in maintaining segregation that the lawyers who argued against the NAACP during the trials that eventually led to *Brown* virtually ignored the social science deployed as evidence. The attorneys, instead, focused on states' rights and judicial precedents (Tucker 2002:11; Baker 1998:205–7).

When Chief Justice Warren crafted his unanimous decision for *Brown*, he relied in part on social science research. Warren explained that separate institutions are inherently unequal, because "to separate [students] solely because of their race generates a feeling of inferiority as to their status in the community that may affect their hearts and minds in a way unlikely ever to be undone . . . this finding is amply supported by modern authority" (*Brown v. Board of Education*, 347 U.S. 494–95 [1954]). The modern authority Warren noted was evidenced in his controversial footnote 11, in which he cited research conducted by psychologists and sociologists, most notably Mamie and Kenneth Clark and E. Franklin Frazier. Warren concludes the footnote, "See generally Gunnar Myrdal *An American Dilemma* (1944)." According to Putnam, the court's reference to Myrdal, "however oblique, was an effective way of saying 'see generally Boas and his disciples' for Myrdal's American Dilemma was Boas from beginning to end" (1967:70).

From Putnam's perspective, this was a conspiracy organized by what he routinely called the "cult of Boas." Although he, like Rockwell, never identified the ringleaders who made this so-called egalitarian dogma first scientific fact and then the law of the land, Putnam was clear on how it came to be: "Indoctrinate a controlling group of scientists in a politically oriented, environmentalist dogma over a period of two generations; make a moral issue out of something immoral; persecute and suppress any dissenters; infiltrate the mass media, and finally persuade the courts by introducing only falsified evidence" (1967:89). Putnam believed that "the ghost of Boas sat on the Supreme Court, put there by 'vociferous minorities' with only the forces of ignorance and intellectual inertia in opposition" (1967:69).

Ironically, Myrdal's work as well as Thurgood Marshall's strategy to argue the case for the NAACP in the cases that culminated with *Brown* was grounded in an unswerving faith that Negroes could and would assimilate once they were integrated into American life. Any discussion of cultural differences between whites and blacks or mention of the fact that some African cultural practices were retained was summarily quashed. For example, Myrdal and Marshall both deferred to Robert Park's student the sociologist E. Franklin Frazier at Howard University, who believed that the behavior of black people that did not conform to a white standard was simply a "pathological phenomenon" that might be changed with the therapy of integration (Frazier 1931:389).

Marshall refused to put Boas's students on the stand to testify on behalf of the NAACP for fear that their association with Carter G. Woodson and the heritage project (see introduction) would lead the justices to believe that African Americans might really be different culturally, like American Indians and other authentic and exotic peoples studied by cultural anthropologists. For example, the Commission of Law and Social Action for the American Jewish Congress wrote to Marshall suggesting that "Ruth Benedict would make a good witness," but Marshall ignored the information because he was interested only in "putting on anthropologists to show that there is no difference between folks."[2] Marshall was interested not in culture, but in the fact that racial inequality in the United States was not the result of biology, and he turned to Robert Redfield at the University of Chicago as a witness to testify about the latest findings in the anthropology of race, not of culture (Baker 1998: 188–207).

Putnam understood the subtleties and nuances of this sociological discourse on assimilation, calling it "a 'sociology' rooted in Boas fantasy" (1967:67). Unlike the NAACP, Putnam was concerned with both sides of the Boasian discourse; he neither believed that people from different racial and cultural backgrounds could achieve and thrive within developed civilizations nor was he pleased with the idea that, during the first half of the twentieth century, Boas, in conjunction with his students and associates, developed research that focused on the environment to explain the plasticity and essential equality of racial groups.

After the Second World War, the discourse on race produced by these anthropologists solidified an academic consensus that racial inequality in the United States was not based on biological inferiority. Facts, not fantasy, drove the majority of American social scientists to consider the impact of racism and the environment as a way of explaining disparities between the races (Jackson 1998). The fact that lawyers for the NAACP employed this relatively new discourse so successfully and that the Southern states' district attorneys never effectively challenged it made Putnam incredulous. As he saw it, precedent, common sense, and "feverish talk about the validity of the 14th Amendment" was the wrong way to argue the case for Jim Crow; he was aghast that "no one challenged the assumption at the root of the whole trouble—the validity of Boas" (1961:20). With the financial backing of the notorious Pioneer Fund, Putnam helped the White Citizens' Councils and prosegregation forces to develop a "plan B," which entailed mounting a scientific campaign to save segregation. Putnam and many others who were not familiar with scientific methods and procedures really did believe they had to first smear Boas's reputation in order to launch their own allegedly scientific evidence.

Although much less acerbic and blatantly anti-Semitic than Rockwell's or Duke's, Putnam's campaign against the cult of Boas was more mainstream, credible, and influential than theirs and was very well organized and well funded. Putnam played to the fears and anxieties of those who were reeling in the wake of the Little Rock crisis and desperately searching for a rationale to continue the fight for states' rights and segregation. He also played to those who were looking for an explanation for the failings of the attorneys who had tried to make white supremacy sound like common sense and precedent. Putnam recounts how he came to mount his campaign against what he called egalitarian dogma in his influential and popular book *Race and Reason: A Yankee View* (1961).

It all started with a simple letter to the editor of the Memphis *Commercial Appeal*, protesting the way the media editorialized about school desegregation after Little Rock. Focusing on an editorial in *Life* magazine, Putnam was incensed that it was "lacking in perception and full of inept analogies and abandoned principles." He received many positive replies, including one that said "it was a comfort . . . that at least one Northerner understood." After reflecting upon the generous support he received, Putnam decided to draft another letter to the "one man who could do more to correct the situation than any other . . . the President of the United States" (1961:4–5).

Putnam's letter to President Eisenhower opened with an explicit attack on the opinion written by Felix Frankfurter, associate justice of the Supreme Court, in *Cooper v. John Aaron* (1958). Putnam argued that "the original desegregation decision was wrong, that it ought to be reversed, and that meanwhile every legal means should be found, not to obey it, but to avoid it. Failing this, the situation should be corrected by constitutional amendment" (1961:6). The rationale for this position was grounded in Putnam's belief that "social status has to be earned . . . it cannot be achieved by legal fiat." Explaining that the court was impinging on "the white man's right to freedom of association," Putnam explained that equality before the law should never be confused with equality (1961:6–7).

Employing a rationale that conflated the potential to achieve a collective civilization with an idea that Negro individuals were racially and morally inferior to whites, Putnam explained that "any man with two eyes in his head can observe a Negro settlement in the Congo" and "can compare this settlement with London or Paris, and can draw his own conclusions regarding relative levels of character and intelligence—or that combination of character and intelligence which is civilization" (1961:7). Putnam closes this rather long-winded and rambling letter to the president with an oft-quoted remark by Abraham Lincoln: "I am not nor ever have been in favor of making voters or jurors of negroes, nor of qualifying them to hold office, nor to intermarry with white people; and I will say in addition to this that there is a physical difference between the white and black races which I believe will forever forbid the two races living together on terms of social and political equality" (1858).

Putnam sent this letter not only to the president, but also to Virginius Dabney, the editor of the *Richmond Times-Dispatch*. "Out of courtesy of the President," Dabney waited three days and then published the entire two-thousand-word letter on October 16, 1958. Putnam's letter was an instant hit among people fearful of desegregated buses, neighborhoods, and schools. It was particularly popular among the members of the White Citizens' Councils and the prosegregationist lobby, who knew Putnam's class position and his status as a New England Brahmin, a businessman, and an intellectual gave them much-needed social capital and intellectual legitimacy.

The letter was printed and reprinted in local Southern papers, was read into the Congressional Record, and was distributed liberally throughout the many citizens' councils. Letters of support came in by the thousands, and within months the Putnam Letter Committee was formed to solicit funds to print the letter as a paid advertisement in Northern and Western papers—it ran in the *New York Times* on January 5, 1959 (Putnam 1959:19). According to Putnam, "Each advertisement, as it appeared, brought in enough money *from the North* to pay for the next. Within five months the fund had passed $37,000 and the letter had been published in eighteen Northern and Western papers with a circulation of nearly seven million. Adding the initial free publication in the South, the total circulation had amounted to over ten million" (1961:14).

Letters from all sides came in, many supporting Putnam's position, but others denouncing it. Many of the letters denouncing his position relied on arguments that turned on the idea that Putnam was purporting a version of Nazism, and the United States should set an example for other nations in the fight between communism and democracy. Although Putnam believed he could dispatch these arguments "without too long a letter in reply," what he "found of larger significance, because it seemed to be the common denominator in a universal misunderstanding, lay in what my correspondents called 'modern' anthropology" (1961:15). After carefully studying the briefs written to support desegregation in *Brown*, Putnam vowed to read up on this so-called modern anthropology and then write a second open letter, this time to William P. Rogers, the U.S. attorney general. Five months after his first open letter, he wrote another one, this time focusing on the hidden issue of Boas and his equalitarian dogma. Like the first letter, the second letter was widely publicized, printed, and reprinted as an editorial and as an advertisement.

After selectively citing Gallup polls to argue that the majority of people in the nation were "against integration," Putnam called into question the fact that the attorney general never challenged "the authorities cited by the Court in Footnote 11 to their opinion of May 17, 1954. . . . They appear, in large measure, to form the foundation of the decision" (1961:22). From Putnam's perspective, "They reflect a point of view rooted in what I may call modern equalitarian anthropology—a school which holds that all races are currently equal in their capacity for culture, and that existing inequalities of status are due solely to inequalities of opportunity" (1961:22). Putnam went on to explain, in this widely circulated letter, "that two generations of Americans have been victimized by a pseudo-scientific hoax in this field, that this hoax is part of an equalitarian propaganda . . . and that it will not stand an informed judicial test" (1961:22). He continued to identify the perpetrator of this hoax as "Franz Boas, a foreign-born Columbia University professor who arrived in the United States in 1886, who was himself a member of a racial minority group, and who may be called the father of equalitarian anthropology in America" (1961:23). Although the Supreme Court never cited Boas in *Brown*, Putnam believed that Boas's propaganda was the "hidden issue," and reiterated that "the entire foundation of the Boas theory rests on sand" (1961:24). Alluding to Boas's findings in *Changes in Bodily Forms of Descendants of Immigrants* (1912), "Human Faculty as Determined by Race" (1895), and *The Mind of Primitive Man* (1911), Putnam countered with research conducted by Audrey Shuey and endorsed by Henry E. Garrett that tried to explain that

differences in IQ between blacks and whites were based on very real racial differences. Putnam was clear, however, that he believed "character to
be more important than intelligence," which he believed was also doled
out along racial lines. Putnam believed in stark and rigid racial lines, and
he deplored the "favorite method used by Boas and [Clyde] Kluckhohn
for throwing dust in the eyes of the public," which was to "create an impression that there is really no such thing as race" (1961:26). The common-
sense argument Putnam put forward combined differences in IQ with his
observation that civilization never developed in Africa; the many examples that contradicted these assertions, he explained, were the result of
white blood and Arab influences.

The second letter was widely published and "enough copies reached
the North by private mailings" to provoke widespread reaction to the so-
called hidden issue, Boas and his equalitarian dogma (Putnam 1961:30).
As the letter began to circulate along the same routes as the first, Putnam
received even more national attention and quickly wrote a short book entitled *Race and Reason: A Yankee View*. The book basically consisted of a
brief narrative that described the context for his two letters; copies of his
two open letters; and then a point-by-point rebuttal of common themes
that arose in the many letters he had received that opposed his views.
"Biological scientists" introduced the book in a one-page statement that
vouched for Putnam's "inescapable scientific validity" (Putnam 1961:viii):

> We, as signatories to this introduction . . . believe that statesmen and judges
> today frequently take positions based upon an inadequate knowledge of the
> facts so far as they relate to the nature of man. Therefore, we have no hesita-
> tion in placing on record our disapproval of what has been all too commonly
> a trend since 1930. We do not believe that there is anything to be drawn from
> the sciences in which we work which supports the view that all races of men,
> all types of men, or all ethnic groups are equal and alike, or likely to become
> equal or alike, in anything approaching the foreseeable future. We believe
> on the contrary that there are vast areas of difference within mankind not
> only in physical appearance, but in such matters as adaptability to varying
> environments, and in deep psychological and emotional qualities, as well as
> in mental ability and capacity for development. (Putnam 1961:vii)

This was the first salvo in dueling scientific statements on race in the aftermath of Little Rock; it was signed by R. Ruggles Gates, Henry E. Garrett, R.
Gayre, and Wesley C. George. This was an explicit effort on the part of

the recently incorporated International Association for the Advancement of Ethnology and Eugenics (IAAEE) and the Putnam Letter Committee to enable Southern lawmakers' plan B by shifting the discourse in favor of segregation away from states' rights, common sense, and precedent to the theater of science. Both the IAAEE and the now "National" Putnam Letters Committee were supported in large part by the reclusive millionaire Wickliffe Draper and his notorious Pioneer Fund (see below) (Jackson 2001:262; Tucker 2002:71, Tucker 1994:160; Winston 1998:180, 2001:1).[3]

Race and Reason sold sixty thousand copies within six months, and many public officials in the South appropriated Putnam's arguments in toto (Tucker 1994:160–61). The Louisiana State Board of Education, for example, hailed Putnam as "an eminent American anthropologist and scholar" and noted that he "exposes the flagrant distortion and perversion of scientific truth by so-called social anthropologists and socialistically oriented sociologists." The board made the book required reading for all deans, professors, and instructors. In addition, the board mandated that professors assign *Race and Reason* in courses pertaining to anthropology, psychology, and sociology as well as in the required course for all students, Americanism vs. Communism (Margolis 1961:1868).

Governor Barnett admired Putnam and his work so much that he invited him to the governor's mansion in Jackson and officially declared October 26, 1961, "Race and Reason Day." As reported in the journal *Science*, Barnett effused that "the people of Mississippi are fortunate to have a scholar of Mr. Putnam's standing visit our state and address our people." The day, he said, should be observed by "reading and discussing *Race and Reason*, calling the book to the attention of friends and relatives in the North, and by participating in appropriate public functions" (Margolis 1961:1868).

The Virginia legislature was so taken by Putnam's book that it held committee hearings and prepared a resolution that "would support a contention that Negroes are inferior to whites in innate ability and that therefore segregation is scientifically supportable." Joseph A. Loftus, writing for the *New York Times*, explained that "the point of the resolution is to call the attention of the State Board of Education to a book 'Race and Reason—A Yankee View.'" Under the section heading "Boas Is Blamed," the *Times* quoted Putnam: "I would go so far as to say that in the last fifty years anthropology has been drafted to serve the demi-goddess of equalitarianism instead of the goddess of truth . . . two generations of

Americans have been victimized by a pseudo-scientific hoax in this field" (Loftus 1962:62).

During the summer of 1961 Governor John Patterson of Alabama addressed the so-called hidden issue by hiring a retired anatomy professor from the University of North Carolina, Wesley Critz George, to investigate the putative scientific basis for white supremacy. George told a reporter from the *Montgomery Advertiser* that "scientific data supports the contention that the white race, intellectually, is superior to the Negro and that is the point we seek to make with this study." Ralph Smith, a lawyer hired by the state of Alabama to fight desegregation cases and assist with the study, told the same reporter that "the rulings of the United States Supreme Court have made it clear that it is no longer an issue of states' rights or interposition but of science. . . . It is the aim of this work to set the record straight. Whatever may be the outcome, the American public and its courts should not be sold a scientific hoax without at least knowing they have bought a hoax" (*NYT*, November 3, 1961:45).

Less than a month after Barnett established "Race and Reason Day" and just days after the story broke that Patterson had commissioned a scientific study to prove the supremacy of whites, the AAA, under the leadership of President Gordon R. Willey, unanimously approved its first statement on race during its sixtieth annual meeting held in Philadelphia. "The American Anthropological Association," the statement read,

> repudiates statements now appearing in the United States that Negroes are biologically and in innate mental ability inferior to whites, and reaffirms the fact that there is no scientifically established evidence to justify the exclusion of any race from the rights guaranteed by the Constitution of the United States. The basic principles of equality of opportunity and equality before the law are compatible with all that is known about human biology. All races possess the abilities needed to participate fully in the democratic way of life and in modern technological civilization. (*NYT*, November 21, 1961:29)

Although the AAA did not link its statement to Putnam's attack on anthropology, the black press made explicit connections.[4]

The Memphis-based *Tri-State Defender* headlined "A Racial Myth Exploded" and cited the AAA statement on race as "a strong reaffirmation of positions which have been taken on the subject of race differences by qualified scientific societies for many years." The paper used the statement to call into question the validity of "Wesley C. George . . . [who]

has been hired by the state of Alabama to prepare this [study] in order
to justify continued segregation of the races in that state, and to dispute
the equalitarian anthropological doctrine of the late Dr. Boaz [*sic*]" (Tri-
State Defender, August 25, 1962:6). The estimable historian J. A. Rogers
used the A A A statement in one of his many missives to the *New Pittsburgh Courier* to explain that the statement was based not on theory but
on "fact established beyond any successful disproof. The descendants of
those African slaves, in spite of severe handicaps, have done all that the
Carleton Putnams, past and present, said they couldn't do. Putnam knows
this, too. So do these Southern lawmakers. But they keep it up" (Rogers
1962:10).

Two weeks after the A A A issued its statement on race, Putnam held
a press conference at which he announced that the A A A should "throw
off the yoke of the hard core radicals" and quit "indulging alien ideologies in their midst" (Margolis 1961:1868). According to a young Howard
Margolis, who covered the story for *Science*, Putnam was asked specifically which "minority group" was responsible for perpetuating this hoax
and silencing scientists who supported his views. Responding directly
to a reporter's question, Putnam explained that it was Jews who were
responsible, but he could "not understand why Jews would want to do
such a thing, since they themselves are not considered inferior" (Margolis
1961:1868). The *New York Times* also covered the press conference, and it
emphasized that Putnam was "acting as counsel for a muzzled group of
scientists" who were silenced by the believers of the equalitarian dogma
(*NYT*, December 2, 1961:47).

Upset with the fact that their colleagues were forced to teach Putnam's
Race and Reason, the American Association of Physical Anthropologists
(A A P A) issued a more pointed statement explicitly indicting Putnam
and his ilk. During the association's annual meeting in May of 1962, they
passed a resolution that stated, "We, the members of the American Association of Physical Anthropologists professionally concerned with differences in man, deplore the misuse of science to advocate racism. We
condemn such writings as *Race and Reason* that urge the denial of basic
rights to human beings. We sympathize with those of our fellow teachers who have been forced by misguided officials to teach race concepts
that have no scientific foundation, and we affirm, as we have in the past,
that there is nothing in science that justifies the denial of opportunities
or rights to any group by virtue of race" (Fried 1962:46). The timing and

quick response of the statements on race by AAA and AAPA were important. The first three years of the 1960s were an exciting, yet turbulent time. Various movements and initiatives to secure human and civil rights gained momentum and began to fuse into what has been termed the civil rights movement. In actuality, the movement was really a convergence of various initiatives articulated by diverse people and organizations.

On February 1, 1960, Ezell Blair Jr., Franklin McCain, Joseph McNeil, and David Richmond, first-year students at North Carolina A&T, decided to take a stand against the indecency and inhumanity of not being allowed to eat at a lunch counter at the F. W. Woolworth's store in Greensboro. They showed the waitress their receipts to prove they had shopped at the store but were curtly refused service. The four young men did not move and by their action launched one of the most effective strategies of nonviolent protest used by the movement, the sit-in. Ultimately, they drew support from local churches and the students and faculty members of the ten historically black colleges between Winston-Salem and Raleigh, North Carolina. Within months, sit-ins were taking place throughout the South. Ella Baker, the executive director of the Southern Christian Leadership Conference (SCLC), sagaciously and shrewdly supported the student movement without trying to contain the students or subordinate them to the more established leadership of the SCLC. With Baker serving as an advisor and mentor, students organized the relatively independent Student Nonviolent Coordinating Committee (SNCC) just months after the Greensboro sit-ins.

The Congress of Racial Equality (CORE), under the direction of James Farmer, organized the famous freedom rides. CORE tried to force Southern states to comply with federal interstate transportation law by sending multiracial groups to ride interstate buses together through Southern states. Facing violence, incarceration, and several firebombs, the intrepid freedom riders successfully forced the Interstate Commerce Commission to enforce its ban on segregated seating in interstate vehicles and terminals in September of 1961. In the autumn of 1962, Governor Barnett encouraged a chaotic battle between prosegregationist militias and the federal marshals sent to protect James Meredith, who had enrolled at the University of Mississippi. President John F. Kennedy quickly deployed over twenty thousand federal troops to Oxford, Mississippi, to quell the unrest, sniper fire, and shotgun blasts that left two people dead.

The SCLC, under the leadership of Martin Luther King Jr., continued to mount specific campaigns against civil and human rights abuses by organizing nonviolent marches and boycotts that were complemented by skillful negotiations. After waging a long, difficult campaign in Albany, Georgia, in 1961–62, the SCLC joined forces with the Alabama Christian Movement for Human Rights in 1963 to mount a sustained protest in Montgomery by using boycotts and marches to chip away at the pillars of white supremacy.

Led by Bull Connor, police officers used attack dogs, high-pressure fire hoses, electric cattle prods, and clubs to disperse picketers and protestors from Birmingham's business district. Later, Governor George Wallace deployed 825 highway patrolmen and troopers, who brandished machine guns and sawed-off shotguns as they launched tear gas to disperse the protesters. King's moving "Letter from Birmingham Jail" and the violent images on television and in newspapers challenged the moral foundation of the nation and emboldened other organizations, while the longtime labor leader A. Philip Randolph organized the March on Washington for Jobs and Freedom in 1963, where King captivated the hearts and minds of many Americans and people around the world with his poignant "I Have a Dream" speech.

The anthropological statements on race were small contributions to these movements. Yet colleges and universities were the training ground for the diverse student bodies who became involved in and led important facets of these movements. Although carefully worded and never declaring outright that the races were equal in ability, the statements were clear that there was no scientific basis to support segregation. More importantly, the membership of the AAA and AAPA eschewed the imaginary line between science and politics and issued these statements just when the various movements were gaining momentum. The statements effectively hobbled the prosegregationist forces' ability to mount an effective social science attack against desegregation and other civil rights. They also were a legitimate and scientific buttress that served to complement the moral, ethical, economic, and legal arguments put forth by the many participants of the civil rights movement. Simply put, this was one theater civil rights leaders could leave to the social psychologists, population geneticists, and anthropologists.

Although hobbled, Putnam and his group of "muzzled scientists" fought tenaciously and fiercely, using fallacious scientific arguments about Negro inferiority in the press and in the scientific journals. And they kept hammering on the Boas conspiracy, a tactic that was never terribly effective within the mainstream press. Who was this group of muzzled scientists? According to Andrew Winston in "Science in the Service of the Far Right," there was a highly organized, politicized, and well-funded group of scientists and policy pundits who circulated within and through the IAAEE, "the neofascist Northern League, and the ultra-right-wing political group, the Liberty Lobby" (1998:179).

Often publishing in the journal *Mankind Quarterly* and other outlets that still valued eugenics in the early 1960s, these scholars worked closely with the National Putnam Letters Committee and its successor, the Patrick Henry Group, to keep the scientific debate over Negro inferiority alive in the press and in front of the public, especially in the South. The Pioneer Fund proved to be an important source of funding for many of these initiatives (Tucker 2002:71; Winston 1998:179). One of the most influential of these social scientists was Henry E. Garrett, to whom the 1960s version of the Boas conspiracy can rightly be credited.

Linking the eighteenth-century word *equalitarianism* to the idea that Boas was its progenitor was a favorite tactic among the people associated with the IAAEE. Although Putnam was at the organization's first conclave, scholars within the scientific community knew he was no academic. Garrett, by contrast, was one of the most respected scientists associated with the IAAEE. He was an academic whose credentials, in the early 1960s, included the past presidency of the American Psychological Association and the former chairmanship of the psychology department at Columbia University; he was a visiting professor at the University of Virginia at the time (Jackson 2001:253; Winston 1998:179). Garrett worked closely with Putnam and Harry Frederick Weyher Jr. (Draper's attorney and operating officer of the Pioneer Fund) to orchestrate the scientific campaign against desegregation (Tucker 2001:71).

In 1961, for example, Garrett published the same article in *Mankind Quarterly*, *Perspectives in Biology and Medicine*, and *U.S. News & World Report*. The title of the article in the two journals was "The Equalitarian Dogma," but apparently *U.S. News* thought it prudent to recast it as "One Psychologist's View of the 'Equality of the Races'" (Garrett 1961a, 1961b, 1961c). In it, Garrett highlights how the dogma "spread through many colleges and universities and is widely accepted by sincere humanitarians, social reformers, crusaders, sentimentalists and—ostensibly—politicians.

Last, but by no means least, the Communists vigorously defend the equalitarian dogma" (1961c:72–73). Garrett used IQ differences between whites and blacks and the fallacious notion that Africans had never developed a civilization as his examples to show that racial segregation should be maintained. He listed five unique sources for this equalitarian propaganda, including the rise of African nationalism, the *Brown* decision, negative reaction to Hitler and the Nazis, and the influence of the communists. Garrett was clear, however, that "by far the most potent assault upon native racial differences from the scientific side has come from the work of Franz Boas, who may be thought of as the 'father' of the equalitarian movement" (1961c:73).

Race Categories Termed Useless

Anthropologists fought this campaign of scientific racism with resolutions and in the pages of *Science, American Anthropologist, Current Anthropology*, and other journals and popular publications. A scathing review of *Race and Reason* was leveled by Theodosius Dobzhansky in the *Journal of Heredity*, and Ashley Montagu continued "as irritatingly as the sound of a clanging door heard in the distance in a wind that will not be shut out, [to] raise the question as to whether, with reference to man, it would not be better if the term 'race' were altogether abandoned" (Montagu 1962:919). *Current Anthropology*, under the editorship of Sol Tax, also played a significant role in the effort at refutation. In the issue of October 1961, Tax published an article entitled "'Scientific' Racism Again" written by Juan Comas, a full-time research professor of anthropology at the National University of Mexico. Comas connected the current regime of scientific racists to an earlier group who had fought against the United Nations Statement on Race in 1952. In addition, Comas put forth a careful scientific rebuttal of Garrett's critiques of Montagu and the theory that racial differences in IQ scores proved that whites were so superior to blacks that racial segregation should be maintained. The broad range of subsequent comments made it clear to the scientific community that careful science—specifically, genetics and informed understandings of the impact of the environment—not equalitarian dogma, had trumped these attempts to use science in the service of segregation. Dobzhansky's comments, for example, explained, "It is . . . a matter of elementary genetics that the capacities of individuals, populations, or races cannot be discovered until they are given an equality of opportunity to demonstrate these capacities" (Comas 1961:317).

In May 1962, the AAA executive board devised a two-pronged attack against racism cloaked as science to turn back the rising tide of continued press coverage, more paid advertisements (in the guise of open letters), and private mailings of offprints of articles published in *Mankind Quarterly*. Financed largely by the Pioneer Fund, this discourse continued to tout both the inferiority of the Negro and the Boas conspiracy. In some respects, the authority of anthropology as a science was being threatened. The approach taken by the AAA leadership consisted of reaching out to the AAAS to develop a broader statement on race and of directing the president of AAA, Sherwood Washburn, to use his presidential address at the November meetings to articulate the scientific position on race (Jackson 2001:267).

By mid-October, however, things had changed. The segregationists had a new arrow in their quiver: a book written by a new New England Brahmin from the distinguished Carleton family. George and Garrett sent that arrow flying in a letter to the editor of the *New York Times* on October 24, 1962. These stalwarts of the IAAEE at first simply rehearsed their familiar refrain about the "influence of Boas as the founder of the so-called subject of cultural anthropology . . . first at Columbia and later at other universities fed from the Boas cult." Then they added something new to the verse that only used IQ test scores and the putative absence of African civilizations on which to hang their scientific arguments about white supremacy. "New evidence has recently come to light," they explained, and it was in "'The Origins of Races,' published Oct. 15 [by] Carleton Coon, one of the foremost physical anthropologists, [who] presents evidence indicating that the white race passed from the stage of Homo erectus to Homo sapiens 200,000 years ahead of the Negro and is therefore 200,000 years ahead of him on the ladder of evolution" (Garrett and George 1962:38).

Carleton Stevens Coon (1904–81) was an early student of Earnest Hooton at Harvard University, where he taught from 1927 until 1948, at which time he moved to Philadelphia to become professor of anthropology at the University of Pennsylvania and curator of ethnology at the University Museum. He was the author of both scholarly and popular books and was a well-respected scholar and public intellectual. "My thesis is, in essence," Coon argued in the conclusion to his book, "that at the beginning of our record, over half a million years ago, man was a single species, *Homo erectus*, perhaps already divided in five geographic races or subspecies. *Homo erectus* then evolved into *Homo sapiens* not once but five times, as each subspecies, living in its own territory, passed a critical threshold from a more brutal to a more *sapient* state" (1962:657). According to Jonathan Marks, "The book made four major claims. First, that the human species was divisible into five fundamental constituent subspecies or races. Second, that these taxonomic entities had a deep presence in prehistory, being discernible as equivalent subunits of *Homo erectus*. Third, that these evolved into *Homo sapiens* at different times. Fourth, that the economic and political dominance of contemporary western Europeans and their descendants (and secondarily, east Asians and their descendants), was simply a consequence of their longevity as members of the species" (2000:2). Alexander Alland, who offers a balanced and informed critique, explains that "Coon stands as an example of a man whose interpretations of the then-available evidence for human evolution were driven by bad theory, the notion that blacks are inferior to whites in intelligence" (2002:58). Coon's seven-hundred-page tome, replete with pictures of bare-breasted pygmies and dark-skinned bushmen interposed with images of lemurs, marmosets, and mandrills, was immediately seized upon by proponents of segregation who took note of Coon's belief that it was a "fair inference" to make that whites who "crossed the evolutionary threshold into the category of *Homo sapiens* the earliest have evolved the most . . . and the levels of civilization attained by some of its populations may be a related phenomena [*sic*]" (Coon 1962:ix–x). Perhaps the most salient feature of Coon's book was the interpretation by many that Negroes were two hundred thousand years behind whites in their collective evolution and quest for civilization. Coon provided proof enough, for many, to try to use it to maintain the bureaucracies and technologies of white supremacy. An article in the *Tri-State Defender* captures the way in which different constituent groups interpreted the book:

> Southern segregationists, who've employed every tactic from murder to economic pressure in their last-gasp effort to maintain a Jim Crow way of life, now are clutching a new weapon. Oddly, it's a book. Stranger still, it's a book written by a "damn Yankee." . . . The book is enjoying wide circulation in Oxford, Miss., scene of the Meredith university case, and other portions of the deep South. Dixiecrats are waving the book aloft and shouting, "The

Negro race is at least 200,000 years behind." Although Dr. Coon himself carefully refrained from applying his theories to American Negroes . . . desperate southern race-haters are making the application for him. (Tri-State Defender, December 1, 1962:7)

The *Defender* reporter went on to cite an article by Frederick S. Hulse in the *American Anthropologist* for October 1962 that stated, "It has become a very common opinion that racial diversity postdates the appearance of *Homo sapiens*" (Hulse 1962:930). Quoting this article, the reporter explained to the paper's primarily black audience that Coon, according to Hulse, represented an "extreme opinion" that "has no evidence of any nature to support it" (Hulse 1962:931; Tri-State Defender, December 1, 1962:7). Although Coon ostensibly was a dispassionate scientist researching the paleontological record and seeking the truth through observing facts, he went to great lengths to mask his rather close relationship to his cousin Carleton Putnam and his colleagues involved with the Pioneer Fund and the IAAEE. Recent work by John P. Jackson Jr., Jonathan Marks, and Rachel Caspari has demonstrated that Coon worked behind the scenes to help segregationists hone their arguments as they attempted to deploy science to serve the cause of white supremacy (Jackson 2001: 250–70; Marks 2000:3–8; Caspari 2003:72).

In the midst of all of the publicity surrounding Coon's new publication, the stakes quickly rose for Washburn and his presidential address, which he reluctantly agreed to deliver at the AAA meetings in Chicago. He opened his remarks by stating, "The Executive Board has asked me to give my address on the subject of race, and, reluctantly and diffidently, I have agreed to do so. . . . The latest information available supports the traditional findings of anthropologists and other social scientists—that there is no scientific basis of any kind for racial discrimination." Although not the strident statement the executive board had hoped for, Washburn emphasized that "our first problem must be the species and the things which have caused the evolution of all mankind, not the races." In a parenthetical swipe at Coon, he added, "A contrary view has recently been expressed by Coon in *The Origin of Races*. I think that great antiquity of human races is supported neither by the record nor by evolutionary theory" (1963:521).

Emphasizing the distinctions between history and evolution, culture and biology, Washburn carefully walked the line between affirming biological diversity and arguing that race "is a very minor concept" (1963:527). He evoked even the founding fathers and their call for life, liberty, and the pursuit of happiness as an argument to foster an enriching environment for all peoples (1963:530). Washburn concluded by suggesting, "We are the primitives living by antiquated customs in the midst of scientific progress. Races are products of the past. They are relics of times and conditions which have long ceased to exist. Racism is equally a relic supported by no phase of modern science" (1963:531).

Washburn's address prompted the *New York Times* to print the headline "Race Categories Termed Useless" and report that "the anthropological position . . . has [a] direct bearing on the segregationist argument that there are inherent racial inequalities favoring whites over Negroes." The article went on to explain how "anthropologists are trying to undercut the argument that the segregationist has science on his side" (*NYT*, November 18, 1962:72).

Slowly yet methodically, anthropologists responded to the Pioneer Fund's plan B, without ever addressing the cult of Boas. Dobzhansky and Montagu, for example, both wrote devastating reviews of Coon's book for *Current Anthropology*. Their reviews were accompanied by Coon's concomitant response, which was mean spirited and frankly pathetic. Dobzhansky demonstrated that a new synthetic approach that used population genetics, cultural anthropology, and the new biological (as opposed to physical) anthropology signaled a paradigm shift away from conceptualizing race in terms of static or essential typologies. This synthesis, he argued, offered a better way to understand the role of human diversity because it emphasized diversity within populations and the relatively small differences between them (Dobzhansky, Montagu, Coon 1963:360–67).

With the financial support of the Pioneer Fund, Putnam, Garrett, and George continued working together to mount a scientific case against desegregation in the courts. They actually won *Stell v. the Savannah Board of Education* (1963) in the lower courts, but it was overturned by the U.S. 5th Circuit and never heard before the Supreme Court (Putnam 1967: 87–93). During the early months of 1963, Mead began working closely with the interdisciplinary AAAS Committee for Science and the Promotion of Human Welfare, chaired by the biologist and early environmental activist Barry Commoner of Washington University. The AAA executive board had approached the AAAS because they wanted to broaden the scope of their statement to include all of the sciences. As well, the AAAS was in a better position to respond to the Boas conspiracy than a group of anthropologists.

In a tersely worded, detailed report entitled "Science and the Race Problem," the committee carefully dissected the work of George and Putnam. The committee believed these two men put forward "in the most coherent form" ideas "regarding scientific evidence of the 'inferiority' of the Negro races" (Commoner 1963:558). Using rather lengthy quotations from Putnam's *Race and Reason* (1961) and George's *Biology of the Race Problem* (1962), the committee indignantly exploded each author's claims with a savvy mix of the principles of democracy and the latest scientific findings. Anthropologists declared they would no longer narrate reliably the story of white supremacy. The committee only tangentially broached the Boas conspiracy by stating, "There is, in our opinion, no evidence to support the claim, advanced by Professor George and Mr. Putnam, that a group of scientists has conspired to mislead the public about the scientific evidence regarding racial differences. This assertion can only reflect a lack of understanding of the nature of the scientific process" (Commoner 1963:559).

The committee reported its findings in *Science* on November 1, 1963. Just days later President Kennedy was assassinated. Within the next year President Lyndon B. Johnson took bold steps by signing the historic Civil Rights Act and the Anti-Poverty Act and asked Congress to pass the Gulf of Tonkin Resolution, which plunged the nation into a protracted war in Vietnam. Medgar Evers was assassinated in June of 1963, and the so-called Freedom Summer of 1964 witnessed the murders of the voting rights activists James Chaney, Andrew Goodman, and Michael Schwerner, while the ever-vocal Stokely Carmichael joined SNCC in Lowndes County, Alabama, to organize voters and create the Lowndes County Freedom Organization, which chose a black panther as the party's mascot. That same year Malcolm X successfully broke away from the Nation of Islam to form his popular Organization of Afro-American Unity and was summarily assassinated in Audubon Ballroom in February 1965.

During the months that followed the AAAS statement on race, the civil rights movement became more violent and bloody and understandably more militant. The movement slowly morphed into Black Power and antiwar movements as hard-core segregationists and white supremacists began to recede from the halls of Congress, statehouses, and governors' mansions when Barry Goldwater's bid for the Oval Office was crushed in 1964. While Democratic segregationists began to leave the structures of civil society or joined the party of Lincoln, others gravitated toward civic and private organizations that continued to promote segregation and traffic in hate and violence.

The Boas conspiracy and the scientific racism of Putnam were rendered insignificant in the mainstream media during the 1960s as much by new understandings of culture, the environment, and population genetics as by the sea change in attitudes and perspectives brought on by that decade's torrent of social change. Racism was taken up, however, with renewed attention by the likes of Rockwell, and it continues to fester in circles that still despise integration.

The historical significance of the efforts by the AAA, AAPA, and AAAS to contribute to the movement toward civil rights by issuing statements on race perhaps pales in comparison to the work of members of such organizations as SCLC and SNCC. Yet the statements are important documents of the civil rights movement because they signaled that science in general and anthropology in particular buttressed the persuasive legal, moral, political, and religious arguments marshaled by so many to effect irrevocable change. Even at the time the statements were issued, however, they were somewhat anachronistic because they were written just as much of anthropology began viewing itself in less scientific as well as less domestic terms. Dell Hymes, Clifford Geertz, Marshall Sahlins, and Stanley Diamond each piloted cultural anthropology in new directions, but less attention was being paid to U.S. racism and African American culture, despite the efforts of scholars like William Willis, St. Clair Drake, and Carol Stack.

Simultaneously, the explicit scientific racism proffered by people associated with the IAAEE along with its Boas conspiracy became anachronistic as William Shockley and Arthur Jensen articulated more sophisticated forms of scientific racism to quietly replace it. Nevertheless, the explicit racist science of Putnam and the IAAEE, together with their Boas conspiracy, continued to find legitimation within groups of neo-Nazis and white supremacists during the late 1960s. As Rockwell so dramatically demonstrated, hard-core white supremacists clung to the simple narratives regarding race mixing and civilization and steeped it in virulent anti-Semitism.

Identifying how the 1960s version of the Boas conspiracy developed and documenting how people like Rockwell appropriated it go a long way toward explaining why Boas makes the list of Americans who have most damaged white interests. However, the story does not begin and end in the 1960s. An equally graphic Boas conspiracy was circulated by Senator Theodore Bilbo of Mississippi in the 1940s when he was involved with the Pioneer Fund's efforts to send blacks back to Africa.

Franz Boas: "A Hypocritical Negrophilistic Quisling"

According to William H. Tucker, Colonel Earnest Sevier Cox and Colonel Wickliffe Preston Draper came to share an almost holy "common cause," namely, a crusade to get the federal government to "return the Negro to his homeland" (Tucker 2001:33; Cox 1937:335). Cox was born in Blount County, Tennessee, in 1880. Before turning thirty, he had pursued such vocations as newspaper reporting, teaching, preaching the gospel, and taking graduate courses in sociology. During his fourth decade, Cox began traveling extensively through Africa and toured the Philippines, Panama, and South America, and he also served in the American Expeditionary Force (Tucker 2002:11).

Draper was born into a prosperous and prestigious New England family. The son of a textile magnate, he attended Harvard College and eventually joined the British Royal Field Artillery. Supported by inherited wealth, Draper traveled the world hunting exotic animals, climbing mountains, and sailing the seas. A bachelor and not particularly close to any of his relatives, Draper searched for a cause to support so he too could leave a lasting legacy like the many members of the Wycliffe and Draper families. By the mid-1920s, Draper became involved in the eugenics and racial purity movements, and he and his wealth, which later was consolidated as the Pioneer Fund, left an important legacy. According to Tucker, "by the time of his death in 1972, Draper's money had become the most important and perhaps the world's only funding source for scientists who still believed that white racial purity was essential for social progress" (2002:23). In the middle of the Depression, the two colonels met and became fast friends, and they remained close associates until Cox's death in 1966. More importantly, as it pertains to the history of anthropology, Cox and Draper serve as the unbroken link between the Boas conspiracy of the 1940s and that of the 1960s.

In 1923, Cox had written a sort of prospectus in the form of a book-length manuscript simply titled *White America* that called for the "repatriation" of the Negro. Although he had difficulty finding a publisher, months after meeting Colonel Draper, a new "Special edition" was published by "a prominent citizen who wishes to promote the cause of 'Repatriation,'" and it was distributed free to members of Congress as well as to state legislators in "certain of the States" (Cox 1937:2).

The congressmen and legislators were treated, compliments of the two colonels, to a troubling racist call for a constitutional amendment to stem the "insane desire of the colored to blot out the color line and bridge the evolutionary chasm between the races by the process of inter-racial marriage" (Cox 1937:19). Deploying even at that time discredited theories of polygenesis and playing on the fears of amalgamation, Cox warned that the United States was soon going to look like Brazil—a country full of mixed-race mulattoes. Cox selectively quoted Presidents Madison, Lincoln, and Jefferson to argue that Congress had the power to decide the fate of the nation, which turned, in Cox's view, on either amalgamation or the complete separation of the races. Jim Crow segregation, in Cox's mind, was not enough.

It was not long after Cox's special edition circulated through the Senate office building that Theodore Bilbo became an enthusiastic supporter of the plan. A former Baptist preacher, Bilbo first won a seat in the State Senate of Mississippi in 1907, running as both an antirailroad populist and a white supremacist. Bilbo had long cultivated the votes of poor rural whites, and he was twice elected governor. In many respects, he was considered a progressive reformer because he brought expanded public services to rural Mississippi and supported Franklin D. Roosevelt's New Deal initiatives. In 1934, his reputation as a friend of the white working class and enemy of the Negro served him well as he successfully campaigned to be the new senator from the Magnolia State.

On the floor of the U.S. Senate, he supported the National Labor Relations Act and the Social Security Act, and he even backed Roosevelt's "court packing plan" (the attempt by Roosevelt in 1937 to add sympathetic justices to the Supreme Court). Bilbo fiercely opposed, however, the Costigan-Wagner Act, which was federal antilynching legislation (Fitzgerald 1997:296). After receiving Cox's book, Bilbo began to fill the hours during which he engaged in filibusters to derail the antilynching bill by quoting long passages of *White America*. Throughout the late 1930s, Cox, Draper, and Bilbo worked hard to secure support for their Greater Liberia bill. In a classic example of how the cultural politics of race can invite strange bedfellows, these explicit and staunch white supremacists worked closely with various black nationalist groups who were engaged in their own back-to-Africa movements. Perhaps the best-known group Cox developed ties with was Marcus Garvey's Universal Negro Improvement Association, but Cox also cultivated the support of others, particularly Mittie Maud Lena Gordon and her Peace Movement of Ethiopia. Cox, Draper, and Bilbo developed broad support for their scheme from many poor blacks who were growing suspicious of the mainstream liberal and integrationist agenda promoted by the NAACP and the Urban League (Guterl 2001:138–40).

The back-to-Africa movements thrust many leaders (black and white) who were committed to self-help and self-reliance briefly into the national limelight. According to Michael W. Fitzgerald, who has written about this chapter in the racial politics of culture, black "supporters of emigration were derided as dupes because they enlisted segregationist allies, but a close examination reveals a more complex reality. The repatriation campaign tapped genuine popular mistrust of middle-class black leaders, even as it highlighted the 'ambivalent legacy' for blacks of the New Deal itself. . . . The 'back-to-Africa' episode thus had important ramifications as African Americans moved into the civil rights era" (1997:294).

Although more than one million signatures were collected from black people in support of the bill, the momentum built by Gordon, Bilbo, and Cox could not be maintained when Germany invaded Poland in 1939. Never dismayed, Bilbo pushed on, writing an invective tract entitled *Take Your Choice: Separation or Amalgamation* (1947). This was Bilbo's last-ditch effort to rally support for his repatriation movement, which amounted to little more than wholesale deportation of African Americans. Bilbo died the year the book was published.

In the preface, he explained that this book is "a S.O.S. call to every white man and white woman within the United States of America for immediate action, and it is also a warning of equal importance to every right-thinking and straight-thinking American Negro who has any regard or respect for the integrity of his Negro blood and his Negro race" (1947:iv). He explained that "for nine years I have read, studied, and analyzed practically all the records and everything written throughout the entire world on the subject of race relations, covering a period of close on to thirty thousand years." According to Bilbo, his plan for the global separation of the races is "an honest attempt to conserve and protect and perpetuate my own white race and white civilization, and at the same time impress especially the black and yellow races with the fact that they must join in an effort to protect the integrity of their own race, blood, and civilization" (1947:iv). Chapter titles such as "The Race Issue—Our Greatest Domestic Problem," "Southern Segregation and the Color Line," and "The Dangers of Amalgamation" capture both the tone and tenor of this work.

Bilbo opens chapter 10, "Astounding Revelations to White America," with an epigram from Shakespeare: "Lord, what fools these mortals be!" and begins as follows:

> Those people in the United States today who advocate a mongrelized Nation may be called disciples of Professor Franz Boas . . . a Jew, [who] brought considerable notoriety to himself during the early years of this century by his efforts to destroy all concepts of race and encourage and promote miscegenation in this country. . . . Yet for some reason which has never been publicized, this German Jew, a newly-arrived immigrant, wanted to destroy the racial stock which had carved this mighty Nation out of the wilderness. Professor Boas frankly and boldly proclaimed that he was in favor of the miscegenation of the races. . . . Professor Boas criticized the South for not promoting a general program of amalgamation so that it would become a land of mulattoes. He wished to lighten the Negro race by an infusion of white blood. . . . His solution was, of course, the intermarriage of the races. (1947:160–61)

Citing passages from Boas's *The Mind of Primitive Man* (1938), *Anthropology and Modern Life* (1928), and "The Real Race Problem" (1910), Bilbo identifies that Boas never states that Negroes or mulattoes were white people's equal and references an article from 1910 Boas wrote for the NAACP's *Crisis Magazine* in which he suggests that "low brain-weights are slightly more frequent among the Negro, high-brain weights slightly more frequent among the whites." Bilbo even cites Boas's early belief that "there is presumably a slight increase of average ability corresponding to a considerable increase in average brain-weight" (Bilbo 1947:161). Bilbo perceived these statements to be glaring contradictions and labeled Boas "a hypocritical negrophilistic Quisling." Boas indeed wrote these statements, and he was clear that he believed both assimilation and amalgamation could help solve the so-called Negro problem (Boas 1921:395). Bilbo was convinced Boas wanted to "make this a Nation of mongrels" and goes on to develop a version of the Boas conspiracy that resonates with the one articulated by Putnam. Bilbo explained,

> We can not dismiss his teachings with a shrug of the shoulders regardless of how much we would like to turn away from them in disgust. . . . Through the tens of thousands of students who came under his influence and teaching and accepted them, he scattered his evil, disastrous, and racial suicidal preachments and his insane and corrupt doctrines of miscegenation, amalgamation, intermarriage, and mongrelization through this broad land. Carefully and deliberately, he sowed the seeds for the undermining and destroying of both the white and Negro races in this Nation. We are today reaping in many ways the evil doctrines and damnable teachings of Professor Boas. . . . In this manner, the damnable and blighting teachings of these disciples of Boas are being disseminated and inculcated into the minds of the pure-blooded Anglo-Saxon students of Dixie. (1947:164–65)

Bilbo goes on to describe "notorious" examples of these doctrines by selectively quoting *Races of Mankind* (1943) by Ruth Benedict and Gene Weltfish and *An American Dilemma* by Gunnar Myrdal (1944). Bilbo relies heavily on Cox's *White America*, Stuart O. Landry's *The Cult of Equality* (1945), and Ira Calvin's *The Lost White Race* (1945) to make many of his arguments. However, his specific assault on Boas, as he reports in a footnote, was inspired by Professor William B. Smith (1850–1934), who "has forcefully and adequately answered the doctrines of Professor Boas in Chapter Four, 'Plea and Counterplea,' of his book, *The Color Line.* Using science and history, this able Southern writer and scientist has refuted what he terms the plea for the 'backward race' which was made by the Jewish professor of Columbia University" (Bilbo 1947:161).

Bilbo remains an icon of white supremacy and white power and an articulate spokesperson for an all-white nation. His book is available online from the Church of True Israel, and he is routinely cited as a paragon of white supremacy. He is perhaps best known, around the white supremacist communities, for a quote that introduces an extremely troubling pamphlet. Reproduced on many Web sites ranging from the Posse Comitatus to David Duke Online, it's called "Whites and Blacks—100 Facts," and it is a fallacious list of spurious facts written by Roger Roots, whose flimsy evidence is drawn from authors that frequently contribute to *American Renaissance, Mankind Quarterly*, and research supported by the Pioneer Fund.

The important point, in terms of tracking down the genealogy of this Boas conspiracy, is that Bilbo's book was tethered to the Pioneer Fund's initial campaign to mount a scheme to deport African Americans during the Great Depression of the 1930s. Virtually all of the elements found in Rockwell's rendition in 1966 were articulated by Bilbo in 1947. Bilbo, in his footnote about Smith's volume from 1905, offers a clue to the actual origin of this critique that blossomed into conspiracy. Throughout *Take Your Choice*, Bilbo references Smith's work and views him as both an inspiration and a sage. As I have researched the origins of this conspiracy, I am well aware that I too am beginning to sound like a conspiracy theorist, using shards of sketchy evidence to build my case—but that is half the fun. The truth is out there! By looking at the work of Smith, however, one gets a better understanding of how Boas was read and interpreted by his contemporaries, which then demonstrates a century-long derision of his work by white supremacists.

A Brief in Behalf of the Unborn

As the nineteenth century closed, Boas was establishing his leadership in the field and moving anthropology in new directions. Content with organizational leadership and debating scholars via scholarly publications and association meetings, Boas remained focused on contributing to the academic arena. By the turn of the century, Boas was trying to challenge the comparative method and rigid racial topologies. As early as 1894, he addressed the Negro problem by bringing together his critique of the comparative method and his understanding that one could not prove racial inferiority. Boas gave this paper, titled "Human Faculty as Determined by Race," at the annual meeting of the AAAS, and it was subsequently published in its annals (Boas 1895). As I documented in the last chapter, this is the address Brinton obliquely challenged when he gave his presidential address "The Aims of Anthropology" the following year. Boas's paper did not get wide circulation and it was not widely cited. A full decade after Boas presented "Human Faculty," Smith gave it national attention when he subjected it, in his popular book *The Color Line: A Brief in Behalf of the Unborn*, to a paragraph-by-paragraph analysis in an effort to "refute it thoroughly" (Smith 1905:xi). Smith committed an entire chapter to challenging Boas's address to the AAAS, calling it "by far the ablest plea yet made for the 'backward races.'" Smith framed his book by asking and then answering what he saw as a central question: *"Is the South justified in this absolute denial of social equality to the Negro, no matter what his virtues or abilities or accomplishments?* We affirm, then, that the South is entirely right in thus keeping open at all times, at all hazards, and at all sacrifices an impassable social chasm between Black and White. This she *must* do in behalf of her blood, her essence, [and] the stock of her Caucasian Race" (1905:7). Smith was one of many early twentieth-century hucksters of white supremacy who peddled, to rich and poor alike, ideological and scientific rationales for lynching, defamation, and the subjugation of the "lesser races." Although he practiced science in the lyceum tradition, he was no amateur. Smith was the chair of the mathematics department at Tulane University, an active participant in the social and intellectual circles of New Orleans, and an author on a wide range of topics for both the scholarly and popular press. Such topics included international trade, disease, and the origins of Christianity. Smith also labored for years to produce a line-by-line translation in dactylic hexameters of *The Iliad of Homer* (Cattell and Brimhall 1921:641; Smith and Miller 1944).

Smith's *The Color Line: A Brief in Behalf of the Unborn* had far-reaching and lasting influence. In 1916, attorneys for the state of Kentucky used it as scientific proof of Negro inferiority when they argued the constitutionality of Louisville's residential segregation before the U.S. Supreme Court in *Buchanan v. Warley* (1917) (Bernstein 1998:849). In 1931, the Church of Jesus Christ of Latter-day Saints used it to scientifically defend their belief in the racial inferiority of Negroes (Roberts 1931:231–33), and even today Smith is cited as an authority on Web sites like Stormfront outlining how interracial dating will ultimately destroy the white race (Fields 1997).

Smith wrote his book about the color line in the South during the first decade of the twentieth century. Awash in racial tension that simply translated into the brutal oppression and repression of African Americans, the omnipresent color line was circumscribed by Jim Crow segregation, disfranchisement, poor sanitary conditions, and little to no wage work. The rationale for the color line had to be constantly described and inscribed by the rich and poor who had a stake in perpetuating split-labor markets, hobbling the Republican Party, and maintaining the "Southern way of life."

Mass media played an integral role in shoring up the ideological demarcation of the color line. Technological advancement and rising literacy rates increased the circulation and decreased the cost of magazines, newspapers, and books. By 1905, stereotypes that had previously been reinforced by folklore and expensive texts were now voraciously consumed by the public.

In *The Color Line*, Smith explored one "of the most important questions that is likely to engage the attention of the American People for many years and even generations to come" (Smith 1905:ix). Like the latter-day authors of *The Bell Curve* (Herrnstein and Murray 1994), he framed his study by suggesting he had made every "effort to make the whole discussion purely scientific, an ethnological inquiry, undisturbed by any partisan or political influence" (1905:x). Smith used what he called "ethnological principles" to defend the South's rigid color line, explaining "that *in the South* the colour line must be drawn firmly, unflinchingly—without deviation or interruption of any kind whatever" (1905:5). Smith was unequivocal that "the Negro is markedly inferior to the Caucasian," which he believed was "proved both craniologically and by six thousand years of planet-wide experimentation; and that the commingling of the inferior with superior must lower the higher is just as certain as that the half-sum of two and six is only four" (1905:12). Like many politicians, tycoons, and Supreme Court justices at the beginning of the twentieth century, he turned to the ideology of social Darwinism to rest his case (Baker 1998:54–81):

> If accepted science teaches anything at all, it teaches that the heights of being in civilized man have been reached along one path and one only—the path of selection, of the preservation of favoured individuals and of favoured races. . . . It is idle to talk of education and civilization and the like as corrective or compensative agencies. All are weak and beggarly as over [sic] against the almightiness of heredity, the omnipotence of the transmitted germ-plasma. . . .
> If this be not true, then history and biology are alike false; then Darwin and Spencer, [Ernst] Haeckel and [August] Weismann, [Gregor] Mendel and [Roger] Pearson, have lived and laboured in vain. (Smith 1905:13–14)

Smith carefully laid out his argument; but it was not necessarily a novel one. He recycled the same rationales that had been routinized in American popular culture and reified within scientific literature by trotting out accounts about cranial capacity, arrested development of children, and higher rates of crime, immorality, and disease (all of which he linked). He devoted much of the book to depicting the horrors of miscegenation and how mulattos receive the worst traits of both races. He couched these dire straits in terms of "the race instinct" and "blood purity," and warned, "The moment the bar of absolute separation is thrown down in the South, that moment the bloom of her spirit is blighted forever . . . the idea of the race is far more sacred than that of the family. It is, in fact, the most sacred thing on earth" (1905:10).

Smith really believed he was acting as a scientist, as did many of his readers. The sociologist Charles Ellwood, for example, highlighted the book's polemic style in a review for the *American Journal of Sociology*, but he emphasized that Smith's style "should not be permitted to obscure its value as a contribution to the study of the Negro problem in the United States" (Ellwood 1906:570).[5] As a good scientist, Smith wanted to test his theories against the strongest counterarguments.

Smith believed, and perhaps rightfully so, that Boas's "Human Faculty" offered the most prestigious and best defense of people of color within the then-current scientific discourse on race. Smith's whole argument rested on the notion that Africans and African Americans were the most inferior of the races both anatomically and culturally. He sought to prove that sub-Saharan Africans had no art, religion, philosophy, or morality and that West Africans in particular had never demonstrated "even one single aspect of civilization or culture or higher humanity" (1905:32).

Smith titled the chapter in which he challenged Boas "Plea and Counter Plea" and opened it by noting, "This distinguished anthropologist, now of Columbia University, New York City, speaks from the pinnacles of science, and his words must not go unregarded. We shall notice every salient point in his twenty-six pages . . . such a formal defense seems to call for an equally formal rejoinder" (1905:111). Smith cited J. C. Nott and George Gliddon, Arthur de Gobineau, and Armand de Quatrefages to challenge Boas's two major claims in "Human Faculty": that various peoples contributed to each major civilization and that the evidence is not conclusive that certain races are inferior to others.

Although Smith exempted the "present backward races," he concurred with Boas that different races contributed to various forms of civilization (1905:113). While Boas viewed the so-called contribution of one race as just as important as the contribution of another toward a civilization, Smith questioned, "But to all in equal measure? Or to some in far higher measure? That is the question. We must not think of the Senate, where all states vote alike; but of the House of Representatives, where "Little Rhody" vanishes by the side of New York or Texas. Even if all races did contribute to the sum total, which is far from true, there is an immense difference between contributions that may vary from a penny to a pound" (1905:115). Smith dismissed Boas as "a penny wise, and a pound foolish" (1905:21) and suggested that "the savant has been unscientific in his procedure; he has gone too far; he has thrown out the baby with the bath" (1905:131).

Smith's *A Brief in Behalf of the Unborn* simply mirrored the pronouncements of many earlier twentieth-century pundits. Yet Smith effectively dragged Boas out of the halls of the academy, where gentleman scholars discussed cultural diffusion and Inca ruins in scholarly tomes, and into the streets, where reformers and racists vociferously debated the problem of the Negro in sensationalist monthlies and newspapers. According to the historian of anthropology William S. Willis, the impact of Smith's chapter on Boas was twofold: it introduced Boas's work to reformers and scholars engaged in so-called racial uplift and formed the basis for lasting labels. Some quickly labeled Boas a "nigger lover," but others viewed him as a much-needed "friend of the Negro."[6]

In the wake of Smith's incendiary text, Boas published his first article about African Americans in a popular magazine. In the autumn of 1905, Boas wrote "The Negro and the Demands of Modern Life: Ethnic and Anatomical Considerations" for the October 7 issue of *Charities*, a special volume addressing Negro migration. A modified version of the article that Smith had challenged, it was sandwiched between articles by W. E .B. Du Bois, Booker T. Washington, and Mary White Ovington, the reformer who initially organized the NAACP (Boas 1905). According to Francille Rusan Wilson, "Boas's article gave white progressives interested in black social problems the scientific basis they needed from a nonblack and presumably disinterested party to legitimate the expansion of their focus from immigrants and poor whites to include black people" (2006:69).

From that point forward, Boas was identified as an important scholar who could be called upon to help uplift the race. Du Bois wasted no time. Four days after the article in *Charities* was published, he wrote Boas a letter inviting him to Atlanta University to address a conference scheduled for May of the next year.[7] That letter, on the heels of Boas's article in *Charities*, which came on the heels of Smith's effort to attack Boas's work, was the beginning of a long and profitable relationship between Du Bois and Boas and the endeavors they pursued (Baker 1994).

Boas's rather muted relationship with the NAACP nevertheless served as a powerful symbol for the organization and others who worked in racial uplift organizations. The relationship also solidified his reputation as a staunch friend of the Negro, which made him suspect just as anthropology began to become an unreliable narrator in the service of white supremacy. His reputation as a friend of the Negro dovetailed with his positions on immigration and war to fuel the allegations made by people like Bilbo who began to believe Boas was the mastermind of some Jewish cabal organized to hoodwink America into believing that there is no such thing as race and that all people have the capacity to participate in modern civilization.

Notably, Thomas Kuhn's *The Structure of Scientific Revolutions* (1962) was first published as the Boas conspiracy flourished in the 1960s. Although politics (of various sorts) play an important role in any paradigm shift, the shaping of a scientific consensus cannot be effectively fashioned through conspiracies, syndicates, and racketeering. Sherwood Washburn never addressed the Boas conspiracy publicly, but he did respond to Carleton Putnam in a letter and tried to explain to him how changes in science actually occur and that anthropology was not the only field involved in rethinking race in the 1960s. According to John P. Jackson Jr., who has analyzed Putnam's correspondence, "'After reading your book,' wrote Washburn to Putnam, 'I believe you greatly exaggerate the role of Boas in American anthropology and social science.' Noting that sociologists and psychologists reached the same conclusions as did anthropologists regarding racial differences, Washburn concluded, 'if there had been no anthropologists at all, the findings would be the same.' In response, Putnam noted that, 'You cannot deceive a child of ten with that sort of *nonsense*, so I wonder what your motives are'" (Jackson 2001:264). Putnam, Cox, Garrett, George, and other scholars associated with the IAAEE and the Pioneer Fund were bent on exposing this so-called hidden issue, first articulated by the notorious senator from Mississippi who was inspired by a reactionary white supremacist who had taken on Boas's essay of 1895. The IAAEE scholars were adamant in their belief about the cult of Boas, but the puerile crowing about a Jewish conspiracy organized by a dead academic never found much traction during the tumultuous change and increasingly social and political complexity that enveloped the world during the mid-1960s. Yet Putnam's ruminations on the race consciousness of the liberal elite served as grist for the mill for the likes of Rockwell and his ANP, who increasingly conflated antiracist research and writing with communism and the supposed Jewish menace. These associations, however, continue to swirl around with remarkable persistence and tenacity in circles and networks committed to white pride worldwide.

A Matter of Time

It is perhaps significant that Boas's preliminary research for both *Changes in Bodily Forms* and *The Mind of Primitive Man* precipitated his debut as a public intellectual or an intellectual in whom the public held interest, albeit hostile interest. Of his hundreds of books, manuscripts, and essays, these two books had the most impact on American history.

It was quite literally just a matter of time before most Americans would begin to view the inherent contradictions in the science underwriting much of the ideology of white supremacy and racial inferiority. Although it took two world wars and protracted campaigns both inside and outside of the academy people eventually incorporated Boas's work on race and culture into the paradigm shift that forever eclipsed mainstream views that certain racial groups were inherently inferior or superior (Baker 1998: 125–26).

In an effort neither to pass down a credulous origin myth nor to bolster conspiracy theories, it is prudent to assess Boas's impact on the public beyond the scope of sympathetic anthropologists and Manhattan intellectuals. In May 1936, an aged Franz Boas graced the cover of *Time* magazine. It was a distinction few anthropologists past or present have received, and it served as a testament, in Boas's own words, to his "task of weaning the people from a complacent yielding to prejudice, and help[ing] them to the power of clear thought, so that they may be able to understand the problems that confront all of us" (Boas 1945:2). The cover story begins with a brief description of the various fields in anthropology and highlights the careers of Sir James Frazer, Lucien Lévy-Brühl, "Harvard's [Earnest] Hooton," and "The Smithsonian Institution's famed Ales Hrdlicka." The article explained that "Franz Boas got into anthropology 53 years ago.

He has invaded almost every branch of this science: linguistics, primitive mentality, folklore, ethnology, growth and senility, [and] the physical effects of environment. He reminds his colleagues of the old-time family doctor who did everything from delivering babies to pulling teeth" (*Time* 1936:37). The story highlighted several key contributions that Boas made as a public figure and as a formidable, but irascible, scholar in the field. It was careful to note, however, that "by no means do all anthropologists share Dr. Boas's belief in the tremendous physical influence of the environment" (*Time* 1936:37). The staff writer and editors devoted several columns of text to Boas's *Changes in Bodily Forms of Descendants of Immigrants* (1912), underwritten by the U.S. Immigration and Naturalization Service in 1908 but initiated in Worcester. The article stated that "over the ensuing 27 years Dr. Boas piled up a mountain of evidence that such changes do occur." The author asked Boas to summarize this research: "'It has been known for a long time,' said Dr. Boas, 'that the bulk of the body as expressed by stature and weight is easily modified by . . . favorable conditions of life. . . . Just in the same way as the proportions of body, head and face of animals born in captivity change when compared to their wild-born ancestors, thus the bodily proportions of man undergo minute changes in new environment[s]'" (1936:37).

For *Time*'s readership, the author asked Boas to "sort out the biological from cultural factors" with regard to the differences between the "motor habits" of various ethnic immigrant groups, particularly the Italians and Jews, and to explain why Americans "do not gesticulate." The author prefaced Boas's explanation with a statement that "the way people use their bodies—seems to be closely linked with the biological make-up." The evidence? Well, the author noted that motor habits "are fairly uniform over wide areas" (1936:38). The author allowed Boas to draw from his years of research to offer rather abstruse elucidation, but the author sardonically summarized, as if the long-winded professor could not get to the point: "Dr. Boas' conclusion from all this is direct and simple: motor habits are cultural, not biological."

When this article was written, Hitler's "New Order," eugenic courts, and the notorious blood purges were swinging into motion. For the first time since the Civil War, Americans began to witness the full sweep of state-sponsored racism. The *Time* article explained that scientists in the United States and England were "engaged in knocking the flimsy props from under Nazi ideas of race purity and race superiority," but it recognized that "a quarter-century ago Franz Boas was attacking the same sort of ideas. At that time the view was popular that different races had their characteristic mentalities which determined their culture. Boas had piled up enough data to convince him that such was not the case" (1936:39).

The article was referring to Boas's *The Mind of Primitive Man* (1911), or what *Time* referred to as the "Magna Charta of the 'lower' races." The author noted that "Boas observed that nowhere on earth was there such a thing as a pure race, and that the term 'race' was vague and approximate at best. [And that he] doubted there were any 'superior' races." Furthermore, the author explained, "Dr. Boas has no confidence in intelligence tests as measures of race superiority, because such tests cannot be divorced entirely from environment and experience" (1936:40). The article also noted Boas's contempt for war and nationalism, citing his optimistic explanation that through anthropology world leaders can "come face-to-face with those forces that will ultimately abolish warfare" (1936:40).

The last section concerned Boas's background as a young scholar in Germany, as an editor of *Science*, an organizer of the World's Fair in Chicago, a leader in the Jesup expedition, a professor at Clark University, and chair of the anthropology department at Columbia University. The article concluded by asking Boas how he felt when the Nazis lit a great bonfire at his beloved Kiel University to burn his books. "Commented 'Papa Franz': if people want to be crazy, what can you do about it?" (1936:42).

This article can actually help one situate and assess Boas's national stature as a public intellectual because it can serve as a reference point on something like a spectrum. On the one hand we have *Time*: driven by its middle-class markets coast to coast, the magazine's editors exemplify how Boas was presented and perceived by a middlebrow American public in 1936. *Time* portrayed him as a purveyor of the equipotential of ethnic and racial groups, a proponent of the nurture side of the nature versus nurture debate, and the quirky and pugnacious father of American anthropology. By the mid-1930s, Boas had earned a reputation as a strict environmentalist, but he was not. By 1936, however, Boas had made such significant contributions to American society that the editors of *Time* knew a cover story about him would cover *their* bottom line.

On the other hand, we have the editors of *The Nation, Charities, The New Republic*, and *The Crisis*. The editors of these magazines targeted a market that was educated, liberal, and located mainly in the Northeast. Quite often the editors of these magazines published or excerpted

Boas's work to help bolster their editorial agendas, which placed Boas shoulder-to-shoulder with reformer-intellectuals of the Progressive Era like Jane Addams, John Dewey, Thorstein B. Veblen, Ida B. Wells, Charles A. Beard, and Louis Brandeis. However, if we limit our view of Boas's public persona to the ways in which he was presented within vehicles of public discourse to which he often contributed, we would perhaps view Boas's contributions as more far-reaching than they were and thus recapitulate the reason for concern voiced by people like the anthropologist Leslie White and even Carleton Putnam. Yet, if we limit our understanding solely to articles like the one in *Time*, we would miss knowing how influential Boas was in shaping the thoughts and actions of the people who were engaged in progressive reform, especially philanthropists, social workers, and the Negro elite. One should conclude that Boas made significant contributions in various public arenas, although his most profound influence was felt among a multiracial and educated elite on the Eastern Seaboard.

By far Boas's and his students' greatest contribution as public intellectuals was helping to solidify the scientific and mass media consensus that ideas about racial inferiority and superiority were, in Boas's words, "Nordic nonsense." Although the consensus did not crystallize until after the ravages of the Jewish Holocaust were widely exposed, its catalyst was the pivotal "Scientists' Manifesto" that was released to the public on December 10, 1938, just as the Nazis' Aryan Nation threatened Europe. It had the signatures of 1,284 scientists from 167 universities—64 were members of the National Academy of Sciences. The *New York Times* reported the next day that Boas wanted "American scientists to take a firm anti-fascist stand," and Boas explained to the paper's readers that "our manifesto declares that we scientists have the moral obligation to educate the American people against all false and unscientific doctrines, such as the racial nonsense of the Nazis" (*NYT*, December 11, 1938:50). The manifesto was the result of a dogged five-year campaign led by Boas, whose explicit goal was to unite scientists and their organizations in an effort to "counteract the vicious, pseudo scientific activity of so-called scientists who try to prove the close relation between racial descent and mental character."[8] Elazar Barkan, in "Mobilizing Scientists against Nazi Racism, 1933–1939" (1988), has detailed this complicated campaign, but he notes that this was Boas's last and most successful campaign outside the academy. Barkan's narrative perhaps best demonstrates that there was nothing even close to a cult of Boas's followers because Boas had to lobby long and hard to individually persuade the many scientists to sign the manifesto.

Following and mapping the Boas conspiracy can actually be instructive in terms of efficiently identifying how various constituent groups have appropriated a counterfactual anthropological narrative to advance particular political agendas. One of the reasons the Boas conspiracy offers such conceptual clarity when it comes to mapping the way anthropology has been appropriated in the United States is that Boas articulated radical views and used unique methods yet was ensconced within elite science. His work and research alarmed and clashed with various movements, beginning with the anti-elitist sentiment in working-class Worcester. In the South, Smith identified Boas as the evil amalgamator and elitist Negro sympathizer. By 1947, Senator Bilbo adds the cult aspect, and Putnam adds the communist aspects, and finally Rockwell makes it a Jewish conspiracy; in the Rockwell version all of the elements come together, and Boas is a leader of an elite cult of communists who are trying to destroy the white race and help the Jews rule the world.

There are significant distinctions to be made between all of these versions, but the Boas conspiracy contrived by Smith runs directly through the work of Bilbo, Putnam, Rockwell, and Duke. Throughout the twentieth century there is a much more robust record of public discourse applauding, even lionizing, Boas and Boasian anthropology. Darnell describes how the "theoretical assessment of Boas's role in the development of the discipline . . . has oscillated between extremes of adulation and vitriolic critique" (2001:33). This oscillation is even more extreme when one looks at the ideological assessment of Boas's work outside of the discipline. While many people within white supremacist circles despised Boas and his work, many more people in African American communities appreciated his work and admired his efforts as the "debunker of racial theories." This was in fact the moniker the Associated Negro Press gave him when it syndicated his obituary, which detailed his efforts to demolish the myth of "the blonde 'superman' and exposing what he called 'this Nordic nonsense'" (Associated Negro Press 1943:24). In a front-page editorial, the *Pittsburgh Courier* eulogized Boas as the man who "fathered a whole school of anthropology which repudiated 'race' as a vicious invention of snobs, exploiters and imperialists" and explained "when Dr. Boas came on the educational stage, the most grotesque fictions were circulating about 'race,' and eminent scholars were prostituting themselves to bolster and justify the enslavement and exploitation of colored nations on the ground that they were 'inferior' and 'not ready for self-government.' He did much to clear away this rubbish and put the old school on the defensive" (Pittsburgh Courier, January 2, 1943:1, 3).

By situating the interpretation and consumption of Boas's work between these two disparate poles one can better demonstrate the overall sweep and power of his message outside the discipline as well as the salience of anthropology within a social history of ideas; finally, it also speaks to the fact that Boas was indeed an intellectual in whom the public took great interest.

Conclusions and Reflections
on the Racial Politics of Culture

Franz Boas continues to be the iconic darling of liberal elites who desire an antiracist yet multicultural society and really want to believe that race does not matter (Pierpont 2004). At the same time, he continues to be the demonic monster of reactionary racists who desire white supremacy and really want to believe that race matters in terms of merit and achievement (MacDonald 1998:27–36). Moreover, the current president of the Pioneer Fund, J. Philippe Rushton, continues to target Boas and paint anthropologists as the real enemy of "race-realist" research in his well-funded campaign to document biological inferiority of black people (Rushton 2002:257; Baker 2004:168). Viewing and interpreting Boas and his work within a rubric framed by these poles helps us gain a better understanding of how anthropology and the history of anthropology continue to be appropriated to articulate very different racial politics of culture. It also helps us better understand the role anthropology has played within the public imaginary over the years.

Throughout the first half of the twentieth century, anthropology was stubbornly resigned to describing exotic cultures while shoring up the idea, in the words of Thurgood Marshall, that "there was not difference between folks." Despite the fact the NAACP Legal Defense and Education Fund, Myrdal's *American Dilemma*, and the National Urban League each leaned on anthropology's scientific contribution to the debate on race relations, intellectuals within these groups often tempered the radical research on race with Frazier's rather conservative view that black people engage in deviant behavior while leavening this rather harsh analysis with an optimistic view that cultural assimilation and integration were the antidote for an ailing culture. By the early 1960s culture and race, at least for people in urban areas in the United States, were severed. Race, racism, and race relations were at issue—not culture, pluralism, self-determination, and relative differences in practices and beliefs.

Even at the height of the Boas conspiracy, for example, no one raised any concerns with regard to anthropology's role in terms of authenticating Indians or describing other exotics in the way Emma Sickels did, in the late nineteenth century, when she alleged Boas, Putnam, and Mooney were engaged in "one of the darkest conspiracies ever conceived against the Indian race" (*NYT*, October 8, 1893:19). On the contrary, during the Second World War and through the Cold War, many anthropologists lent their support, expertise, and knowledge to various government agencies, and even more anthropologists received financial support for ethnographic research from both public and private sources to describe and document out-of-the-way people (Price 2004:4). Anthropology's role as the salvager of exotic cultures and describer of wild people was firmly ensconced within America's imagination during the late 1950s and early 1960s, hewing closely to *National Geographic*'s Cold War photographic conventions and Theodora Kroeber's popular story, *Ishi in Two Worlds: A Biography of the Last Wild Indian in North America* (1961) (Starn 2004; di Leonardo 1998; Lutz and Collins 1993:87–118).

In some respects, describing exotic, out-of-the-way peoples was what anthropologists were supposed to be doing, not trying to pass resolutions regarding racial equality. Moreover, there was little concern over paucity of anthropological descriptions and explorations of African Americans' rich, unique, creative, and expressive culture because the sociology of black folks dominated academic and even popular discourse, although that began to change in the late 1960s with the advent of black studies programs.

David H. Price in *Threatening Anthropology: McCarthyism and the FBI Surveillance of Activist Anthropologists* (2004) describes in detail how J. Edgar Hoover and his FBI agents routinely surveyed and compiled dossiers on many anthropologists. However, Price makes a compelling case that the anthropologists who were subjected to the most virulent FBI harassment and subpoenaed to perform in what he calls Senator Joseph McCarthy's "public show trials" were usually activists who used anthro-

pology to fight for U.S. civil rights and racial equality and were not necessarily Marxists scholars or people with close ties to the Communist Party
(Price 2004:34–168).

During the late 1960s and early 1970s, mainstream sociology was still
influenced by the Chicago school, where Myrdal's and Frazier's thesis regarding Negroes' pathological culture was only slightly modified into a
belief that African Americans articulated a problematic culture of poverty and that structural issues perpetuated the underclass; an individual's
dysfunctional behavior was thus a product of culture even as it fixed one's
class position—the underclass was imprisoned by a culture of poverty
(Kelley 1997:19). Despite the fact that sociology proved to be a reliable
narrator in the story about the deviance of black folks, anthropology remained an unreliable narrator in the story of white supremacy. Boas and
subsequently the field of anthropology generally got implicated as instiga-
tors of a new racial politics of culture that was largely articulated by the
Black, Chicano, and Red power movements within a context of greater
appreciation of multiculturalism. Associating Boas with multiculturalism within the United States is quite curious in that he was a strict assimilationist, to the point of advocating amalgamation as a way to solve
the Negro problem, while he went about salvaging what he perceived as
disappearing indigenous cultures. The black press and the NAACP as well
as the promoters of the Boas conspiracy had one thing in common: each
focused on Boas's research and writings on race, not those on culture.

This very concept of race emerged from an articulation of culture
grounded in the Americanist tradition that categorized languages and documented customs of American Indians. Race and culture in the United
States have slipped back and forth and doubled back on each other.

Anthropology and its relationship to the racial politics of culture and
the cultural politics of race have been recycled, refurbished, reinvented,
and even sucked into the vortex of a twisted Jewish conspiracy. The
Hampton notebooks serve as an apt metaphor for anthropology's flexible
role in the racial politics of culture in the United States. First written by
proponents of racial uplift and used in the service of the civilizing mission, it was quickly recycled by proponents of cultural pluralism and re-
used in the service of the heritage project. Even when anthropologists like
James Mooney tried to use his science in the service of the betterment
of American Indians, progressive reformers and American Indian intellectuals turned his science against him, suggesting he was trying to keep

the Indian down, uncivilized, and mired in pathology and uncivilized behavior. Although Daniel G. Brinton was hailed as a stellar man of science,
a public intellectual, and the first professor of anthropology, the work
that began with such promise quickly became anachronistic when the
terms and conditions of the production of knowledge changed under his
feet. And while a dogged and determined Boas positioned anthropology
squarely within leading universities, the fact that he trained graduate students and influenced social sciences outside of anthropology was grist for
angry conspiracy theories that threatened the work of so many who tried
to transform the meaning of race in America. Although an outgrowth of
Boas's culture concept, Putnam was correct about one thing: Boas's most
important legacy was his influence over the science of race that influenced the *Brown* decision, which was predicated on assimilation, racial
uplift, and the argument that blacks were racially and culturally no different from whites.

The anthropological discourse about black culture was so marginalized
during the early 1960s that it did not warrant much attention from either
white supremacists or African American intellectuals. Like the reemer-
gence of those Hampton notebooks, the celebration, engagement, and
even marketing of black culture moved center stage as dashiki-clad, Afro-
sporting activists began to articulate Black Power in the late 1960s. The
scholarly exploration of diasporic cultures within postcolonial regimes,
under the aegis of the nascent black studies movement, drew heavily
from the work of Zora Neale Hurston, Melville Herskovits, Arthur Fauset,
St. Clair Drake, John Gwaltney, Carol Stack, and other anthropologists.
The inability of a critical mass of anthropologists to develop a sustained
critique of race as a social construct and of racism as an integral part of
the colonial project, however, muted the role it could play in the new
interdisciplinary field of black studies. Anthropology—the science of
race and culture—demonstrated, as Washburn declared, that "race isn't
very important biologically" (1963:548), since the species was the important unit when it came to evolution. When Washburn telescoped seventy
years of Boasian anthropology on race to conclude race was an unimportant biological category, he closed the door on anthropologists who saw
race as an important social fact. He opened the door, however, for shrewd
pundits to offer a seductive line of thought that race does not matter and
racism was just a form of old-fashioned ethnocentrism that could be
surmounted (as the Poles, Italians, and the Irish did) through behavior

modification and the assimilation of mainstream culture (Glazer and Moynihan 1963). Boas's initial scientific move was important in terms of promulgating public policy, bolstering court decisions, and forcing many Americans to rethink notions of inferiority, but the idea that race was an unimportant biological category obscured the idea that race and racism are very important socially, culturally, economically, and politically (see Baker 2001; Harrison 1995). This legacy still fuels the colorblind bind and forms the basis of arguments against, among a host of other instances, affirmative action, ordinances that ban baggy pants, and strict dress codes for players in the National Basketball Association sitting on the sidelines.

Nevertheless, it was Boas's so-called equalitarian dogma that created the most anxiety in white supremacists. Despite the fact that Boas was routinely equivocal when it came to discussions of racial equality, his work on race served as an important scientific bulwark for civil rights advocates and was ultimately responsible for landing him on that list with Lyndon B. Johnson, John F. Kennedy, Abraham Lincoln, Earl Warren, and Martin Luther King Jr.—not bad company to keep.

Notes

Introduction

1. Andrew Carnegie, for example, rejected a request from Boas to fund an African Museum. See F. Boas to Andrew Carnegie, 11/30/1906. Professional Correspondence of Franz Boas, American Philosophical Society Library. Philadelphia. For an excellent discussion of the politics of playing Indian, see Deloria 1998: 95–97, and for playing Sambo, see Lott 1993:1–12.

2. Peyote Hearings Before the Subcommittee of the Committee on Indian Affairs regarding House Resolution 2614, February 21, 1918, House Committee of Indian Affairs. Subcommittee Chaired by John N. Tillman, Representing Arkansas Third District [hereafter cited as PH].

3. Luke Eric Lassiter, who has collaborated with Kiowa writers and musicians for years, reminds me that many members of the Kiowa speak highly of Mooney and deeply appreciate his support and advocacy, which complicates Mooney's position even more because he was sincerely fighting for the best interest of the people with whom he worked. See Lassiter 1998:47 and Lassiter 2005a:32–33.

4. For a sophisticated and helpful discussion about how Boas's concept of culture was different from W. E. B. DuBois's notion of race, see Evans 2005:152–89.

5. Several scholars offer detailed analyses of this complicated approach. See Platt 1991, J. Holloway 2002, and Gaines 2005.

6. F. Boas to D. S. Andron, 10/26/1933. Professional Correspondence of Franz Boas, American Philosophical Society Library. Philadelphia.

(1) Research, Reform, and Racial Uplift

1. The story I used as an epigraph (Bacon and Parsons 1922:251) was written by Andrew W. C. Bassette, who, according to Waters (1983:105), was a member of the class of 1903.

2. He succeeded in having the indigenous Hawaiians build much of the island's infrastructure, although they probably engaged in various forms of resistance, as Mary Armstrong suggests: "The natives were awkward and very destructive,

breaking their tools and ox-carts and always relying upon their 'kumu' to repair them" (Armstrong 1887:21).

3. Richard Armstrong to C. Armstrong, 10/06/1844, Personal Memories and Letters of S. C. Armstrong, Compiled by Helen Ludlow. Williams College Archives and Special Collections. Williamstown, Mass.

4. Richard Armstrong to R. C. Armstrong, 02/18/1844. Richard Armstrong Papers, Manuscript Division, Library of Congress. Washington.

5. Samuel Chapman Armstrong to Archibald Hopkins, 12/08/1862. Personal Memories and Letters of S. C. Armstrong, Compiled by Helen Ludlow. Williams College Archives and Special Collections. Williamstown, Mass.

6. Like many of the letters to the editor in the *Southern Workman*, some of these are signed, some are initialed, and some are anonymous. For these letters addressing the papers on conjuring, I note them all under the editorship of Armstrong because he clearly chose which submissions to print and which to respond to.

7. William Wells Newell to Franz Boas, 03/26/1889. Professional Correspondence of Franz Boas, American Philosophical Society Library. Philadelphia.

8. William Wells Newell to Franz Boas, 12/10/1890. Professional Correspondence of Franz Boas, American Philosophical Society Library. Philadelphia.

9. Curtis Hinsley offers a compelling analysis that connects Mary T. Hemenway's philanthropic support of Hampton and Tuskegee to her support of ethnology and archaeology, which is not intuitive on the surface but is explained well by Hinsley, who links it to her own sense of loss nationally, spiritually, and personally as a result of the Civil War (Hinsley 2002:18).

10. Erica Brady in *A Spiral Way: How the Phonograph Changed History* (1999) provides a detailed explanation of the complex roles the phonograph played in developing ethnography and folklore around the beginning of the twentieth century.

11. William Wells Newell to Franz Boas, 12/09/1898. Professional Correspondence of Franz Boas, American Philosophical Society Library. Philadelphia.

12. William Wells Newell to Franz Boas, 12/14/1898. Professional Correspondence of Franz Boas, American Philosophical Society Library. Philadelphia.

13. William Wells Newell to Franz Boas 12/16/1898. Professional Correspondence of Franz Boas, American Philosophical Society Library. Philadelphia.

14. Alice M. Bacon to William Wells Newell, carbon copy to Franz Boas, 12/16/1898. Professional Correspondence of Franz Boas, American Philosophical Society Library. Philadelphia. Davis's paper was quickly published in the *Southern Workman* (Davis 1899).

15. William Wells Newell to Franz Boas, 2/21/1899. Professional Correspondence of Franz Boas, American Philosophical Society Library. Philadelphia.

16. William Wells Newell to Franz Boas, 3/08/1899. Professional Correspondence of Franz Boas, American Philosophical Society Library. Philadelphia.

17. The HFS was not the first group of nineteenth-century black Americans to find anthropology conducive to their progressive and explicitly modernist efforts

for racial uplift. For example, Frederick Douglass wrote *The Claims of the Negro Ethnologically Considered* in 1854, and in 1879 Martin Delany put forth *Principia of Ethnology: The Origin of Races and Color, with an Archeological Compendium of Ethiopian and Egyptian Civilization, from Years of Careful Examination and Enquiry.*

(2) Fabricating the Authentic and the Politics of the Real

1. Gertrude Bonnin to R. H. Pratt, 01/29/1919. Richard Henry Pratt Papers, Yale Collection of Western Americana, Beinecke Rare Book and Manuscript Library. WA MSS S-1174, series 1, box 1, folder 35.

2. T. J. Davis to Rev. Bruce Kinney, 11/18/1918. Richard Henry Pratt Papers, Yale Collection of Western Americana, Beinecke Rare Book and Manuscript Library. WA MSS S-1174, series 1, box 1, folder 35.

3. Zitkala-Ša to Carlos Montezuma, 09/04/1901. Carlos Montezuma Papers, Division of Archives and Manuscripts, State Historical Society of Wisconsin, Madison.

4. The original appropriation and authorization was part of the Sundry Civil Appropriation Bill of March 3, 1879. 59 H.R. 6140; 45 Cong. 3 Sess. H2361. Originally, it was called Bureau of Ethnology, but in 1894 the name was changed to Bureau of American Ethnology.

5. Powell took scores of pictures that were deposited at the Library of Congress. Or, as he noted, "Entered according to Act of Congress, in the year 1874, by J. W. Powell, in the Office of the Librarian of Congress at Washington." A stunning collection of these images is available at www.memory.loc.gov.

6. Thomas W. Kavanagh (2003), a curator at the William Hammond Mather Museum at Indiana University, has documented how Mooney edited, deleted, doctored, and added elements to the images in *Ghost Dance Religion and the Sioux Outbreak.* Available on Kavanagh's Web page at Indiana University. Mooney was a technological pioneer and brought cameras and sound recorders into the field. He made twelve recordings for the E. Berliner's Gramophone Company in July 1894. According to René Bache, however, "the Bureau of Ethnology sent Mr. James Mooney" to the offices of Berliner, a leader in recording industry technology. Mooney actually recorded the Ghost Dance songs not on the plains, but in a recording studio in Washington, D.C., "for the purpose of making permanent records of the songs of the famous ghost dance, popular among the Sioux Indians and certain other of our aborigines. Mr. Mooney has spent years among these savages, living their life and learning their songs. These chants of a dying people, which have historical value, he sang into the gramophone, and the records are now preserved in a safe at the Smithsonian Institution" (Bache 1895:424). The Library of Congress, in the catalog records of these recordings, notes that the "performance is probably by Mooney and not by authentic Native Americans.

Bibliographic information lists performers as Charles and James Mooney, but no data has been found to verify the existence of Charles." The following is an excerpt from the Library of Congress Catalog listing Mooney's Ghost Dance songs:

1. Arapaho No. 52. Ghost dance
2. Caddo No. 2. Ghost dance
3. Kiowa No. 12. Ghost dance
4. Arapaho No. 1. Ghost dance
5. Arapaho No. 73. Ghost dance
6. Caddo No. 15. Ghost song
7. Comanche No. 1. Ghost dance
8. Arapaho No. 9, 28. Ghost dance
9. Arapaho No. 44, 45. Ghost dance
10. Kiowa. Mescal song. Daylight song
11. Paiute. Gambling song; Arapaho No. 67. Ghost dance
12. Kiowa No. 15. Ghost song; Caddo No. 12. Ghost song
MEDIUM 12 sound tapes: analog, 10 in., CALL NUMBER LWO 8861
REPOSITORY

Library of Congress. Motion Picture, Broadcasting and Recorded Sound Division. Washington, D.C. 20540 USA.

7. Instead of science, Mooney turned to literature and used the popular stories of Joel Chandler Harris, whose framing of the fictional and avuncular "Remus" served to shore up an idyllic memory of the plantation South, while lynching and mob violence tore at the seams of the South during the years preceding *Plessy v. Ferguson* (1896). Mooney could have just been following the lead of J. W. Powell. Powell questioned the perspective of Joel Chandler Harris who, like Samuel Chapman Armstrong and Alice Bacon, comfortably identified an African provenance for these stories. Brad Evans, in his chapter "Circulating Culture: Reading the Harris-Powell Folklore Debate," details this tug of war over whether or not Negroes "influence" American Indian culture (Evans 2005:51–81). It is interesting that Mooney chose Joel Chandler Harris, whose own fabrication of an ideal type helped to authenticate minstrelsy. Harris's popular stories, especially in the South, were serialized in the *Atlanta Constitution* and *Century Magazine*. *Uncle Remus* was a "Book of the Month" for *Atlantic Monthly*. Many editions were printed and circulated widely; it is quite possible that the story that struck Mooney as identical to Harris's rendition was from *Uncle Remus* directly. Mooney did not compare the Cherokee stories he recorded to the stories or collections of the HFS or to the many reports of Negro folklore published in the JAF during the same years he was publishing in it (Ritterhouse 2003:585–600; Harris 1883, 1880; *Atlantic Monthly* 1881:304; Lott 1993:31; Vest 2000:36; Dundes 1990:114–25; F. Utley 1974:5–27; McLoughlin 1984:253–60). Harris's stories did shine a spotlight on Negro folklore during the 1890s, which forced the AFS to address the obvious parallels between Indian and Negro tales. A bit of a debate ensued within the journal, and Mooney weighed in decidedly on the side that the stories diffused in one direction, from

the Indians to Negroes (Boas 1891a; Gerber 1893; Mason 1891). In his article about Cherokee myths in the *JAF*, Mooney conceded that many "resemble the Uncle Remus stories" but immediately countered, "which I hope yet to prove are of Indian origin" (1888:106).

8. Obviously, this is a complicated history, and many people, including Mooney, wrote extensively about the various details. I can offer only some facts and dates regarding this tragic chapter in American history; for a more detailed account, see Coleman 2000; Harriman 2000; DeMallie 1995:327–42; Utley 1963; Kehoe 1989; Mooney 1896:843–94.

9. In an interesting chapter entitled "The Cherokee Ghost Dance Movement of 1811–1813," William G. McLoughlin takes Mooney to task for calling a Cherokee religious revival in 1811–13 a "Ghost Dance Movement" (McLoughlin 1984:111–52). Scholars still seriously engage the content of Mooney's writing in a way that most scholars today do not engage the content of Mooney's peers at the bureau.

10. The total population of the United States was around sixty-eight million in 1893, and regardless of how many people got counted twice a rather large percentage of the overall population was directly influenced by the fair.

11. Boas reported and exhibited not only the anthropometric measurements of particular races, but also the measurements of "people of the same race living under different conditions." He was trying to demonstrate to the public that the environment plays an important role in the actual bodily form of so-called racial types (Boas 1893:609). He put forward this important thesis in his influential book *Changes in Bodily Forms of Descendants of Immigrants* (1912). Also see Cole 1999:152–61.

12. Franz Boas worked closely with George Hunt, his Kwakiutl collaborator, to invite fifteen adults and two children. "The visiting Kwakiutl were housed temporarily in three small rooms in the stock pavilion, with mattresses, bed clothing, chairs, and two stoves . . . until they moved into one of the traditional beam-and-plank houses on the ethnological grounds" (Cole 1999:155).

13. Joy Kasson notes, however, that the American Indians who performed in Buffalo Bill's Wild West were encouraged to be accessible and wear their costumes offstage to function as a walking advertisement for the show, and also "to endorse the Wild West's claims to authenticity and its view of history" (Kasson 2001:162). I realize that the World's Fair of 1893 is well-trod terrain, and several scholars have explored the agency and the production of images of these performers within these so-called native habitations. No one, however, has explicitly compared the work these images did when sandwiched between the production of menial images of Negroes and the opulence of the White City (Moses 1991, 1999; Rydell 1984; Ellis 2003:55–99; Parezo and Troutman 2001:3–43; Bank 2002). My view of production and consumption here is influenced by Curtis Hinsley, who offers a compelling argument that "at Chicago in 1893, public curiosity about other peoples, mediated by the terms of the market place, produced an early form of touristic consumption" (1991:363). Parezo and Troutman look specifically at similar exhibits at the Louisiana Purchase Exposition of 1904 in St. Louis and explain

that "native peoples formed their own opinions of the fairgoers they met and controlled and manipulated their own experience at the fair as best they could. They retained control over the manufacture and marketing of their individual works of art, and tried, sometimes successfully, sometimes not, to limit and bound the taking of photographs and the arenas in which the touristic encounters took place" (Parezo and Troutman 2001:7). For a comprehensive view of anthropology at the 1904 World's Fair, see Parezo and Fowler (2007). Clyde Ellis also makes a critical point that, despite the fabrication of the exotic, many of these American Indians were performing dances that the federal government prohibited. Ellis notes that this production was far from naked exploitation, and indeed many American Indians viewed it as subversive because they were given permission to perform what so many others wanted to destroy because not only agents of the BIA, but missionaries, local citizens, reformers, and philanthropists alike joined the chorus and placed their combined influence behind policies designed to destroy every ritual, ceremony, and dance that reinforced Indianness and therefore stood in opposition to federal aims (Ellis 2003:57).

14. Of course one of Cody's agents could have simply said to these performers, "Cody and Burke will pay you, Putnam won't." The early ethnomusicologist John C. Fillmore took the opportunity to study the tones and rhythms of exotic others exhibited at the fair. He made no distinction between "commercial" and "ethnological" and reported his research on the various "villages" along the midway at the International Congress of Anthropology. He was particularly struck by the "complicated rhythms" of the "Dahomey village" and noted how he "watched them for hours" (Fillmore 1894:174). In addition, Mary Hemenway underwrote the research of Benjamin Gilman, who made wax cylinder recordings of the music performed by those who made up the various contingents of international performers who lived and worked on the midway (Mark 1988:237).

15. Barnum was extending an even longer tradition of exhibiting exotic people in museums, zoos, and theaters (Kirshenblatt-Gimblett 1991).

16. See Jacknis 1985 and Hinsley 1991.

17. Carl Hagenbeck was at the Chicago World's Fair, but his exhibit was much more of a circus, with animals performing tricks, etc. At the Louisiana Purchase Exposition in 1904, however, Carl Hagenbeck's Zoological Paradise and Animal Circus combined displaying animals in their native habitats and a circus element (Bancroft 1894:844; St. Louis Public Library, exhibits Web page). It was these living ethnological exhibits that Hagenbeck found so profitable, the science societies found so educational, and the German people found so entertaining, and they animated the so-called Hagenbeck revolution (Rothfels 2002:8). Moreover, it was Boas's rendition of the life group in 1893, both static and dynamic, that would form the basis of the familiar life-group diorama of indigenous people that still dominates the depiction of "little brown people" in U.S. natural history museums. These dioramas remain popular and often uncritical testimonies and trophies to imperial expansion and a belief in the advance of civilization.

18. Franz Boas to Parents, 10/21/1893, in Cole 1999:156. Boas continued to be involved in bringing people from the field to New York to study. For example, Boas asked the Arctic explorer Robert Peary to bring him back "a middle aged Eskimo." In 1898, Peary brought Boas a whole family, who lived in the American Museum of Natural History but quickly died of tuberculosis (Thomas 2000:81).

19. Ida B. Wells and Frederick Douglass composed and edited a free pamphlet entitled *The Reason Why the Colored American is not in the World's Columbian Exposition* with an introduction written in German and French. This controversial pamphlet detailed the many achievements blacks had made in spite of the convict lease system, lynchings, and segregation statutes (Wells and Douglass 1999). Similarly, Simon Pokagon wrote a scathing critique of American progress and civilization entitled "The Red Man's Greeting." Printed on birch-bark paper, he sold many copies at the fair. In the pamphlet, Pokagon referred to whites as the "pale faces" who, like ravens, "were soon to pluck out our eyes and the eyes of our children." Challenging the notion of progress, Pokagon documented the disease and environmental degradation wrought by the "cyclone of civilization" (2001:31–32).

20. T. J. Morgan to Harriet Lucas, 03/30/1892. Yale University Beinecke Rare Book and Manuscript Library, Yale Collection of Western Americana, WA MSS S-1174, series 1, box 2, folder 46.

21. Perhaps the seeds were sown during the 1893 World's Fair for an interpretation of practices that would blossom into the very idea of particular cultures, which would later inform the Wheeler-Howard Act of 1934. Nancy Scheper-Hughes somberly reminds anthropologists how "modern anthropology was built up in the face of colonial and post-colonial genocides, ethnocides, population die-outs, and other forms of mass destruction visited on non-western peoples whose lives, suffering and deaths provide the raw material for much of our work" (Scheper-Hughes 2001:12).

22. Two very good books explore these contested issues from somewhat different approaches. They are Steven Conn's excellent work *History's Shadow: Native Americans and Historical Consciousness in the Nineteenth Century* (2004) and Alan Trachtenberg's engaging *Shades of Hiawatha: Staging Indians, Making Americans, 1880–1930* (2004). Both authors carefully and thoroughly document the role American Indian images and history have played in shaping ideas of the American and America.

23. Like many of the American Indian leaders, George Sword combined various offices of leadership: he became a renowned *wicasa wakan* and *pejuta wicasa* (spiritual leader and spiritual healer) as well as a diplomat and war hero. He became a major and the commander of agency police, served as an ordained deacon in the Episcopal Church, and eventually served as a judge on the reservation's Court of Indian Offenses. However, he is also known for working closely with James R. Walker, a government doctor who tirelessly compiled traditional Oglala beliefs and practices (Parks and DeMallie 1992). Around 1908, Ella Deloria

became one of George Sword's translators, translating narratives that he had written during the 1890s (Weatherford 1991:269).

24. In a letter dated January 15, 1891, and sent to General Colby, "Commander of Nebraska State Troops," Sickels offered him what she considered important intelligence, informing him that, "This has been defeated in two ways: The hostile Ogalallas [*sic*] have been detected and outwitted. The confidence of the progressive Indians has been obtained and the plots of their real enemies (the hostiles), have been shown to them and they have emphatically placed themselves on the side of the government. The soldiers have been so managed and placed that the friendlies have been defended and supported while all felt the hopelessness of an attack" (Colby 1892:181). Brigadier General L. W. Colby explained that Sickels "probably knows as much as any person about the different factions and feuds existing among the Indians" of Pine Ridge (1892:185). Fiercely protective of the industrial school she founded and deeply committed to the civilizing mission, Sickels actually fueled tensions between two important Oglala leaders, Chief Little Wound and Chief Red Cloud, during the confusion that followed the massacre.

(3) Race, Relevance, and Daniel G. Brinton's Ill-Fated Bid for Prominence

1. "From Appleton's Cyclopaedia of American Biography, 1887, vol. 1," Culin Archival Collection [9.1.0001], Brooklyn Museum Libraries and Archives, Brooklyn.

2. D. G. Brinton to Sara Stevenson, 01/30/1893, Director's Office Records, Dept. of A&P—Pres. C. Tower, 1892–1894, Brinton, American Section Folder, the University of Pennsylvania Museum of Archaeology and Anthropology Archives. Philadelphia.

3. Auguste Comte devised a scheme of social evolution based on both cooperation and competition, and the scientist played one of the most important roles in this progressive movement. From Comte's perspective, people have an instinct to understand their world and control it. In this process of gaining a better understanding, people pass from a theological understanding through a metaphysical understanding and finally reach a scientific way of thinking. One of the specific roles that Comte identified for the scientific thinker was identifying the "chain of successive transformations [of] the human race." "Starting from a condition barely superior to that of a society of great apes," Comte argued, scientists should help find out how the human race "has been gradually led up to the present stage of European civilization" (1911[1877]:237–38).

4. Brinton envisioned, for example, that the mind of man was "everywhere different yet everywhere the same," concluding that the condition of savages was the product of "the same great natural forces [that] are eternally at work, above, around and beneath us, producing similar results in matter, educing like conceptions in mind" (1859:126). Yet the "peninsular tribes of the sixteenth century," he

explained, were sparsely "peopled by a barbarous and quarrelsome race of savages, rent asunder into manifold petty clans, with little peaceful leisure wherein
to better their condition, wasting their lives in aimless and unending internecine
war" (1859:111).

5. Almost forty years later, even after distilling Darwin's theories, Brinton hung
onto virtually the same admixture of ideas: "We must accept ethnic characteristics as originally acquired traits, slowly strengthened by repetition and natural
selection in some more plastic stage of the life of the species than the present, and
hence impressed indelibly upon its members" (1898:275).

6. "A Circular to the Resident Members of the American Philosophical Society," Brinton Biography File, the University of Pennsylvania Museum of Archaeology and Anthropology Archives. Philadelphia.

7. In a review of Regna Darnell's biography of Brinton, Curtis Hinsley noted,
"The key to understanding Brinton lies in his self-definition as an 'Americanist.'" He questioned the way Darnell labeled Brinton simply as an anthropologist
(Hinsley 1989:775). The evidence is clear that Brinton was committed to advancing anthropology as a science that would identify and explain problems for American society. However, he had a passion and an unusual skill for classifying and
analyzing American languages. He knew that this alone would not help advance
the field of anthropology and elevate him as a leading intellectual. Brinton was
quite fluid with regard to his identities as an Americanist, an anthropologist, and
a general scientist. I think the key to understanding Brinton is how flexible he
was with his scholastic identities. When he was on Independence Mall he was
the resident Americanist at the APS. When he crossed the Schuylkill River to the
University of Pennsylvania he embraced his role as an anthropologist, but on 13th
and Race streets he emerged as a great man of science to give popular lectures at
the ANSP.

8. William W. Newell to Franz Boas, 05/09/1890. Professional Correspondence
of Franz Boas, American Philosophical Society Library. Philadelphia.

9. D. G. Brinton to Franz Boas, 06/06/1887. Professional Correspondence of
Franz Boas, American Philosophical Society Library. Philadelphia.

10. William Pepper to D. G. Brinton, 04/25/1892, Director's Office Records,
Dept. of A&P—Pres. C. Tower, 1892–1894, Brinton, American Section Folder.
University of Pennsylvania Museum of Archaeology and Anthropology Archives.
Philadelphia.

11. C. Tower, 1895, Report from the President of the Board of Managers of
the Department of Archaeology and Paleontology to the Board of Trustees of
the University of Pennsylvania, Director's Office Records, Dept. of A&P—Pres.
C. Tower, 1892–1894, Brinton, American Section Folder. University of Pennsylvania Museum of Archaeology and Anthropology Archives. Philadelphia.

12. C. Howard Colket to Stewart Culin, 03/06/1894, Director's Office Records,
Dept. of A&P—Pres. C. Tower, 1892–1894, Brinton, American Section Folder.
University of Pennsylvania Museum of Archaeology and Anthropology Archives.
Philadelphia.

13. D. G. Brinton to Sara Stevenson, 07/11/1894, Director's Office Records, Dept. of A&P—Pres. C. Tower, 1892–1894, Brinton, American Section Folder. University of Pennsylvania Museum of Archaeology and Anthropology Archives. Philadelphia.

14. D. G. Brinton to Sara Stevenson, 07/08/1894, Director's Office Records, Dept. of A&P—Pres. C. Tower, 1892–1894, Brinton, American Section Folder. University of Pennsylvania Museum of Archaeology and Anthropology Archives. Philadelphia.

15. Frederic Ward Putnam was the next person appointed professor of anthropology at Harvard University in 1887.

16. D. G. Brinton to Rev. Dr. M.C.L.[??]K., Committee on Instruction, April 24, 1884, Collection 567, ANSP Correspondence. Ewell Sale Stewart Library, Academy of Natural Sciences of Philadelphia.

17. D. G. Brinton to Angelo Heilprin, 09/06/1889, Collection 567, ANSP Correspondence. Ewell Sale Stewart Library, Academy of Natural Sciences of Philadelphia.

18. D. G. Brinton to Angelo Heilprin, 12/17/1890, Collection 567, ANSP Correspondence. Ewell Sale Stewart Library, Academy of Natural Sciences of Philadelphia.

19. D. G. Brinton to Franz Boas, 12/30/1888, Professional Correspondence of Franz Boas, American Philosophical Society Library. Philadelphia.

20. If the gendered form of address was not specified by the student who signed the roll, Brinton dutifully marked "Miss." or "Mrs." in the margin. See "List of Lectures and Lecturers 1881–1898," Collection 289D, ANSP Education. Ewell Sale Stewart Library, Academy of Natural Sciences of Philadelphia.

21. D. G. Brinton to Angelo Heilprin, n.d., Collection 567, ANSP Correspondence. Ewell Sale Stewart Library, Academy of Natural Sciences of Philadelphia.

22. For a detailed discussion of Brinton's ideas about the racial stratigraphy within the white race, see Patterson's and Spencer's (1994) excellent discussion of "buffer races."

23. "Crane, Agnes. 1890. *Races and Peoples*. Brighton Herald, October 11, 1890," Culin Archival Collection [9.1.0002], Brooklyn Museum Libraries and Archives. Brooklyn.

24. The one difference between these sentences was that in the *JAF* Boas used "This" and in *Science* he used "His."

25. It was the data generated from this study that Corey Sparks and Richard Jantz used to go head to head with Clarence Gravlee, Russell Bernard, and William Leonard in dueling reanalyses (Sparks and Jantz 2002; Gravlee, Bernard, and Leonard 2003).

26. F. Boas to Parents 4/19/1891 (Cole 1999:143). Although Boas's professional correspondence is somewhat incomplete during this period of his life, there is no evidence the so-called caliper question had any impact on his research, writing, or day-to-day activities. There is no mention in his professional correspondence of

this affair or of anything related to his public school research or the issues raised by the *Telegram*. Quite to the contrary, during the weeks of this local scandal he corresponded with many people and neither he nor the people who wrote to him mentioned the attention he received in the press.

27. F. Boas to W. W. Newell, 5/12/1890. Franz Boas Professional Correspondence, American Philosophical Society Library. Philadelphia.

28. Although Brinton was not cited in *Plessy*, his book *Races and Peoples* was cited as an authority as late as 1925 in *United States v. Cartozian*, 6F 2d 919 (1925), which was a District of Columbia appellate case about who was considered a "free white" with regard to naturalization laws. Charles A. Lofgren in *The Plessy Case: A Legal-Historical Interpretation* (1988) makes a compelling argument that Brinton influenced the legal-racial matrix of the 1890s, from which the case emerged (Lofgren 1987:104–5).

29. There is some debate about how much social Darwinism and Lamarckism informed this style of jurisprudence (Ely 1995:57–82; Lofgren 1987:102–4). I have found evidence to suggest, however, that certain anthropologists who advanced ideas of racial inferiority interacted with the justices who decided *Plessy*. In 1893, a member of the Anthropological Society of Washington, Robert H. Lamborn, offered cash prizes to the two anthropologists who could write the "clearest statements of the *elements* that go to make up the most useful citizen of the United States" (emphasis added). Because Brinton was the expert on the "elements" of ethnography, he was selected as one of the judges to decide the winners. The prize committee that deliberated upon the specific ethnological elements of useful U.S. citizens comprised Brinton, Daniel Gilman (president of Johns Hopkins University), Adlai E. Stevenson (vice president of the United States under Grover Cleveland), and Melville W. Fuller (chief justice of the U.S. Supreme Court, who concurred with *Plessy*) (Lamb 1906:573–74). Circles of power in Washington during the 1890s were tight knit and intimate, scientists and explorers serving as central figures within informal networks of power. A particularly vibrant hub of social activity among the nation's power elite was the Cosmos Club. John Wesley Powell was the founder and inspiration of this influential club, which sought to cultivate conversation among influential men in the arts, sciences, and politics. Associate Justice Henry Billings Brown, the author of *Plessy*, and Associate Justice Oliver Wendell Holmes both belonged to the Cosmos Club, where people from the Anthropological Society of Washington played billiards with members of the U.S. Senate at their clubhouse at the Dolley Madison House on Lafayette Square. Ely makes the argument that the justices were not in contact with people who were articulating these scientific ideas of racial hierarchy, but the Cosmos Club at that time was dominated by scientists who explicitly articulated these ideas (Cosmos Club 1968:14, 56; Washburn 1978:15–25).

30. Helen Abbott Michael to Stewart Culin, 12/27/1899, Culin Archival Collection [9.1.0003], Brooklyn Museum Libraries and Archives. Brooklyn. For biographical information about Helen Abbott Michael, see Michael (1907:3–107).

31. Brinton was an intimate friend of Walt Whitman and his confidant and biographer Horace L. Traubel. In volume 9 of Traubel's *With Walt Whitman in Camden* (1996), Traubel includes some charming and personal remembrances of Brinton within the intellectual milieu of the Delaware Valley.

32. Each time someone dials 703-528-1902 to reach the American Anthropological Association in Arlington, Virginia, it is a wink to the culmination, in 1902, of contentious processes that finally led to a sustainable national organization.

33. Of course, Boas was an intellectual in the public interest and was often involved in public affairs. However, he actively engaged in issues outside the academy only after 1905, once he had a firm institutional foundation. Although Columbia promoted Boas from lecturer to professor in 1898, he joined Columbia's faculty full time in 1905, when he left the American Museum of Natural History. Faculty members at colleges in the early twentieth century did not have the security of tenure, which was first proposed in 1925 when representatives of the American Association of University Professors (founded in 1919) and of the Association of American Colleges outlined a set of guidelines for Academic Freedom and Tenure. In 1940, these organizations agreed upon a restatement of principles set forth earlier. The restatement, widely known as *The 1940 Statement of Principles on Academic Freedom and Tenure*, standardized guidelines and protocols for procedures to ensure academic freedom and grant tenure across universities and colleges.

(4) The Cult of Franz Boas

1. The Internet is full of spoof or parody sites, like www.whitehouse.com, which for years was a pornography site. During 2005, Google page-ranked it number five when "white house" was queried. This King site, hosted by Stormfront, seems qualitatively more pernicious to me because it explicitly targets students in secondary school.

2. Maslow to Marshal, 04/28/1947, NAACP Papers, group II, box 206, file "Sweatt v. Painter Correspondence," Manuscript Division, Library of Congress, Washington; Marshal to Hastie, 04/03/1947, NAACP Papers, group II, box 205, file "Sweatt v. Painter Correspondence," Manuscript Division, Library of Congress, Washington.

3. William H. Tucker, John P. Jackson Jr., and Andrew Winton are each superb intellectual historians who have published important work outlining the relationships between the Pioneer Fund and the IAAEE. Together, they have outlined how members of these organizations supported Southern segregation, Putnam's popularity, and the perpetuation of the Boas conspiracy. Their collective research on the history of science has really enabled me, in writing this chapter, to focus specifically on the history of anthropology.

4. For a review of the scientific reviews, see Jackson (2001:259–62).

5. Charles Ellwood notes the high sales volume as well as comments on the publisher's marketing practices (Ellwood 1906:570).

6. Mss. Coll. 30. William S. Willis Papers, American Philosophical Society, folder "Research Notes" Franz Boas—Boas Goes to Atlanta.

7. F. Boas to W. E. B. Du Bois 10/11/1905, Franz Boas Professional Correspondence, American Philosophical Association, Philadelphia.

8. F. Boas to P. Baerwals 02/12/1933, Franz Boas Professional Correspondence, American Philosophical Association, Philadelphia.

Works Cited

Manuscript Sources

Boston Public Library, Central Library Newspaper Room. Boston.
Carlos Montezuma Papers, Division of Archives and Manuscripts, State
  Historical Society of Wisconsin. Madison.
Collection 567, ANSP Correspondence. Ewell Sale Stewart Library, Academy of
  Natural Sciences of Philadelphia.
Culin Archival Collection, Brooklyn Museum Libraries and Archives. Brooklyn.
Director's Office Records, University of Pennsylvania Museum of Archaeology
  and Anthropology Archives. Philadelphia.
Elsie Clews Parsons Papers, Collection 29, American Philosophical Society
  Library. Philadelphia.
Personal Memories and Letters of S. C. Armstrong, Compiled by Helen Ludlow.
  Williams College Archives and Special Collections. Williamstown, Mass.
Professional Correspondence of Franz Boas, American Philosophical Society
  Library. Philadelphia.
Richard Armstrong Papers, Manuscript Division, Library of Congress.
  Washington.
Richard Henry Pratt Papers, Yale Collection of Western Americana, Beinecke
  Rare Book and Manuscript Library. New Haven.
Worcester Daily Telegram. Worcester, Mass.: Telegram Newspaper Co.,
  1888–1989.

Works Cited

Abu-Lughod, Lila. 1991. "Writing Against Culture." *Recapturing Anthropology*,
  edited by Richard Fox, 137–62. Santa Fe: School of American Research
  Press.
Adams, David W. 1995. *Education for Extinction: American Indians and the
  Boarding School Experience, 1875–1928*. Lawrence: University Press of
  Kansas.

Adams, William Y. 1998. *The Philosophical Roots of Anthropology*. Stanford,
    Calif.: CSLI Publications.
Alexander, Elizabeth. 1997. "'We Must Be about Our Father's Business': Anna
    Julia Cooper and the In-Corporation of the Nineteenth-Century African-
    American Woman Intellectual." *In Her Own Voice: Nineteenth-Century
    American Women Essayists*, edited by Sherry L. Linkon, 61–80. New York:
    Garland.
Alland, Alexander, Jr. 2002. *Race in Mind: Race, IQ, and Other Racisms*. New
    York: Palgrave Macmillan.
American Anthropologist. 1906. "Recent Progress in American Anthropology:
    A Review of the Activities of Institutions and Individuals from 1902 to 1906."
    American Anthropologist 8(3):441–554.
Anderson, Eric, and Alfred A. Moss Jr. 1999. *Dangerous Donations: Northern
    Philanthropy and Southern Black Education, 1902–1930*. Columbia: University
    of Missouri Press.
Anderson, Warwick. 2006. *Colonial Pathologies: American Tropical Medicine,
    Race, and Hygiene in the Philippines*. Durham: Duke University Press.
Anti-Defamation League. 2000. "Poisoning the Web: Hatred Online Poisoning
    the Web: Hatred Online, Internet Bigotry, Extremism and Violence."
    Electronic document, http://www.adl.org/poisoning_web/introduction.asp,
    accessed April 8, 2008.
Appadurai, Arjun. 1988. "Putting Hierarchy in Its Place." *Cultural Anthropology*
    3(1):36–49.
Armstrong, Mary F. M. 1887. *Richard Armstrong: America, Hawaii*. Hampton,
    Va.: Normal School Press Print.
Armstrong, Mary F. M., and Helen W. Ludlow. 1874. *Hampton and Its Students
    with Fifty Cabin and Plantation Songs*. New York: G. P. Putnam and Sons.
Armstrong, Samuel C. 1878. "Editorials about Papers on Conjuring." *Southern
    Workman* 7(4):26–35.
———. 1909. "From the Beginning." *Memories of Old Hampton: The Armstrong
    League of Hampton Workers*, 1–15. Hampton, Va.: Hampton Institute Press.
Associated Negro Press. 1943. "Dr. Franz Boas Dead." *Pittsburgh Courier*, January
    2:24.
Atlantic Monthly. 1881. "Books of the Month." *Atlantic Monthly* 47(280):
    300–304.
Bache, René. 1895. "Wonders of the Gramophone." *Current Literature* 18(5):
    422–24.
Bacon, Alice M. 1890. "Silhouettes." *Southern Workman* 19(11):124–25.
———. 1891. *Japanese Girls and Women*. Boston: Houghton Mifflin.
———. 1893. "Folk-Lore and Ethnology." *Southern Workman* 22(12):179–81.
———. 1895a. "Folk Lore and Ethnology: Conjuring and Conjure-Doctors."
    Southern Workman 24(11):193–94.
———. 1895b. "Folk Lore and Ethnology: Conjuring and Conjure-Doctors."
    Southern Workman 24(12):209–11.

———. 1898. "Work and Methods of the Hampton Folk-Lore Society." *Journal of American Folk-Lore* 11(40):17–21.

———. 1909. "A Child's Impressions of Early Hampton." *Memories of Old Hampton: The Armstrong League of Hampton Workers*, 85–86. Hampton, Va.: Hampton Institute Press.

Bacon, Alice M., and Elsie C. Parsons. 1922. "Folk-Lore from Elizabeth City County, Virginia." *Journal of American Folk-Lore* 35:250–327.

Baker, Lee D. 1994. "Location of Franz Boas within the African-American Struggle." *Critique of Anthropology* 14(2):199–217.

———. 1996. "Review of *Rethinking Race: Franz Boas and His Contemporaries*." *American Journal of Sociology* 102:909–10.

———. 1998. *From Savage to Negro: Anthropology and the Construction of Race, 1896–1954*. Berkeley: University of California Press.

———. 2002. "Frederic Ward Putnam." *Celebrating a Century of the American Anthropological Association: Presidential Portraits*, edited by Regna Darnell and Frederick Gleach, 5–9. Lincoln: University of Nebraska Press.

———. 2004. "Franz Boas Out of the Ivory Tower." *Anthropological Theory* 4(1):29–51.

Baltimore Sun. 1897. "Queer Traditions: Popular Ideas Concerning Hell, Earth and Heaven Told by Folk-Lore Collectors." *Baltimore Sun*, December 30:8.

Bancroft, Hurbert H. 1894. *The Book of the Fair: An Historical and Descriptive Presentation of the World's Science, Art, and Industry, As Viewed Through the Columbian Exposition*. Chicago: Bancroft.

Bank, Rosemarie K. 2002. "Representing History: Performing the Columbian Exposition." *Theater Journal* 54(4):589–607.

Banks, Frank D. 1894. "Plantation Courtship." *Journal of American Folk-Lore* 7(25):147–49.

Barkan, Elazar. 1988. "Mobilizing Scientists against Nazi Racism, 1933–1939." *Bones, Bodies, Behavior*, edited by George Stocking, 180–205. Madison: University of Wisconsin Press.

Barkun, Michael. 2003. *A Culture of Conspiracy: Apocalyptic Visions in Contemporary America*. Berkeley: University of California Press.

Beals, Melba P. 1994. *Warriors Don't Cry: A Searing Memoir of the Battle to Integrate Little Rock's Central High School*. New York: Washington Square Books.

Beardsley, Edward H. 1973. "The American Scientist as Social Activist: Franz Boas, Burt G. Wilder, and the Cause of Racial Justice, 1900–1915." *Isis* 64(1):50–65.

Bell, Michael J. 1973. "William W. Newell and American Folklore Scholarship." *Journal of the Folklore Institute* 10:7–21.

Bender, Thomas. 1993. *Intellect and Public Life: Essays on the Social History of Academic Intellectuals in the United States*. Baltimore: Johns Hopkins University Press.

Benedict, Ruth, and Gene Weltfish. 1943. *The Races of Mankind*. New York: Public Affairs Committee.

Bergstrom, Bill. 2002. "Race Has Major Effect on Skull Shape: Study. Findings Go Against Century-Old Belief, But Have No Relationship to Brain Size, Researchers Insist." *Ottawa Citizen*, November 1:A11.

Bernstein, David E. 1998. "Philip Sober Controlling Philip Drunk: *Buchanan v. Warley* in Historical Perspective." *Vanderbilt Law Review* 51(4):798–879.

Bernstein, Jay H. 2002. "First Recipients of Anthropological Doctorates in the United States, 1891–1930." *American Anthropologist* 104(2):551–64.

Beyer, C. K. 2007. "The Connection of Samuel Chapman Armstrong as Both Borrower and Architect of Education in Hawai'i." *History of Education Quarterly* 47(1):23–48.

Bilbo, Theodore G. 1947. *Take Your Choice, Separation or Mongrelization*. Poplarville, Miss.: Dream House Publishing.

Bishop, E. C. 1911. *Twenty-First Biennial Report of the State Superintendent of Public Instruction (1909–1911)*. Lincoln, Nebraska.

Blakey, Michael L. 1997. "The New York African Burial Ground Project: An Examination of Enslaved Lives, a Construction of Ancestral Ties." Paper presented at Sub-commission on Prevention of Discrimination and Protection of Minorities, Commission on Human Rights, United Nations. Delivered on August 19 at Palais des Nations, Geneva, Switzerland.

———. 1999. "Scientific Racism and the Biological Concept of Race." *Literature and Psychology* 45(1/2): 29–43.

Boas, Franz. 1887a. "The Occurrence of Similar Inventions in Areas Widely Apart." *Science* 9(224):485–86.

———. 1887b. "Museums of Ethnology and Their Classification." *Science* 9(228):587–89.

———. 1887c. "Poetry and Music of Some North American Tribes." *Science* 9(220):383–85.

———. 1889. "On Alternating Sounds." *American Anthropologist* 2(1):47–53.

———. 1891a. "Dissemination of Tales Among the Natives of North America." *Journal of American Folk-Lore* 4(12):13–20.

———. 1891b. "Review of *Races and Peoples*, by Daniel G. Brinton." *Journal of American Folk-Lore* 4(12):87–88.

———. 1893. "Ethnology at the Exposition." *Cosmopolitan* 15(9):607–9.

———. 1895. "Human Faculty as Determined by Race." *Proceedings of the American Association for the Advancement of Science* 43:301–27.

———. 1896a. The Limitations of the Comparative Method of Anthropology. *Science* 4: (103):901–9.

———. 1896b. "The Growth of Indian Mythologies." *Journal of American Folk-Lore* 9(32):1–11.

———. 1905. "The Negro and the Demands of Modern Life: Ethnic and Anatomical Considerations." *Charities: A Review of Local and General Philanthropy* 15(1):86–88.

————. 1907. "Some Principles of Museum Administration." *Science* 25(650): 921–33.

————. 1910. "The Real Race Problem." *Crisis Magazine* 1(5):22–25.

————. 1911a. "Introduction." *Handbook of American Indian Languages*, Bulletin 40, Bureau of American Ethnology, Smithsonian Institution, 1–85. Washington: Government Printing Office.

————. 1911b. *The Mind of Primitive Man*. New York: Macmillan.

————. 1912. *Changes in Bodily Forms of Descendants of Immigrants*. New York: Columbia University Press.

————. 1921. "The Problem of the American Negro." *Yale Quarterly Review* 10(2):384–95.

————. 1928. *Anthropology and Modern Life*. New York: Norton.

————. 1938 [1911]. *The Mind of Primitive Man*. New York: Macmillan.

————. 1945. *Race and Democratic Society*. New York: J. J. Austin.

————. 1978 [1935]. "Preface." *Mules and Men*, edited by Zora Hurston, x. Bloomington: Indiana University Press

Boas, Franz, et al. 1891. "Second Annual Meeting of the American Folk-Lore Society." *Journal of American Folk-Lore* 4(12):1–5.

Boas, Franz, and William H. Dall. 1887. "Museums of Ethnology and Their Classifications." *Science* 9(229):587–89.

Borofsky, Robert. 2000. "Public Anthropology: Where To? What Next?" *Anthropology News* 45(5):9–10.

Bourguignon, Erika 1996. "American Anthropology: A Personal View." *General Anthropology* 3(1):1, 7–9.

Bowditch, Henry P. 1877. *The Growth of Children*. Boston: A. J. Wright.

Brand, Chris. 2003. "The Great Social Anthropology Scam: Multiculturalism's Scandal-Ridden Academic Discipline." Electronic document, http://theoccidentalquarterly.com/archives/vo13no2/cb-boasa.html, accessed April 11, 2008.

Briggs, Charles. 2002. "Linguistic Magic Bullets in the Making of a Modernist Anthropology." *American Anthropologist* 104(2):481–98.

Brinton, Daniel G. 1859. *Notes on the Floridian Peninsula, Its Literary History, Indian Tribes and Antiquities*. Philadelphia: J. Sabin.

————. 1866a. "The Shawnees and Their Migrations." *Historical Magazine* 10:1–4.

————. 1866b. "Artificial Shell Depositions in the United States." *Annual Report of the Smithsonian Institution for the Year 1866*, 356–58. Washington: Smithsonian Institution.

————. 1866c. "Mound-Builders of the Mississippi." *Historical Magazine* 11:33–37.

————. 1890a. *Races and Peoples: Lectures on the Science of Ethnography*. New York: Hodges.

————. 1890b. *Essays of an Americanist*. Philadelphia: Porter and Coates.

————. 1891. *The American Race*. Philadelphia: David McKay.

———. 1892a. *Anthropology: As a Science and As a Branch of University Education in the United States*. Philadelphia: D. G. Brinton.

———. 1892b. "Address Delivered on Columbus Day, October 21, 1892 at the Library and Museum Building of the University of Pennsylvania, Philadelphia." Pamphlet 32 (572.A), American Philosophical Society.

———. 1896a. "The Relation of Race and Culture to Degenerations of the Reproductive Organs and Functions in Women." Reprinted from the *Medical News*, January 18:1–6.

———. 1896b. "The Aims of Anthropology." *Popular Science Monthly* 48:59–72.

———. 1898. "The Factors of Heredity and Environment in Man." *American Anthropologist* 11(9):271–77.

Brinton, Daniel G., and Livingston Farrand. 1902. *Basis of Social Relations*. New York: G. P. Putnam and Sons.

Brinton, Daniel G., and John W. Powell. 1892. "The Nomenclature and Teaching of Anthropology." *American Anthropologist* 5:263–71.

Bronner, Simon J. 1986. *American Folklore Studies*. Lawrence: University Press of Kansas.

Browman, David L. 2002. "The Peabody Museum, Frederic W. Putnam, and the Rise of U.S. Anthropology, 1866–1903." *American Anthropologist* 104(2): 508–19.

Brown, Elspeth H. 2005. "Racialising the Virile Body: Eadweard Muybridge's Locomotion Studies, 1883–1887." *Gender and History* 17(3):627–56.

Brownell, Herbert. 1957. "Text of 'Petition and Order on Faubus.'" *New York Times*, September 11:24.

Bunzl, Matti. 1996. "Franz Boas and the Humboldtian Tradition: From Volksgeist and Nationalcharakter to an Anthropological Concept of Culture." *History of Anthropology*, Vol. 8, *Volksgeist as Method and Ethic: Essays on Boasian Ethnography and the German Anthropological Tradition*, edited by George W. Stocking Jr., 17–78. Madison: University of Wisconsin Press.

———. 2004. "Boas, Foucault, and the 'Native Anthropologist': Notes toward a Neo-Boasian Anthropology." *American Anthropologist* 106(3):435–42.

Caffrey, Margaret M. 1989. *Ruth Benedict: Stranger in This Land*. Austin: University of Texas Press.

Calvin, Ira. 1945. *The Lost White Race*. Brookline, Mass.: Countway-White.

Camic, Charles, and Yu Xie. 1994. "The Statistical Turn in American Social Science: Columbia University, 1890 to 1915." *American Sociological Review* 59:773–805.

Carnegie, Andrew. 1889. "Wealth." *North American Review* 148(391):653–65.

Carter, Edward C. 1993. *"One Grand Pursuit": A Brief History of the American Philosophical Society's First 250 Years, 1743–1993*. Philadelphia: American Philosophical Society.

Caspari, Rachel. 2003. "From Types to Populations: A Century of Race, Physical Anthropology, and the American Anthropological Association." *American Anthropologist* 105(1):65–76.

Cattell, J. M., and Dean R. Brimhall. 1921. *American Men of Science: A Biographical Directory*. Garrison, N.Y.: Science Press.

Chamberlain, Alexander F. 1899. "In Memoriam: Daniel Garrison Brinton." *Journal of American Folklore* 12(46):215–25.

———. 1903. "Review of *Nineteenth Annual Report of the Bureau of American Ethnology to the Secretary of the Smithsonian Institution, 1897–98* by J. W. Powell." *American Anthropological Association* 5(2):336–45.

Cherokee Phoenix. 2002. "Anthropologist James Mooney." *Cherokee Phoenix and Indian Advocate* 26(4):58.

Cheyney, Edward P. 1940. *History of the University of Pennsylvania*. Philadelphia: University of Pennsylvania Press.

Churchill, Ward. 1997. *A Little Matter of Genocide: Holocaust and Denial in the Americas, 1492 to the Present*. San Francisco: City Lights Books.

Clifford, James. 1988. *The Predicament of Culture: Twentieth-Century Ethnography, Literature, and Art*. Cambridge, Mass.: Harvard University Press.

Clifton, James A. 1987. "Simon Pokagon's Sandbar." *Michigan History* 71(5): 12–19.

Colby, L. W. 1892. "The Sioux Indian War of 1890–91." *Transactions and Reports of the Nebraska State Historical Society*, edited by J. S. Morton, 144–90. Fremont: Hammond Brothers Printers.

Cole, Douglas. 1999. *Franz Boas: The Early Years, 1858–1906*. Seattle: University of Washington Press.

Coleman, William S. E. 2000. *Voices of Wounded Knee*. Lincoln: University of Nebraska Press.

Comaroff, Jean, and John Comaroff. 1991. *Of Revelation and Revolution: Christianity, Colonialism, and Consciousness in South Africa*. Chicago: University of Chicago Press.

Comas, Juan. 1961. "'Scientific' Racism Again?" *Current Anthropology* 2(4): 303–40.

Commoner, Barry. 1963. "Science and the Race Problem: A Report of the AAAS Committee on Science in the Promotion of Human Welfare." *Science* 142(3592):558–61.

Comte, Auguste. 1911 [1877]. *Early Essays on Social Philosophy*. London: Routledge.

Conn, Steven. 1998. *Museums and American Intellectual Life, 1876–1926*. Chicago: University of Chicago Press.

———. 2003. "Archaeology, Philadelphia, and Understanding Nineteenth-Century American Culture." *Philadelphia and the Development of Americanist Archaeology*, edited by Don D. Fowler and David R. Wilcox, 165–80. Tuscaloosa: University of Alabama Press.

———. 2004. *History's Shadow: Native Americans and Historical Consciousness in the Nineteenth Century*. Chicago: University of Chicago Press.

The Conservator. 1900. "Daniel Brinton." *The Conservator*, February:189.

Cook-Lynn, Elizabeth. 2001. *Anti-Indianism in Modern America: A Voice from Tatekeya's Earth.* Urbana: University of Illinois Press.

Cook, Samuel R. 2003. "Anthropological Advocacy in Historical Perspective: The Case of Anthropologists and Virginia Indians." *Human Organization* 62(2):191–201.

Coon, Carleton S. 1962. *The Origin of Races.* New York: Knopf.

Cooper, Anna J. 1892. *A Voice from the South by a Black Woman of the South.* Xenia, Ohio: Aldine Printing House.

Corbey, Raymond. 1993. "Ethnographic Showcases, 1870–1930." *Cultural Anthropology* 8(3):338–69.

Cosby, Bill, and Alvin Poussaint. 2007. *Come On People: On the Path from Victims to Victors.* Nashville: Thomas Nelson.

Cosmos Club. 1968. *Membership of the Cosmos Club.* Washington: Cosmos Club.

Cox, Earnest S. 1937 [1923]. *White America.* Richmond, Va.: White American Society.

Culin, Stewart. 1900. "In Memoriam: Daniel G. Brinton." *Bulletin of the Free Museum of Science and Art* 2(3):199–200.

Dall, William. 1893. "The Columbian Exposition—IX: Anthropology." *Nation* 57(1474):224–26.

Danien, Elin C., and Eleanor M. King. 2003. "Unsung Visionary: Sara Yorke Stevenson and the Development of Archaeology in Philadelphia." *Philadelphia and the Development of Americanist Archaeology,* edited by Don D. Fowler and David R. Wilcox, 36–47. Tuscaloosa: University of Alabama Press.

Darnell, Regna. 1970. "The Emergence of Academic Anthropology at the University of Pennsylvania." *Journal of the History of the Behavioral Sciences* 6:80–92.

———. 1971. "The Professionalization of American Anthropology." *Social Science Information* 10(2):83–103.

———. 1973. "American Anthropology and the Development of Folklore Scholarship." *Journal of the Folklore Institute* (10):23–39.

———. 1982. "The History of Anthropology in the Undergraduate Curriculum." *Journal of the History of the Behavioral Sciences* 18:265–71.

———. 1988. *Daniel Garrison Brinton: The "Fearless Critic" of Philadelphia.* Philadelphia: Department of Anthropology, University of Pennsylvania.

———. 1998. *And Along Came Boas: Continuity and Revolution in Americanist Anthropology.* Amsterdam: John Benjamins.

———. 2000. "Reenvisioning Boas and Boasian Anthropology." *American Anthropologist* 102(4):896–900.

———. 2001. *Invisible Genealogies: A History of Americanist Anthropology.* Lincoln: University of Nebraska Press.

———. 2003. "Toward Consensus on the Scope of Anthropology: Daniel Garrison Brinton and the View from Philadelphia." *Philadelphia and the*

Development of Americanist Archaeology, edited by Don D. Fowler, and David R. Wilcox, 21–25. Tuscaloosa: University of Alabama Press.

————. 2008. "North American Traditions in Anthropology: The Historiographic Baseline." *A New History of Anthropology*, edited by Henrika Kuklick, 35–51. Malden, Mass.: Blackwell.

Darrah, William C. 1951. *Powell of the Colorado*. Princeton: Princeton University Press.

Darwin, Charles R. 1988 [1859]. *On the Origin of Species by Means of Natural Selection; or, The Preservation of Favoured Races in the Struggle for Life*. New York: New York University Press.

Davis, Daniel W. 1899. "Echoes from a Plantation Party." *Southern Workman* 28:54–59.

Deacon, Desley. 1997. *Elsie Clews Parsons: Inventing Modern Life*. Chicago: University of Chicago Press.

Degler, Carl N. 1991. *In Search of Human Nature: The Decline and Revival of Darwinism in American Social Thought*. New York: Oxford University Press.

Delany, Martin R. 1879. *Principia of Ethnology: The Origin of Races and Color, with an Archeological Compendium of Ethiopian and Egyptian Civilization, from Years of Careful Examination and Enquiry*. Philadelphia: Harper and Brothers.

Deloria, Philip J. 1998. *Playing Indian*. New Haven: Yale University Press.

Deloria, Vine. 1969. *Custer Died for Your Sins: An Indian Manifesto*. New York: Macmillan.

DeMallie, Raymond J. 1995. "The Lakota Ghost Dance: An Ethnohistorical Perspective." *Religion and American Culture*, edited by David Hackett, 327–42. New York: Routledge.

Dennis, Michael. 1998. "Schooling along the Color Line: Progressives and the Education of Blacks in the New South." *Journal of Negro Education* 67(2): 142–56.

Dexter, Ralph W. 1966. "Putnam's Problems Popularizing Anthropology." *American Scientist* 54(3):315–32.

Di Leonardo, Micaela. 1998. *Exotics at Home: Anthropologies, Others, American Modernity*. Chicago: University of Chicago Press.

Dilworth, Leah 1996. *Imagining Indians in the Southwest: Persistent Visions of a Primitive Past*. Washington: Smithsonian Institution Press.

Dobzhansky, Theodosius, Ashley Montagu, and Carleton Coon. 1963. "Two Views of Coon's Origin of Races with Comments by Coon and Replies." *Current Anthropology* 4(4):360–67.

Douglas, Mary. 1966. *Purity and Danger: An Analysis of Concepts of Pollution and Taboo*. London: Routledge and Kegan Paul.

Douglass, Frederick. 1999 [1854]. "The Claims of the Negro Ethnologically Considered." *Frederick Douglass: Selected Speeches and Writings*, edited by Philip S. Foner and Taylor Yuval, 282–97. Chicago: Lawrence Hill Books.

———. 2000 [1893]. "Speech at Colored American Day (25 August 1893)." *All the World Is Here: The Black Presence at White City*, edited by Christopher R. Reed, 193–94. Bloomington: Indiana University Press.

Du Bois, W. E. B., and Augustus G. Dill. 1968 [1910]. "The College-Bred Negro American: Report of a Social Study Made by Atlanta University under the Patronage of the Trustees of the John F. Slater Fund; with Proceedings of the 15th Annual Conference for the Study of Negro Problems, Held at Atlanta University, on Tuesday, May 24th, 1910." *The Atlanta University Publications*, edited by William L. Katz, 1–136. New York: Arno Press and the New York Times.

Duke, David. 1998. *My Awakening: A Path to Racial Understanding*. Mandeville, La.: Free Speech Press.

Dundes, Alan. 1990. "African Tales among the North American Indians." *Mother Wit from the Laughing Barrel*, edited by Alan Dundes, 114–25. Jackson: University Press of Mississippi.

Eagle, Mary K. O., ed. 1894. *The Congress of Women Held in the Woman's Building, World's Columbian Exposition, Chicago, U.S.A., 1893*. Chicago: Monarch Book Company.

Eastman, Elaine. 1896. "Address of Mrs. Eastman." *Proceedings of the Thirteenth Annual Meeting of the Lake Mohonk Conference of the Friends of the Indian, 1895*, edited by William J. Rose, 92–94. Lake Mohonk, N.Y.: Lake Mohonk Conference.

Eisenhower, Dwight D. 1957. "Text of Eisenhower Address on Little Rock Crisis." *New York Times*, September 25:14.

Elliott, Michael A. 1998. "Ethnography, Reform, and the Problem of the Real: James Mooney's Ghost-Dance Religion." *American Quarterly* 50(2): 201–33.

Ellis, Clyde. 2003. *A Dancing People: Powwow Culture on the Southern Plains*. Lawrence: University Press of Kansas.

Ellwood, Charles A. 1906. "Review of *The Color Line: A Brief in Behalf of the Unborn*." *American Journal of Sociology* 11(4):570–75.

Ely, James W. 1995. *The Chief Justiceship of Melville W. Fuller, 1888–1910*. Columbia: University of South Carolina Press.

Engs, Robert F. 1999. *Educating the Disfranchised and Disinherited: Samuel Chapman Armstrong and Hampton Institute, 1839–1893*. Knoxville: University of Tennessee Press.

Evans, Brad. 2005. *Before Cultures: The Ethnographic Imagination in American Literature, 1865–1920*. Chicago: University of Chicago Press.

Evans, Stephanie. 2007. *Black Women in the Ivory Tower, 1850–1954: An Intellectual History*. Gainesville: University Press of Florida.

Eversley, Shelly. 2004. *The Real Negro: The Question of Authenticity in Twentieth-Century African American Literature*. New York: Routledge.

Fabian, Johannes. 1983. *Time and the Other: How Anthropology Makes Its Subjects*. New York: Columbia University Press.

Faubus, Orval. 1957. "Text of Faubus Address of Little Rock Controversy." *New York Times*, September 27:10.

Fields, Ed. 1997. "Inter-Racial Dating, Inter-Racial Marriage, Judgement Day." Electronic document, http://www.stormfront.org/truth_at_last/archives/interracial.htm, accessed April 14, 2008.

Filmore, John C. 1894. "Primitive Scales and Rhythms." *Memoirs of the International Congress of Anthropology*, edited by G. S. Wake, 158–75. Chicago: Schulte.

Fine, Benjamin. 1957. "Students Unhurt." *New York Times*, September 24:1.

Finger, John R. 1984. *The Eastern Band of Cherokees, 1819–1900*. Knoxville: University of Tennessee Press.

Fisher, Donald. 1986. "Rockefeller Philanthropy and the Rise of Social Anthropology." *Anthropology Today* 2(1):5–8.

Fitzgerald, Michael W. 1997. "'We Have Found a Moses': Theodore Bilbo, Black Nationalism, and the Greater Liberia Bill of 1939." *Journal of Southern History* 63(2):293–320.

Flagg, John. 1897. "Anthropology: A University Study." *Popular Science Monthly* 51(4):510–13.

Fletcher, Alice C., and Francis La Flesche. 1911. *The Omaha Tribe*. Washington: Government Printing Office.

Francis, Sam. 2002. "Franz Boas—Liberal Icon, Scientific Fraud." Electronic document, http://www.vdare.com/francis/boas.htm, accessed April 8, 2008.

Frank, Gelya. 1997. "Jews, Multiculturalism, and Boasian Anthropology." *American Anthropologist* 99(4):731–45.

Frazier, E. F. 1927. "Is the Negro Family a Unique Sociological Unit?" *Opportunity* 5:155–68.

———. 1931. "The Changing Status of the Negro Family." *Social Forces* 9(3): 386–93.

———. 1939. *The Negro Family in the United States*. Chicago: University of Chicago Press.

Fredrickson, George M. 1965. *The Black Image in the White Mind: The Debate on African American Character and Destiny, 1817–1914*. New York: Harper and Row.

———. 1971. *The Black Image in the White Mind*. Middletown, Conn.: Wesleyan University Press; distrib. by University Press of New England, Hanover, N.H.

———. 2002. *Racism: A Short History*. Princeton: Princeton University Press.

Freeman, Derek. 1983. *Margaret Mead and Samoa: The Making and Unmaking of an Anthropological Myth*. Cambridge, Mass.: Harvard University Press.

———. 1999. *The Fateful Hoaxing of Margaret Mead: A Historical Analysis of Her Samoan Research*. Boulder: Westview Press.

Fried, Morton. 1962. "Racial Differences Denied: Anthropologists Quoted on Negroes' Biological Equality." *New York Times*, October 10:46.

Gaines, Kevin. 2005. "E. Franklin Frazier's Revenge: Anticolonialism, Nonalignment, and Black Intellectuals' Critiques of Western Culture." *American Literary History* 17(3):506–29.

———. 1996. *Uplifting the Race: Black Leadership, Politics, and Culture in the Twentieth Century*. Chapel Hill: University of North Carolina Press.

Garrett, Henry E. 1961a. "The Equalitarian Dogma." *Mankind Quarterly* 1:253–57.

———. 1961b. "The Equalitarian Dogma." *Perspectives in Biology and Medicine* 4:480–84.

———. 1961c. "One Psychologist's View of the 'Equality of the Races.'" *U.S. News & World Report*, August 14:72–74.

Garrett, Henry E., and Wesley C. George. 1962. "Findings on Race Cited: White Man Declared 200,000 Years Ahead on Ladder of Evolution." *New York Times*, October 24:38.

Gates, Merrill E. 1900. "President's Address." *Proceedings of the Seventeenth Annual Meeting of the Lake Mohonk Conference of Friends of the Indian, 1899*, edited by Isabel Barrows, 8–13. Ulster County, N.Y.: Lake Mohonk Conference.

George, Wesley C. 1962. *Biology of the Race Problem*. New York: National Putnam Letters Committee.

Gerber, A. 1893. "Uncle Remus Traced to the Old World." *Journal of American Folk-Lore* 6(23):245–57.

Gershenhorn, Jerry. 2004. *Melville J. Herskovits and the Racial Politics of Knowledge*. Lincoln: University of Nebraska Press.

Glazer, Nathan, and Daniel P. Moynihan. 1963. *Beyond the Melting Pot: The Negroes, Puerto Ricans, Jews, Italians, and Irish of New York City*. Cambridge, Mass.: MIT Press.

Glick, Leonard B. 1982. "Types Distinct from Our Own: Franz Boas on Jewish Identity and Assimilation." *American Anthropologist* 84(3):545–65.

Godfrey, Phoebe. 2003. "Bayonets, Brainwashing, and Bathrooms: The Discourse of Race, Gender, and Sexuality in the Desegregation of Little Rock's Central High." *Arkansas Historical Quarterly* 62(1):42–67.

Goodyear-Ka'opua, Jennifer N. 2005. "K I Ka Mana: Building Community and Nation through Contemporary Hawaiian Schooling." PH.D. diss., University of California, Santa Cruz.

Gravlee, Clarence C., H. R. Bernard, and William R. Leonard. 2003. "Heredity, Environment, and Cranial Form: A Reanalysis of Boas's Immigrant Data." *American Anthropologist* 105(1):125–38.

Greene, John C. 1959. "Biology and Social Theory in the Nineteenth Century: Auguste Comte and Herbert Spencer." *Critical Problems in the History of Science*, edited by Marshall Clagett, 419–46. Madison: University of Wisconsin Press.

Griffin, John H. 1961. *Black Like Me*. Boston: Houghton Mifflin.

Guterl, Matthew P. 2001. *The Color of Race in America, 1900–1940*. Cambridge, Mass.: Harvard University Press.

Gutman, Herbert G. 1973. "Work, Culture, and Society in Industrializing America, 1815–1919." *American Historical Review* 78(3):531–88.

Haley, Alex. 1966. "George Lincoln Rockwell: A Candid Conversation with the Fanatical Führer of the American Nazi Party." *Playboy* 13(4):71–74, 76–82, 154, 156.

———. 1976. *Roots: The Saga of an American Family*. Garden City, N.Y.: Doubleday.

Haller, John S. 1971a. *Outcasts from Evolution; Scientific Attitudes of Racial Inferiority, 1859–1900*. Urbana: University of Illinois Press.

———. 1971b. "Race and the Concept of Progress in Nineteenth-Century American Ethnology." *American Anthropologist* 73:710–22.

Hallowell, A. I. 1960. "Introduction." *Selected Papers from the American Anthropologist (1888–1920)*, edited by Frederica De Laguna, 1–99. Lincoln: University of Nebraska Press.

Hampton Normal and Agricultural Institute. 1893. *Twenty-Two Years' Work of the Hampton Normal and Agricultural Institute at Hampton, Virginia: Records of Negro and Indian Graduates and Ex-Students*. Hampton, Va.: Normal School Press.

Harjo, Susan S. 2003. "Scalp Lock on Internet Auction Block and a Burial Ground Headed That Way." *Indian Country Today* 22(52):A5.

Harper, Thomas. 1957. "For the Record." *New York Times*, September 22:191.

Harriman, Peter 2000. "Turning Tragedy into Strength." Electronic document, http://www.ouachitalk.com/wounded.htm, accessed July 1, 2009.

Harris, Joel C. 1880. *Uncle Remus, His Songs and His Sayings*. New York: Appleton.

———. 1883. "Nights with Uncle Remus." *Century: A Popular Quarterly* 26(3):340–49.

Harrison, Faye V. 1994. "Racial and Gender Inequalities in Health and Health Care." *Medical Anthropology Quarterly* 8(1):90–95.

———. 1995. "The Persistent Power of 'Race' in the Cultural and Political Economy of Racism." *Annual Review of Anthropology* 24:47–74.

Harrison, Ira E., and Faye V. Harrison. 1999. *African-American Pioneers in Anthropology*. Urbana: University of Illinois Press.

Hartigan, John. 1999. *Racial Situations: Class Predicament of Whiteness in Detroit*. Princeton: Princeton University Press.

Hawthorne, Julian. 1893a. "On the Way." *Lippincott's Monthly Magazine*, July: 70–77.

———. 1893b. "Foreign Folk at the Fair." *Cosmopolitan* 15(9):567–76.

Hayes, Rutherford B. 1966 [1879]. "Third Annual Message (State of the Union Address to the 46th Congress)." *The State of the Union Messages of the Presidents*, edited by Fred L. Israel, 1371–95. New York: Chelsea House.

Herrnstein, Richard, and Charles Murray. 1994. *The Bell Curve: Intelligence and Class Structure in American Life*. New York: Free Press.

Herron, Leonora, and Alice M. Bacon. 1896a. "Conjuring and Conjure Doctors in the Southern United States." *Journal of American Folklore* 9(33):143–47.

———. 1896b. "Conjuring and Conjure Doctors in the Southern United States (Continued)." *Journal of American Folklore* 9(34):224–26.

Herskovits, Melville J. 1925 [1999]. "The Negro's Americanism." *The New Negro: Voices of the Harlem Renaissance*, edited by Alain Locke, 353–60. New York: Touchstone.

———. 1953. *Franz Boas: The Science of Man in the Making*. New York: Scribner and Sons.

Hertzberg, Hazel W. 1971. *The Search for American Indian Identity*. Syracuse: Syracuse University Press.

Higginbotham, Evelyn B. 1993. *Righteous Discontent: The Women's Movement in the Black Baptist Church, 1880–1920*. Cambridge, Mass.: Harvard University Press.

Hinsley, Curtis M. 1981. *Savages and Scientists: The Smithsonian Institution and the Development of American Anthropology, 1846–1910*. Washington: Smithsonian Institution.

———. 1989 "Zunis and Brahmins: Cultural Ambivalence in the Gilded Age." *Romantic Motives: Essays on Anthropological Sensibility*, edited by George Stocking, 169–207. Madison: University of Wisconsin Press.

———. 1990. "Authoring Authenticity." *Journal of the Southwest* 32(Winter): 462–78.

———. 1991. "The World as Market Place: Commodification of the Exotic at the World's Columbian Exposition, Chicago 1893." *Exhibiting Cultures: The Poetics and Politics of Museum Display*, edited by Ivan Karp and Steven D. Lavine, 345–65. Washington: Smithsonian Institution Press.

———. 2002. "Introduction: The Lost Itinerary of Frank Hamilton Cushing." *The Lost Itinerary of Frank Hamilton Cushing*, edited by Curtis M. Hinsley and David R. Wilcox. Tucson: University of Arizona Press.

———. 2003. "Drab Doves Take Flight: The Dilemmas of Early Americanist Archaeology in Philadelphia, 1889–1900." *Philadelphia and the Development of Americanist Archaeology*, edited by Don D. Fowler and David R. Wilcox, 1–20. Tuscaloosa: University of Alabama Press.

Hinsley, Curtis M., and David R. Wilcox. 2002. *The Lost Itinerary of Frank Hamilton Cushing*. Tucson: University of Arizona Press.

Hoffman, Frederick L. 1896. "Race Traits and Tendencies of the American Negro." *American Economic Association* 11(1, 2, 3):1–329.

Hofstadter, Richard. 1955. *Social Darwinism in American Thought*. Boston: Beacon Press.

Holden, Constance. 2002. "Going Head-to-Head over Boas's Data." *Science* 298(5595):942–45.

Holloway, Jonathan. 2002. *Confronting the Veil: Abram Harris, Jr., E. Franklin Frazier, and Ralph Bunch, 1919–1941*. Chapel Hill: University of North Carolina Press.

Holloway, Ralph. 2002. "Head to Head with Boas: Did He Err on the Plasticity of Head Form?" *Proceedings of the National Academy of Sciences* 99(23): 14622–623.

Hoxie, Frederick E. 1984. *A Final Promise: The Campaign to Assimilate the Indians, 1880–1920*. Lincoln: University of Nebraska Press.

———. 1992. "Exploring a Cultural Borderland: Native American Journeys of Discovery in the Early Twentieth Century." *Journal of American History* 79(3):969–96.

———. 2001. *Talking Back to Civilization: Indian Voices from the Progressive Era*. Boston: Bedford.

Huggins, Nathan. 1977 [1971]. *Harlem Renaissance*. New York: Oxford University Press.

Hulse, Frederick. 1962. "Race as an Evolutionary Episode." *American Anthropologist* 64(5):929–45.

Hunter, Tera W. 1997. *To 'Joy My Freedom: Southern Black Women's Lives and Labors after the Civil War*. Cambridge, Mass.: Harvard University Press.

Hutchinson, George. 1995. *The Harlem Renaissance in Black and White*. Cambridge, Mass.: Belknap Press of Harvard University Press.

Hyatt, Marshall. 1985. "Franz Boas and the Struggle for Black Equality: The Dynamics of Ethnicity." *Perspectives in American History*, n.s. 2:269–95.

———. 1990. *Franz Boas, Social Activist*. Westport, Conn.: Greenwood Press.

Inscoe, John C. 1989. *Mountain Masters, Slavery, and the Sectional Crisis in Western North Carolina*. Knoxville: University of Tennessee Press.

Irwin, Lee. 1997. "Freedom, Law, and Prophecy: A Brief History of Native American Religious Resistance." *American Indian Quarterly* 21(1):35–56.

Jacknis, Ira. 1985. "Franz Boas and Exhibits: On the Limitations of the Museum Method of Anthropology." *Objects and Others: Essays on Museums and Material Culture*, edited by George W. Stocking Jr., 75–111. Madison: University of Wisconsin Press.

———. 2002. "The First Boasian: Alfred Kroeber and Franz Boas, 1896–1905." *American Anthropologist* 104(2):520–32.

Jackson, John P. 1998. "Creating a Consensus: Psychologists, the Supreme Court, and School Desegregation, 1952–1955." *Journal of Social Issues* 54:143–77.

———. 2001 "'In Ways Unacademical': The Reception of Carleton S. Coon's *The Origin of Races*." *Journal of the History of Biology* 34:247–85.

Jacobs, Margaret D. 1999. *Engendered Encounters: Feminism and Pueblo Cultures*. Lincoln: University of Nebraska Press.

Jacobson, Mathew F. 2001. *Barbarian Virtues: The United States Encounters Foreign Peoples at Home and Abroad, 1876–1917*. New York: Hill and Wang.

————. 1998. *Whiteness of a Different Color: European Immigrants and the Alchemy of Race.* Cambridge, Mass.: Harvard University Press.

Jewell, Joseph O. 2007. *Race, Social Reform, and the Making of the Middle Class.* Lanham, Md.: Roman and Littlefield.

Journal of American Folk-lore. 1895. "Sixth Annual Meeting of the American Folk-Lore Society." *Journal of American Folk-lore* 8(28):1–6.

Kaplan, Amy. 1993. "Left Alone with America: The Absence of Empire in the Study of American Culture." *Cultures of United States Imperialism*, edited by Amy Kaplan and Donald E. Pease, 3–20. Durham: Duke University Press.

Kaplan, Carla. 2002. *Zora Neale Hurston: A Life in Letters.* New York: Doubleday.

Kasson, Joy S. 2000. *Buffalo Bill's Wild West: Celebrity, Memory, and Popular History.* New York: Hill and Wang.

Kavanagh, Thomas W. 2003. "Imaging and Imagining the Ghost Dance: James Mooney's Illustrations and Photographs, 1891–1893." Electronic document, http://php.indiana.edu/~tkavanag/visua15.html, accessed November 1, 2003.

Kehoe, Alice B. 1989. *The Ghost Dance: Ethnohistory and Revitalization.* Fort Worth, Texas: Holt, Rinehart.

Kelley, Robin D. G. 1997. *Yo' Mama's Disfunktional! Fighting the Culture Wars in Urban America.* Boston: Beacon Press.

Kelly, Brian 2003. "Sentinels for New South Industry: Booker T. Washington, Industrial Accommodation, and Black Workers in the Jim Crow South." *Labor History* 44(3):337–57.

Kirshenblatt-Gimblett, Barbara. 1991. "Objects of Ethnography." *Exhibiting Cultures: The Poetics and Politics of Museum Display*, edited by Ivan Karp, and Steven D. Lavine, 386–443. Washington: Smithsonian Institution Press.

Klineberg, Otto. 1931. "The Question of Negro Intelligence." *Opportunity* 9:366–67.

Knight, Peter. 2001. *Conspiracy Culture: From Kennedy to the X-Files.* New York: Routledge.

Koelsch, William A. 1987. *Clark University 1887–1987: A Narrative History.* Worcester, Mass.: Clark University Press.

Kroeber, Theodora. 1961. *Ishi in Two Worlds: A Biography of the Last Wild Indian in North America.* Berkeley: University of California Press.

Kuhn, Thomas S. 1962. *The Structure of Scientific Revolutions.* Chicago: University of Chicago Press.

Kuklick, Bruce. 1996. *Puritans in Babylon: The Ancient Near East and American Intellectual Life, 1880–1930.* Princeton: Princeton University Press.

Kusz, Kyle W. 2001. "'I Want to Be a Minority': The Politics of Youthful White Masculinities in Sport and Popular Culture in 1990s America." *Journal of Sport and Social Issues* 25(4):390–416.

Lamb, Daniel S. 1906. "The Story of the Anthropological Society of Washington." *American Anthropologist* 8(3):564–79.

Lamothe, Daphne. 2008. *Inventing the New Negro: Narrative, Culture, and Ethnography*. Philadelphia: University of Pennsylvania Press.

Lamphere, Louise. 2004. "The Convergence of Applied, Practicing, and Public Anthropology in the 21st Century." *Human Organization* 63(4):431–43.

Landry, Stuart O. 1945. *The Cult of Equality: A Study of the Race Problem*. New Orleans: Pelican Publishing.

Langhorne, Orra. 1878. "Correspondence." *Southern Workman* 7(9):67.

Laslett, Barbara, Sally G. Kohlstedt, Helen Longino, and Evelynn Hammonds. 1996. "Introduction." *Gender and Scientific Authority*, edited by Barbara Laslett, Sally G. Kohlstedt, Helen Longino, and Evelynn Hammonds, 1–16. Chicago: University of Chicago Press.

Lassiter, Luke E. 1998. *The Power of Kiowa Song: A Collaborative Ethnography*. Tucson: University of Arizona Press.

———. 2005a. *The Chicago Guide to Collaborative Ethnography*. Chicago: University of Chicago Press.

———. 2005b. "Collaborative Ethnography and Public Anthropology." *Current Anthropology* 46(1):83–106.

Leacock, Elenore. 1963. "Introduction." *Ancient Society*, edited by Lewis H. Morgan, i–xx. New York: Meridian Books.

Lears, T. J. 1981. *No Place of Grace: Antimodernism and the Transformation of American Culture, 1880–1920*. New York: Pantheon Books.

Lee, Harper. 1960. *To Kill a Mockingbird*. London: William Heinemann.

Lewis, David L. 1997 [1981]. *When Harlem Was in Vogue*. New York: Penguin Books.

Lewis, Herbert S. 2001. "The Passion of Franz Boas." *American Anthropologist* 103(2):447–67.

Lindsey, Donald. 1995. *Indians at Hampton Institute, 1877–1923*. Urbana: University of Illinois Press.

Liss, Julia E. 1996. "German Culture and German Science in the *Bildung* of Franz Boas." *History of Anthropology*, Vol. 8, *Volksgeist as Method and Ethic: Essays on Boasian Ethnography and the German Anthropological Tradition*, edited by George W. Stocking, 155–84. Madison: University of Wisconsin Press.

Locke, Alain LeRoy, ed. 1968 [1925]. *The New Negro*. Boston: Atheneum.

Loewenberg, Bert J. 1928. "Darwinism Comes to America, 1859–1900." *Mississippi Valley Historical Review* 3:339–68.

Lofgren, Charles A. 1987. *The Plessy Case: A Legal-Historical Interpretation*. New York: Oxford University Press.

Loftus, Joseph. 1962. "Virginia Debates Negro Abilities." *New York Times*, February 18:62.

Lott, Eric. 1993. *Love and Theft: Blackface Minstrelsy and the American Working Class*. New York: Oxford University Press.

Ludlow, Helen W. 1909. "The Hampton Student Singers." *Memories of Old Hampton*. The Armstrong League of Hampton Workers, 105–28. Hampton, Va.: Hampton Institute Press.

Lutz, Catherine, and Jane Collins. 1993. *Reading National Geographic*. Chicago: University of Chicago Press.

Lyman, Stanford M. 1968. "The Race Relations Cycle of Robert E. Park." *Pacific Sociological Review* 11(1):16–22.

Lyon-Callo, Vincent, and Susan B. Hyatt. 2003. "Introduction: Anthropology and Political Engagement." *Urban Anthropology* 32(2):133–46.

MacDonald, Kevin. 1998. *The Culture of Critique: An Evolutionary Analysis of Jewish Involvement in Twentieth-Century Intellectual and Political Movements*. Westport, Conn.: Praeger.

Maddox, Lucy. 2005. *Citizen Indians: Native American Intellectuals, Race, and Reform*. Ithaca: Cornell University Press.

Makofsky, Abraham. 1989. "Experience of Native Americans at a Black College: Indian Students at Hampton Institute, 1878–1912." *Ethnic Studies* 17(3):31–46.

Malcolm X and Alex Haley. 1965. *The Autobiography of Malcolm X*. New York: Grove Press.

Manning, M. M. 1998. *Slave in a Box: The Strange Career of Aunt Jemima*. Charlottesville: University of Virginia Press.

Margolis, Howard. 1961. "Science and Segregation: The American Anthropological Association Dips into Politics." *Science* 134(3493):1868.

Mark, Joan. 1980. *Four Anthropologists: An American Science in Its Early Years*. New York: Science History Publications.

———. 1982. "Francis La Flesche: The American Indian as Anthropologist." *Isis* 73(4):497–510.

———. 1988. *A Stranger in Her Native Land: Alice Fletcher and the American Indians*. Lincoln: University of Nebraska Press.

Marks, Jonathan. 2000. "Human Biodiversity as a Central Theme of Biological Anthropology: Then and Now." *Racial Anthropology: Retrospective on Carleton Coon's* The Origin of Races *(1962)*, edited by Jonathan Marks, 1–10. Berkeley, Calif.: Kroeber Anthropological Society Papers, no. 84.

Mason, Otis T. 1891. "The Natural History of Folk-Lore." *Journal of American Folk-Lore* 4(13):97–105.

———. 1894. "Ethnological Exhibit of the Smithsonian Institution." *Memoirs of the International Congress of Anthropology*, edited by G. S. Wake, 208–16. Chicago: Schulte.

Massa, Ann. 1974. "Black Women in the 'White City.'" *Journal of American Studies* 8:319–37.

McCabe, Linda R. 1893. "The 'Indian Man.'" *Daily Inter Ocean*, August 20.

McCain, Robert Stacy. 2001. "The Godfather of the Multicult Nightmare." Electronic document, http://www.ety.com/HRP/race/boasianmulcult.htm, accessed April 8, 2008.

McCormick, Richard L. 1993. "Evaluating the Progressives." *Major Problems in the Gilded Age and the Progressive Era*, edited by Leon Fink, 315–29. Lexington, Mass.: D. C. Heath.

McGee, W. J. 1903. "The American Anthropological Association." *American Anthropologist* 5(1):178–92.

McLoughlin, William G. 1984. *The Cherokee Ghost Dance: Essays on the Southeastern Indians, 1789–1861*. Macon, Ga.: Mercer University Press.

Mead, Margaret, and Ruth L. Bunzel. 1960. *The Golden Age of American Anthropology*. New York: George Braziller.

Meagher, Timothy J. 2001. *Inventing Irish America: Generation, Class, and Ethnic Identity in a New England City, 1880–1928*. Notre Dame, Ind.: University of Notre Dame Press.

Medicine, Bea. 1998. "American Indians and Anthropologists: Issues of History, Empowerment, and Application." *Human Organization* 57(3):253–58.

Meltzer, David J. 2003. "In the Heat of Controversy: C. C. Abbott, the American Paleolithic, and the University Museum, 1889–1893." *Philadelphia and the Development of Americanist Archaeology*, edited by Don D. Fowler and David R. Wilcox, 48–87. Tuscaloosa: University of Alabama Press.

Meriam, Lewis. 1928. *The Problem of Indian Administration*. Baltimore: Johns Hopkins University Press.

Michael, Helen A. 1899. "Daniel Garrison Brinton." *The Conservator*, September:102–3.

———. 1907. *Studies in Plant Chemistry and Literary Papers*. Cambridge, Mass.: Riverside Press.

Montagu, Ashley M. F. 1952 [1942]. *Man's Most Dangerous Myth: The Fallacy of Race*. New York: Harper Brothers.

———. 1962. "The Concept of Race." *American Anthropologist* 64(5):919–28.

Moody, Shirley C. 2006. "By Custom and by Law: Black Folklore and Racial Representation at the Birth of Jim Crow." PH.D. diss., University of Maryland, College Park.

Mooney, James. 1888. "Myths of the Cherokees." *Journal of American Folk-Lore* 1(2):97–108.

———. 1889. "Folk-Lore of the Carolina Mountains." *Journal of American Folk-Lore* 2(5):95–104.

———. 1890. "Cherokee Theory and Practice of Medicine." *Journal of American Folk-Lore* 3(8):44–50.

———. 1891a. "Notes and News." *American Anthropologist* 4(4):393–94.

———. 1891b. "Sacred Formulas of the Cherokee." *Seventh Annual Report of the Bureau of Ethnology, 1885–86*, edited by John W. Powell, 307–97. Washington: Government Printing Office.

———. 1896. "The Ghost Dance Religion and the Sioux Outbreak of 1890." *Fourteenth Annual Report of the Bureau of American Ethnology, 1892–1893*, edited by John W. Powell, 645–1136. Washington: Government Printing Office.

———. 1897. "The Kiowa Peyote Rite." *Der Urquell* 1:329–33.

———. 1898. "Calendar History of the Kiowa Indians." *Seventeenth Annual Report of the Bureau of American Ethnology, 1896*, edited by John W. Powell, 129–445. Washington: Government Printing Office.

————. 1899. "The Indian Congress at Omaha." *American Anthropologist* 1(1):126–49.

————. 1900. *Myths of the Cherokee: Nineteenth Annual Report of the Bureau of American Ethnology, 1897–98*, edited by John W. Powell, 5–576. Washington: Government Printing Office.

Morgan, Thomas J. 1890. *Annual Report of the Commissioner of Indian Affairs*. Washington: Government Printing Office.

————. 1891. *Annual Report of the Commissioner of Indian Affairs*. Washington: Government Printing Office.

Moses, L. G. 1991. "Indians on the Midway: Wild West Shows and the Indian Bureau at World's Fairs, 1893–1904." *South Dakota History* 21(3):205–29.

————. 1999. *Wild West Shows and the Images of American Indians, 1883–1933*. Albuquerque: University of New Mexico Press.

————. 2002. *The Indian Man: A Biography of James Mooney*. Lincoln: University of Nebraska Press.

Moton, Robert R. 1976 [1895]. "Negro Folk Songs." *Black Perspective in Music* 4(2):145–51.

————. 1895. "Negro Folk-Songs." *Southern Workman* 24(2):30–32.

Moynihan, Daniel Patrick. 1965. "The Negro Family: The Case for National Action." Electronic document, http://www.dol.gov/oasam/programs/history/webid-moynihan.htm, accessed December 20, 2007.

Mullin, Molly H. 2001. *Culture in the Marketplace: Gender, Art, and Value in the American Southwest*. Durham: Duke University Press.

Mullings, Leith. 2005. "Interrogating Racism: Toward an Antiracist Anthropology." *Annual Review of Anthropology* 34(1):667–93.

Myrdal, Gunnar. 1964 [1944]. *An American Dilemma: The Negro in a White Nation*. New York: McGraw-Hill.

National Association of the Deaf. 2000. "Cochlear Implants: NAD Position Statement." Electronic document, http://www.nad.org/ciposition, accessed September 17, 2007.

National Parks Service. 2005. *Little Rock Central High School National Historic Site, Lesson #3, "Great Things Happen in Small Places . . .": Government Authority and Civil Rights Activism in Arkansas (1954–1959)*. Little Rock: U.S. Department of the Interior.

New York Age. 1891. "Women and the World's Fair." *New York Age*, October 24.

New York Times. 1890. "Desperate Chief's Career." *New York Times*, December 16:1.

————. 1890. "The Worst Indian of Them All. That Is How Buffalo Bill Characterizes Sitting Bull." *New York Times*, November 25:5.

————. 1892. "The Study of Mankind." *New York Times*, May 8:4.

————. 1893. "Miss Sickels Makes Charges: Tells Why There Are No Civilized Indians at the Fair." *New York Times*, October 8:19.

————. 1893. "Miss Sickels's Daring Work." *New York Times*, April 21:12.

————. 1893. "Prof. Putnam's Hard Luck." *New York Times*, May 22:9.

————. 1903. "Did Not Buy Torture; Prof. Mooney Denies that He Paid Indians to Go through Sun Dance with Its Cruelties." *New York Times*, August 26:8.

————. 1931. "Ninety 'Great Souls' Placed in Church." *New York Times*, March 8:19.

————. 1938. "Nazi's Conception of Science Scored." *New York Times*, December 11:50.

————. 1958. "Little Rock Called 'Excuse' for North." *New York Times*, November 21:19.

————. 1961. "Alabama Orders Study of Races." *New York Times*, November 3:45.

————. 1961. "Experts Affirm Race's Equality." *New York Times*, November 21:29.

————. 1961. "Gag on Racial Issue Charged by Writer." *New York Times*, December 2:47.

————. 1962. "Race Categories Termed Useless." *New York Times*, November 18:72.

Newell, William W. 1983 [1894]. "The Importance and Utility of the Collection of Negro Folklore." *Strange Ways and Sweet Dreams: Afro-American Folklore from the Hampton Institute*, edited by Donald Waters, 186–90. Boston: G. K. Hall.

————. 1883. *Games and Songs of American Children*. New York: Harper and Brothers.

————. 1888. "On the Field and Work of a Journal of American Folk-Lore." *Journal of American Folk-Lore* 1(1):3–7.

————. 1890. "First Annual Meeting of the American Folk-Lore Society." *Journal of American Folk-Lore* 3:1–16.

————. 1895. "Theories of Diffusion of Folk-Lore." *Journal of American Folk-Lore* 8:7–19.

————. 1891. "Bibliographic Notes." *Journal of American Folk-Lore* 4:87–93.

Ngai, Mae M. 2003. *Impossible Subjects: Illegal Aliens and the Making of Modern America*. Princeton: Princeton University Press.

Oliver, Revilo P., and Francis P. Yockey. 2003. *The Enemy of Europe: The Enemy of Our Enemies*. Florissant, Mo.: Liberty Bell Publications.

Omi, Michael, and Howard Winant 1986. *Racial Formation in the United States*. New York: Routledge.

Parezo, Nancy J., and Don D. Fowler. 2007. *Anthropology Goes to the Fair: The 1904 Louisiana Purchase Exposition*. Lincoln: University of Nebraska Press.

Parezo, Nancy J., and John W. Troutman. 2001. "The 'Shy' Cocopa Go to the Fair." *Selling the Indian: Commercializing and Appropriating American Indian Cultures*, edited by Carter J. Meyer and Diana Royer, 3–43. Tucson: University of Arizona Press.

Park, Robert E. 1914. "Racial Assimilation in Secondary Groups with Particular Reference to the Negro." *American Journal of Sociology* 19(9):606–23.

————. 1919. "The Conflict and Fusion of Cultures with Special References to the Negro." *Journal of Negro History* 4(2):111–33.

Parks, Douglas R., and Raymond J. DeMallie. 1992. "1492–1992: American Indian
    Persistence and Resurgence." *Boundary 2* 19(3):105–47.
Patterson, Thomas C. 2001. *A Social History of Anthropology in the United
    States*. New York: Berg.
Patterson, Thomas C., and Frank Spencer. 1994. "Racial Hierarchies and Buffer
    Races." *Transforming Anthropology* 5:20–27.
Patterson, Vivian. 2000. *Carrie Mae Weems: The Hampton Project*.
    Williamstown, Mass.: Aperture.
Perdue, Theda. 2003. *"Mixed Blood" Indians: Racial Construction in the Early
    South*. Athens: University of Georgia Press.
Pierpont, Claudia R. 2004. "The Measure of America: How a Rebel
    Anthropologist Waged a War on Racism." *New Yorker*, March 8:48–63.
Platt, Anthony M. 1991. *E. Franklin Frazier Reconsidered*. New Brunswick, N.J.:
    Rutgers University Press.
Pokagon, Simon. 1897. "The Future of the Red Man." *Forum* (August):698–709.
———. 1898. "The Future of the Red Man." *Current Literature* 24(3):254–56.
———. 1899. *O-Gî-Mäw-Kwe Mit-i-Gwä-Kî (Queen of the Woods)*. Hartford,
    Mich.: C. H. Engle.
Porter, Joy. 2001. *To Be Indian: The Life of Iroquois-Seneca Arthur Caswell
    Parker*. Norman: University of Oklahoma Press.
Possnock, Ross. 2000. *Color and Culture: Black Writers and the Making of the
    Modern Intellectual*. Cambridge, Mass.: Harvard University Press.
Powdermaker, Hortense. 1993 [1939]. *After Freedom: A Cultural Study of the
    Deep South*. Madison: University of Wisconsin Press.
Powell, John W. 1874. "Statement of Major J. W. Powell Made before the House
    Committee on Indian Affairs as to the Condition of the Indian Tribes West of
    the Rocky Mountains." January 13, 1874. House Miscellaneous Document
    no. 86 43rd Cong. 1st Sess. Ser. Set 1618, pp. 1–11.
———. 1878. *Report on the Methods of Surveying the Public Domain*.
    Washington: Government Printing Office.
———. 1885. "From Savagery to Barbarism, Annual Address of the President,
    Delivered February 3, 1885." *Transactions of the Anthropological Society of
    Washington* 3:173–96.
———. 1888. "From Barbarism to Civilization." *American Anthropologist* 1(2):
    97–123.
———. 1891. "Report of the Director." *Seventh Annual Report of the Bureau
    of Ethnology*, 1885–86, edited by John W. Powell, xiii–xl. Washington:
    Government Printing Office.
———. 1896. "Report of the Director." *Fourteenth Annual Report of the Bureau
    of Ethnolology, 1892–93*, edited by John W. Powell, lx–lxi. Washington:
    Government Printing Office.
Pratt, Richard H. 1973 [1892]. "The Advantages of Mingling Indians with Whites."
    Americanizing the American Indians, edited by Francis P. Prucha, 260–71.
    Lincoln: University of Nebraska Press.

———. 1900. "Zitkala Sa in the Atlantic Monthly." *Red Man and Helper* 6(3):2.

———. 1964. *Battlefield and Classroom: Four Decades with the American Indian, 1867–1904*. New Haven: Yale University Press.

Price, David H. 2004. *Threatening Anthropology: McCarthyism and the FBI's Surveillance of Activist Anthropologists*. Durham: Duke University Press.

Putnam, Carleton. 1958. *Theodore Roosevelt: A Biography*. New York: Scribner.

———. 1959. "Distinguished New Englander Discusses High Court's Decision on Public Schools." *New York Times*, January 5:19.

———. 1961. *Race and Reason: A Yankee View*. Washington: Public Affairs Press.

———. 1967. *Race and Reality: A Search for Solutions*. Washington: Public Affairs Press.

Putnam, Frederic W. 1890. "An Interesting Suggestion for the Columbian Exposition." *Chicago Tribune*, May 31:13.

Rabinow, Paul. 1992. "For Hire: Resolutely Late Modern." *Recapturing Anthropology*, edited by Richard Fox, 59–72. Santa Fe: School of American Research Press.

Ralph, Julian. 1892. "Our Exposition at Chicago." *Harper's New Monthly* 84(500): 205–14.

Redfield, Robert. 1950. "[Testimony in] Transcript of Record." *Sweatt v. Painter* 399 U.S. 629:192–205.

Reed, Christopher R. 2000. *"All the World Is Here!": The Black Presence at the White City*. Bloomington: Indiana University Press.

Rice, Franklin. 1889. *Dictionary of Worcester and Vicinity*. Worcester, Mass.: F. S. Blanchard.

Ridgeway, James. 1995. *Blood in the Face: The Ku Klux Klan, Aryan Nations, Nazi Skinheads, and the Rise of a New White Culture*. New York: Thunder's Mouth Press.

Ritterhouse, Jennifer. 2003. "Reading, Intimacy, and the Role of Uncle Remus in White Southern Social Memory." *Journal of Southern History* 69(3):585–622.

Roberts, Brigham H. 1931. *The Seventy's Course in Theology*. Salt Lake City: Deseret Book Company.

Robinson, William H. 1977. "Indian Education at Hampton Institute." *Stony the Road: Chapters in the History of Hampton Institute*, edited by Keith L. Schall, 1–33. Charlottesville: University Press of Virginia.

Rockwell, George L. 1966. "From Ivory Tower to Privy Wall: On the Art of Propaganda." *National Socialist World* 1(1):8–12.

Rogers, J. A. 1962. "History Shows." *New Pittsburgh Courier* [March 10] 2(49):10.

Roscoe, Gerald, and David Larkin. 1995. *Westward: The Epic Crossing of the American Landscape*. New York: Monacelli Press.

Rosenzweig, Roy. 1983. *Eight Hours for What We Will: Workers and Leisure in an Industrial City, 1870–1920*. New York: Cambridge University Press.

Rothfels, Nigel. 2002. *Savages and Beasts: The Birth of the Modern Zoo*. Baltimore: Johns Hopkins University Press.

Rushton, J. Philippe. 2002. "The Pioneer Fund and the Scientific Study of Human Differences." *Albany Law Review* 66(1):207–62.

Rydell, Robert W. 1984. *All the World's a Fair: Visions of Empire at the American International Expositions*. Chicago: University of Chicago Press.

Sanday, Peggy Reeves. 2002. "Science and Engagement in Public Interest Anthropology: Lessons from Boas and Bourdieu." Paper presented at Annual Meeting of the American Anthropological Association, New Orleans, December.

Sapir, Edward. 1924. "Culture, Genuine and Spurious." *American Journal of Sociology* 29(4):401–29.

Scheper-Hughes, Nancy. 2001. "Ishi's Brain, Ishi's Ashes: Anthropology and Genocide." *Anthropology Today* 17(1):12–18.

Schmaltz, William H. 1999. *Hate: George Lincoln Rockwell and the American Nazi Party*. Washington: Brassey's.

Schomburg, Arthur. 1968 [1925]. "The Negro Digs Up His Past." *The New Negro*, edited by Alain Locke, 231–37. Boston: Atheneum.

Science. 1890. "Review of *Races and Peoples*." *Science* 16(406):276–77.

———. 1905. "Mr. Rockefeller's Endowment for Higher Education." *Science* 22(549):28–29.

Segal, Daniel, and Sylvia J. Yanagisako. 2005. "Introduction." *Unwrapping the Sacred Bundle: Reflections on the Disciplining of Anthropology*, edited by Daniel Segal and Sylvia J. Yanagisako, 1–24. Durham: Duke University Press.

Serling, Rod. 1966. "Nazi Rockwell." *Playboy Magazine* 13(7):7.

Shaler, Nathan S. 1890. "Science and the African Problem." *Atlantic Monthly* 66:36–45.

Sharps, Ronald L. 1991. "Happy Days and Sorrow Songs: Interpretations of Negro Folklore by Black Intellectuals, 1893–1928." PH.D. diss., George Washington University.

Shaw, Albert. 1898. "The Trans-Mississippians and Their Fair at Omaha." *Century: A Popular Quarterly* 56(6):836–53.

Showers, Susan. 1898. "Two Negro Tales Concerning the Jay." *Journal of American Folk-Lore* 11(40):74.

Sickels, Emma C. 1892. "The Story of the Ghost Dance: Written in the Indian Tongue by Major George Sword, An Ogallala Sioux, Captain of the Indian Police." *Folk-Lorist* 1(1):28–36.

Siegel, Robert, Mellissa Block, and Howard Berks. 2003. "Analysis: John Wesley Powell's Vision for Water Use in the Western United States." *All Things Considered from National Public Radio*, August 26.

Silva, Noenoe K. 2004. *Aloha Betrayed: Native Hawaiian Resistance to American Colonialism*. Durham: Duke University Press.

Sioux City Journal. 1898. "Lo and All His Relatives: Congress of Redmen at Omaha a Feature of the Exposition." *Sioux City Journal* (July 9):2.

Sklar, Kathryn Kish, and Erin Shaghnessy. 1997. "How Did African-American
    Women Define Their Citizenship at the Chicago World's Fair in
    1893?" Electronic document, http://www.alexanderstreet6.com/wasm/
    wasmrestricted/ibw/intro.htm, accessed February 24, 2008.
Smedley, Audrey. 1993. *Race in North America: Origin and Evolution of a
    Worldview.* Boulder: Westview.
Smith, William B. 1905. *The Color Line: A Brief in Behalf of the Unborn.* New
    York: McClure, Phillips.
Smith, William B., trans., and Walter Miller (joint trans.). 1944. *The Iliad of
    Homer, a Line for Line Translation in Dactylic Hexameters.* New York:
    Macmillan.
Smithson, James. 1826. "The Will of James Smithson (in His Own Hand)."
    Electronic document, http://www.sil.si.edu/Exhibitions/Smithson-to-
    Smithsonian/labels/021c_high.html, accessed February 23, 2008.
Smyth, Albert. 1900. *Brinton Memorial Meeting.* Philadelphia: American
    Philosophical Society.
Southern Workman. 1874. "Labor." *Southern Workman* 2(3):166.
———. 1876. "Dear Teacher." *Southern Workman* 5(6):46.
———. 1894. "More Letters Concerning the 'Folk-Lore Movement' at Hampton."
    Southern Workman 23(1):5.
———. 1895. "Folk-Lore and Ethnology." *Southern Workman* 30(24):30.
———. 1899. "Dr. Campbell's Address." *Southern Workman* 28(9):362–65.
Southwick, Albert B. 1998. *150 Years of Worcester: 1848–1998.* Worcester, Mass.:
    Chandler House.
Spack, Ruth. 2001. "Dis/Engagement: Zitkala-Sa's Letters to Carlos Montezuma,
    1901–1902." *MELUS* 26(1):173–205.
Sparks, Corey, and Richard Jantz. 2002. "A Reassessment of Human Cranial
    Plasticity: Boas Revisited." *Proceedings of the National Academy of Sciences*
    99(23):14636–639.
Spivey, Donald. 1978. *Schooling for the New Slavery: Black Industrial Education,
    1868–1915.* Westport, Conn.: Greenwood Press.
Spivey, Richard. 2003. *The Legacy of Maria Poveka Martinez.* Santa Fe: Museum
    of New Mexico Press.
Starn, Orin. 2004. *Ishi's Brain: In Search of America's Last "Wild" Indian.* New
    York: W. W. Norton.
Stegner, Wallace E. 1954. *Beyond the Hundredth Meridian: John Wesley Powell
    and the Second Opening of the West.* Boston: Houghton Mifflin.
Steinberg, Stephen. 2007. *Race Relations: A Critique.* Palo Alto: Stanford Social
    Sciences.
Stewart, Kathleen, and Susan Harding. 1999. "Bad Endings: American
    Apocalypsis." *Annual Review of Anthropology* 28:285–310.
Stocking, George W., Jr. 1962. "Lamarckianism in American Social Science:
    1890–1915." *Journal of the History of Ideas* 23(2):239–56.

———. 1966. "Franz Boas and the Culture Concept in Historical Perspective." *American Anthropologist* 68(4):867–82.

———. 1968. *Race, Culture, and Evolution: Essays in the History of Anthropology*. New York: Free Press.

———. 1974. *A Franz Boas Reader*. Chicago: University of Chicago Press.

———. 1987. *Victorian Anthropology*. New York: Free Press.

———. 1992. *The Ethnographer's Magic and Other Essays in the History of Anthropology*. Madison: University of Wisconsin Press.

———. 2001. *Delimiting Anthropology: Occasional Inquiries and Reflections*. Madison: University of Wisconsin Press.

Sturm, Circe. 2002. *Blood Politics: Race, Culture, and Identity in the Cherokee Nation of Oklahoma*. Berkeley: University of California Press.

Swan, Daniel C. 1999. *Peyote Religious Art: Symbols of Faith and Belief*. Jackson: University Press of Mississippi.

Talbot, Edith A. 1969 [1904]. *Samuel Chapman Armstrong*. New York: Negro Universities Press.

Taylor, Jared. 1997. "Who Reads American Renaissance?" *American Renaissance* 8(7&8):8–11.

Tenenbaum, Shelly. 2003. "The Vicissitudes of Tolerance: Jewish Faculty and Students at Clark University." *Massachusetts Historical Review* 5:7–27.

Thomas, David H. 2000. *Skull Wars: Kennewick Man, Archaeology, and the Battle for Native American Identity*. New York: Basic Books.

Thomas, Robert M., Jr. 1998. "Carleton Putnam Dies at 96; Led Delta and Wrote on Race." *New York Times*, March 16:B7.

Thomas, Sabrina L. 2001. "Review of *Slave in a Box: The Strange Career of Aunt Jemima*." *Transforming Anthropology* 10(1):58–60.

Thomson, Rosemarie G. 1996. "From Wonder to Error—A Genealogy of Freak Discourse in Modernity." *Freakery: Cultural Spectacles of the Extraordinary Body*, edited by Rosemarie G. Thomson, 1–18. New York: New York University Press.

Tierney, Patrick. 2000. *Darkness in El Dorado: How Scientists and Journalists Devastated the Amazon*. New York: Norton.

Time Magazine. 1936. "Franz Boas: Environmentalist." *Time*, May 11:37–42.

Trachtenberg, Alan. 2004. *Shades of Hiawatha: Staging Indians, Making Americans, 1880–1930*. New York: Hill and Wang.

Traubel, Horace L. 1899. "Editorial on D. G. Brinton." *The Conservator* 10(9): 131–32.

———. 1996. *With Walt Whitman in Camden*. Vol. 9. Oregon House, Calif.: W. L. Bentley.

Trennert, Robert A. 1987. "Selling Indian Education." *American Indian Quarterly* 11(3):203–20.

Tri-State Defender. 1962. "Dixie Finds Yankee Book to Uphold Jim Crow." *Tri-State Defender* 7(54) (December 1):7.

Trouillot, Michel-Rolph. 1995. *Silencing the Past: Power and the Production of History*. Boston: Beacon Press.

———. 2003. *Global Transformations: Anthropology and the Modern World*. New York: Palgrave Macmillan.

Tucker, William H. 1994. *The Science and Politics of Racial Research*. Urbana: University of Illinois Press.

———. 2002. *The Funding of Scientific Racism: Wickliffe Draper and the Pioneer Fund*. Urbana: University of Illinois Press.

Tylor, Edward B. 1920 [1871]. *Primitive Culture: Researches into the Development of Mythology, Philosophy, Religion, Art, and Custom*. London: J. Murray.

Utley, Francis L. 1974. "The Migration of Folktales: Four Channels to the Americas." *Current Anthropology* 15(1):5–27.

Utley, Robert M. 1963. *The Last Days of the Sioux Nation*. New Haven: Yale University Press.

———, ed. 1964. *Battlefield and Classroom: Four Decades with the American Indian, 1867–1904*. New Haven: Yale University Press.

Van Brunt, Henry. 1893. "The Columbian Exposition and American Civilization." *Atlantic Monthly* 71(427):577–88.

Vest, Jay H. C. 2000. "From Bobtail to Brer Rabbit: Native American Influences on Uncle Remus." *American Indian Quarterly* 24(1):19–43.

Visweswaran, Kamala. 1998a. "Race and the Culture of Anthropology." *American Anthropologist* 100(1):70–83.

———. 1998b. "Wild West Anthropology and the Disciplining of Gender." *Gender and American Social Science*, edited by Helen Silverberg, 86–124. Princeton: Princeton University Press.

Wade, Nicholas. 2002. "A New Look at Old Data May Discredit a Theory on Race." *New York Times*, October 8:F3.

Wake, G. Staniland, ed. 1894. *Memoirs of the International Congress of Anthropology*. Chicago: Schulte.

Warrior, Robert. 1995. *Tribal Secrets: Recovering American Indian Intellectual Traditions*. Minneapolis: University of Minnesota Press.

Washburn, Sherwood. 1963. "The Study of Race." *American Anthropologist* 65(3):521–31.

Washburn, Wilcomb E. 1978. *The Cosmos Club of Washington: A Centennial History, 1878–1978*. Washington: Cosmos Club of Washington.

Washington, Booker T. 1902 [1901]. *Up From Slavery: An Autobiography*. New York: Doubleday.

Washington Times. 1918. "Indian Woman in Capital to Fight Growing Use of Peyote Drug by Indians." *Washington Times*, February 17:1,9.

Waters, Donald J. 1983. *Strange Ways and Sweet Dreams: Afro-American Folklore from the Hampton Institute*. Boston: G. K. Hall.

Weatherford, Jack. 1991. *Native Roots: How Indians Enriched America*. New York: Crown.

Wells, Ida B., and Frederick Douglass. 1999 [1893]. *The Reason Why the Colored American Is Not in the World's Columbian Exposition*. Urbana: University of Illinois Press.

Wells-Barnett, Ida B. 1899. *Lynch Law in Georgia*. Chicago: Chicago Colored Citizens.

White, Ackrel E. 1878. "To the Hampton Alumni Association." *Southern Workman* 7(7):54.

White, Max E. 2001. "Anthropologists and the Eastern Cherokees." *Anthropologists and Indians in the New South*, edited by Rachel A. Bonney, and J. A. Paredes, 11–16. Tuscaloosa: University of Alabama Press.

Wiecek, William M. 1992. "Laissez-Faire Constitutionalism." *Oxford Companion to the Supreme Court of the United States*, edited by Kermit T. Hall, 492–93. New York: Oxford University Press.

Wiegman, Robyn. 1995. *American Anatomies: Theorizing Race and Gender*. Durham: Duke University Press.

Willard, William. 1991. "The First Amendment, Anglo-Conformity, and American Indian Religious Movement." *Wicazo Sa Review* 7(1):26–30.

Williams, Brackette. 1989. "A Class Act: Anthropology and the Race to Nation across Ethnic Terrain." *Annual Review of Anthropology* 18:401–44.

Williams, Vernon J., Jr. 1989. *From a Caste to a Minority: Changing Attitudes of American Sociologists toward Afro-Americans, 1896–1945*. Westport, Conn.: Greenwood Press.

———. 1996. *Rethinking Race: Franz Boas and His Contemporaries*. Lexington: University Press of Kentucky.

———. 2006. *The Social Sciences and Theories of Race*. Urbana: University of Illinois Press.

Willis, Arlette I. 2002. "Literacy at Calhoun Colored School, 1892–1945." *Reading Research Quarterly* 37(1):8–44.

Wilson, Francille R. 2006. *The Segregated Scholars: Black Social Scientists and the Creation of Black Labor Studies, 1890–1950*. Charlottesville: University of Virginia Press.

Winston, Andrew S. 1998. "Science in the Service of the Far Right: Henry E. Garrett, the IAAEE, and the Liberty Lobby." *Journal of Social Issues* 54(1): 179–211.

———. 2001. "'The Boas Conspiracy': The History of the Behavioral Sciences as Viewed from the Extreme Right." Paper presented at the 33rd Annual Meeting of CHEIRON, International Society for the History of Behavioral and Social Sciences, Indiana University, Bloomington, June 21–24, 2001. Electronic document, http://htpprints.yorku.ca/archive/00000012/00/boasforarchive.htm, accessed April 11, 2008.

Wissler, Clark. 1942. "The American Indian and the American Philosophical Society." *Proceedings of the American Philosophical Society* 86:189–204.

Worcester Daily Spy. 1891. "Dr. Franz Boas: Worcester." *Worcester Daily Spy* 46(April 17):4.

————. 1891. "The School Committee: Dr. Boas Allowed to Make Head
    Measurements." *Worcester Daily Spy* 46(March 4):1.
Worster, Donald. 2001. *A River Running West: The Life of John Wesley Powell.*
    New York: Oxford University Press.
Yanagisako, Sylvia J. 2005. "Flexible Disciplinarity: Beyond the Americanist
    Tradition." *Unwrapping the Sacred Bundle: Reflections on the Disciplining
    of Anthropology*, edited by Daniel Segal and Sylvia J. Yanagisako, 78–98.
    Durham: Duke University Press.
Zitkala-Ša. 1900. "An Indian Teacher among Indians." *Atlantic Monthly*
    85(509):381–87.

Index

Big Foot (Si Tank), 85–86
Bilbo, Theodore, 168, 199, 200–
204, 214
Biology of the Race Problem
(George), 197
Black, Don, 171, 172
Black Fox (Inâli), 78
boarding school movement, 67,
100–101
Board of Lady Managers (Chicago
World's Fair), 106–8
Boas, Franz: AAA address of, 147–49,
204–5, 207; AFLS and, 54, 55, 57, 61–62;
Americanist anthropology and,
10–12; on *American Renaissance* list,
156–57; anthropometric measurements by, 92, 138–46, 225n11; on assimilation, 24, 202–3, 217; authenticity and, 16, 115; Brinton vs., 136–37,
146–48; Chicago World's Fair and,
92–97, 103; controversies over, 159;
culture separated from race by, 6,
7–8, 12; Du Bois and, 208–9; emergence of race position of, 137–38;
German influence on, 11; intertextu-
ality and, 160–61; legacy of, 217, 219;
on museums, 16; on Negroes, 23–25;
as public intellectual, 208, 210–15,
232n33; retrospective significance
of, 154–55; in *Time*, 210–12. *See also
under titles of specific works by*
Boas conspiracy: AAA, AAAS, and
AAPA statements on race and,
187–90, 196–97, 198; academic
facets of, 164; back-to-Africa movements and, 199–204; *Brown v.
Board of Education* and, 158, 175,
179–82, 218; civil rights movement
and, 189–90, 197–98; conspiracy
culture and, 165; Coon's *The Origin
of Races* and, 193–96; Duke's *My
Awakening* and, 172–74; equalitarianism debate and, 184, 191–92, 219;
Internet and alleged evidence in,

162–63; Little Rock and Putnam in,
175–78; mapping of appropriation
of anthropology and, 214; Pioneer
Fund and IAAEE and, 182, 186, 191,
193, 196, 198, 204, 209, 232n3; public
intellectuals and, 165–66; Putnam
letters and, 182–86; Putnam's influence in Southern states and, 186–87;
racial politics of culture and, 164–65;
rebuttals by anthropologists and,
188–89, 192–93, 195–96; Rockwell
interview and American Nazi
Party and, 166–71; Stormfront and,
171–72; "the truth is out there" and,
160, 163, 204; white men as victims
and, 161–62; white supremacism and
public consumption of anthropology
and, 156–61
Bonnin, Gertrude. *See* Zitkala-Ša
Bourguignon, Erika, 12
Bowditch, Henry P., 141
Brady, Erica, 222n10
Briggs, Charles, 29
Brinton, Daniel G.: AAAS presidential
address of (1895), 149–50, 204; AFLS
and, 55, 59; "The Aims of Anthropology," 149–50; as Americanist,
229n7; *The American Race*, 133;
American School of anthropology
and, 11; at APS, 125–26; background
to, 121–23; *The Basis of Sexual
Relations*, 152–53; Boas vs., 136–37,
146–48; Chicago World's Fair and,
94; Columbus Day address of (1892),
127–28; influence of, on legislation
and jurisprudence, 150, 231nn28–29;
institutionalization of anthropology
and, 118, 120–21, 154; Lamarckianism and, 123, 124, 135; methodology
of, 134–35; Mooney compared to,
68; "Mound-Builders of the Mississippi Valley," 122; *Notes on the Floridian Peninsula*, 122, 123; on origin
of races, 228n4; popularity of, 151;

Lee D. Baker

is an associate professor of cultural anthropology and African
American studies and Dean of Academic Affairs, Trinity College
of Arts and Sciences, Duke University. He is the author of *From
Savage to Negro: Anthropology and the Construction of Race,
1896–1954* (1998) and the editor of *Life in America: Identity and
Everyday Experience* (2003).

Library of Congress Cataloging-in-Publication Data
Baker, Lee D., 1966–
Anthropology and the racial politics of culture / Lee D. Baker.
p. cm.
Includes bibliographical references and index.
ISBN 978-0-8223-4686-9 (cloth : alk. paper)
ISBN 978-0-8223-4698-2 (pbk. : alk. paper)
1. Race. 2. Culture. 3. Anthropology. 4. Sociology.   I. Title.
GN320.B25 2010
305.8—dc22   2009041447